D0823013

"Hope you will find the book an enjoyable read"

Raj gupta

EIGHT DOLLARS AND A DREAM

MY AMERICAN JOURNEY

RAJ GUPTA WITH SYD HAVELY

Copyright © 2016 Raj Gupta.

All rights reserved. No part of this book may be reproduced, stored, or
transmitted by any means—whether auditory, graphic, mechanical, or
electronic—without written permission of both publisher and author, except
in the case of brief excerpts used in critical articles and reviews. Unauthorized
reproduction of any part of this work is illegal and is punishable by law.

ISBN: 978-1-4834-4756-8 (sc)
ISBN: 978-1-4834-4755-1 (e)

Library of Congress Control Number: 2016903281

Because of the dynamic nature of the Internet, any web addresses or links contained in
this book may have changed since publication and may no longer be valid. The views
expressed in this work are solely those of the author and do not necessarily reflect the
views of the publisher, and the publisher hereby disclaims any responsibility for them.

Any people depicted in stock imagery provided by Thinkstock are models,
and such images are being used for illustrative purposes only.
Certain stock imagery © Thinkstock.

Lulu Publishing Services rev. date: 03/10/2016

To my parents, Rukmini Sahai and Phool Prakash, my wife, Kamla, and my daughters, Amita and Vanita

Contents

Acknowledgments ix

Foreword xi

Introduction xv

Part I.   From India to America

Chapter 1   A Boy's Life in Northern India.. 3
Chapter 2   The Pull of America and the Lure of the American
Dream 26

Part II.   My Career at Rohm and Haas

Chapter 3   On the Way to CEO.. 45
Chapter 4   Anxiety and the High Bar of Self-Imposed Expectations 59
Chapter 5   The Best Lessons and Advice are Based on Negatives 66
Chapter 6   Being CEO: A Cauldron of Change 90
Chapter 7   Planning for Succession and Then Acquisition 108

Part III.   Moving On—My Career after Rohm and Haas, My Family, and Reflections on the Lessons of My Life

Chapter 8   A New Life in Private Equity—
Not All PE Firms Are Alike 139
Chapter 9   Boards: Their Importance and Role in Corporate
Governance...145
Chapter 10 Back to the Family...163

Chapter 11   Reflections on My Life and Lessons Learned 199
Chapter 12   The Summing Up.. 224

Index.. 227
Raj Gupta 233
Syd Havely 235

Acknowledgments

There were both selfish and unselfish reasons for telling my story. First, I wanted to understand what made me tick as a human being, and by writing and thinking about my life, I was hoping to come to some deeper understanding of what made me who I am and what I accomplished. I am now perhaps closer to and clearer about that amalgam of race, ethnicity, family, fortune, hard work, personality, and luck that makes people who they are.

The second reason was to offer thanks to those people who, in fact, really did make me who I am. Our parents and friends are the mirrors of our personality. As the sociologist Charles Horton Cooley said in his "looking glass theory" of self-development, we grow out of our interactions with others and how they perceive us. I am a product of my parents' upbringing; the influence of my brother and sisters; my school mates; my wife, Kamla; daughters Amita and Vanita; and my professional colleagues and social network. I am that person in addition to the values I have learned and internalized along the way.

And I would be remiss if I didn't acknowledge those whose efforts, kindness, patience, and belief in me paved the way for the professional and personal opportunities I have enjoyed. Among the very many who influenced and guided my life are Phil Lippincott at Scott Paper; Fred Shaffer, who hired me at Rohm and Haas; Vince Gregory, who mentored me by allowing access and providing guidance when he was chairman and CEO of Rohm and Haas; Larry Wilson, who taught me leadership and decision-making; Basil Vassiliou, who helped me navigate often politically-rocky assignments while in Europe and offered candid insights and suggestions that only a caring and objective mentor could; and of course John C. Haas and the Haas family and in particular John's son, David, who supported me throughout my tenure as chairman and CEO of Rohm and Haas Company.

Other business leaders figure into my story. Sandy Moose, leader of Rohm and Haas's board of directors, provided strong and steady counsel throughout my tenure; Jack Brennan and Bill McNabb of Vanguard, on whose board I have served for 12 years, watching the company grow and lead the investment management industry; Jack Krol, former chairman and CEO of DuPont and board member of several large companies, including Tyco and Delphi where I serve, who provided the kind of no-nonsense example of board leadership I am continually looking to adopt; Ed Breen, former chairman and CEO of Tyco International, who set the kind of leadership example needed not only by Tyco International but also by any other company; Steve Klinsky, founder and Chief Executive of New Mountain Capital, the private equity firm that recruited me, where I now make my home and where Steve's leadership and temperament set a standard that all private equity firms should follow; and the myriad friends and colleagues at the former Rohm and Haas Company, the American Chemistry Council, and the boards of Tyco, The Vanguard Group, Hewlett-Packard Company, and Delphi Automotive as well as the Ujala Foundation and its commitment to health care and education.

FOREWORD

Raj Gupta's story is a tiny but significant thread in the Indian-American tapestry. More than three million Americans were either born in India or are of Indian descent. They represent one of the most educated and productive demographic slices of the American pie—71 percent of adults have bachelor's degrees, and their median household income is the highest of any ethnic group. Yet Indian-Americans have long been subsumed in the great American melting pot with very few well-known, high profile personalities, particularly in the world of business. This is the story of just one highly successful, influential, and generous Indian immigrant.

Raj Gupta came to the United States in 1968 at age 22 with $8 in his pocket and a degree from the elite Indian Institute of Technology (IIT). At 24, with a wife and a child and a graduate degree in operations research from Cornell, he joined Scott Paper. By 26, having earned an MBA, he was hired into an entry-level job by the specialty chemicals company, Rohm and Haas.

After nearly 30 years of learning the ropes, taking advantage of opportunities as they were offered at each step, listening to the advice of mentors, and trusting in the system, in 1998 Mr. Gupta was named chairman and CEO of Rohm and Haas Company, by then a Fortune 500 company. He was the first foreign-born executive and person of color to lead the century-old company, which was still owned to a significant degree by the founding Haas family.

As a result of both Mr. Gupta's tenure and his predecessor's, Rohm and Haas grew from a mid-size hybrid chemical company in 1988 to a global leader in specialty chemicals and electronic materials by 2008. Total shareholder return outpaced industry competitors and overall market performance during Mr. Gupta's last five years at the helm, achieving a Total Shareholder Return of 17.3 percent compared to the S&P 500's -4.8 percent. That is an amazing achievement. Rohm and Haas did well by his leadership.

Retired from Rohm and Haas, Mr. Gupta is now senior advisor at New Mountain Capital, a New York-based private equity firm. He is board chairman at Delphi Automotive and also sits on the boards of Tyco International, Hewlett-Packard, The Vanguard Group, and the IRI Group. In addition, he leads a philanthropic effort—the Ujala Family Foundation—that promotes children's health care and educational initiatives in the United States and India.

He is also a loving husband and the father of two daughters who have inherited their parents' American dream of working hard, playing by the rules, trusting the system, and trying to make a better life for themselves and others.

On the global stage as of this writing, 13 companies in the Fortune 500 are headed by executives born in India, which means India has produced more CEOs than any other country but the U.S. And while Indians lead such Indian giants as Tata and Mital, they also lead non-Indian giants such as Microsoft, MasterCard, and Pepsi. There are many reasons why these companies chose Indian-Americans—their competence, strategic acumen, and fluency in English for sure, but also because they brought a skill and experience few other non-American CEOs bring. They cut their teeth on India's intensely competitive home markets, laden with regulatory red tape and corruption. They know what happens when the playing field is tilted and what happens to competitiveness when fair play isn't part of the game. But just as important, they succeeded because they also knew and appreciated the importance of diversity in leadership, whether in race, religion, language, or culture. They know and appreciate the value of building teams of individuals with multiple perspectives that lead to significantly better decision-making and organizational resiliency. Raj Gupta is part of the Indian-American diaspora, bringing those qualities and embodying those same values in his life and work.

Yet no ethnic class or group comes without examples of greed, temptation, and law-breaking, including several high-profile professionals of Indian origin in the Wall Street investment and consulting world.

Their trials and convictions for insider trading cast a harsh light on a group of Indian-Americans and other South Asians who formed an illicit network to capitalize on their membership in America's business elite. Testimony about Wall Street greed, boardroom leaks, and government wiretaps resulted in convictions for those individuals, becoming the subject of a well-received book called *The Billionaire's Apprentice: The Rise of the Indian-American Elite and the Fall of the Galleon Hedge Fund,* by Anita Raghavan (2013).

Raj Gupta's is the story of another Indian-American businessman who rose to the pinnacle of corporate America but who made his name and his good fortune by playing it straight, albeit in a career filled with personal challenges and boardroom drama. By any business measure, Raj is a huge success, but he measures his life according to a different metric. He asks himself if he has been true to his values, to what his parents and family taught him, his ideals of being a good husband and father, and if he is giving back in a meaningful way to those who do not have the opportunities he did. He's still working it out.

What perhaps separates Raj's account from other CEOs who never saw a challenge they couldn't conquer or a goal not achieved, is that Raj is amazingly candid about both his business life and the lessons it taught him and what he is still coming to learn about himself. It's an inside story of one man's life lessons in a refreshing, insightful, and deeply personal way, showing us what it means to be Indian, American, a leader, and a sentient human being. It is the story of modesty from a man who has mastered both business and what is important in life.

Jack Krol
Former Chairman and CEO of
DuPont and director of numerous
corporate boards

Ram Charan
Advisor to Fortune 500 Boards,
business speaker, and author of
The Attacker's Advantage

INTRODUCTION

There is a Hindu proverb that says "a man becomes like those whose society he loves." I am both the son of India who did everything he could to become an American and the American who wants to extend to the people he left back home the same advantages that he found in his new world. I therefore have a foot, and a heart, in both societies and cultures.

I came to the United States in the late 1960s because I loved what America stood for and what I hoped she would give me. I was 22. Together with my wife Kamla we built a life here that we could not have had in India. Our daughters' accomplishments in this country —Amita is a physician who is Associate Professor and Deputy Director of the Center for Clinical Global Health Education at Johns Hopkins, and Vanita is head of the United States Justice Department's Civil Rights Division—could not have been attained in India. We are all grateful for the opportunities.

In many ways, my adopted country made me a better person, a more caring husband and father, and a more qualified colleague and leader. I have benefited from opportunities extended to me throughout my career by my superiors, mentors, and friends and am in that sense a true participant in the American dream—if you work hard, play by the rules, and have some breaks along the way, you can make a good life for yourself and your family. I have accomplished that and more.

My own story is that of the journey to potential writ small, a personal account and life report that I offer to illustrate the promise and opportunity, based on meritocracy, that I believe is America's greatest gift to itself and to the world. I am now at the point where I must understand how fortunate I have been, to give back, and not to assume that the fortune and gifts that came my way are there for everyone just for the taking.

My narrative is neither a tale of a slum dog millionaire nor of a privileged Brahmin. It is of a member of India's middle class who, like many others in the world, wanted a piece of the American dream and spent his life trying to achieve it. My life is not a fairy tale—my decade as the CEO of the Rohm and Haas Company was a highly stressful one, beginning with the dot-com collapse and ending with the near implosion of America's, and the world's, financial systems. It is a story of a man still with dreams and desires, along with some demons and even a few deep regrets, but also many proud achievements and accomplishments. In some ways, I have lived a double life—as both an Indian and as an American— and in the process I have learned lessons and gathered unique insights and observations that could be useful to others.

But I am also a man in the third and final segment of his life, on life's graying edge. I have been spared an earlier mortality from prostate cancer by the advances of medical science and the expertise and diligence of the American health care system, not to mention the love and care of my family. The late Senator Arlen Specter, a man I knew and greatly respected, said the hardest thing he ever did was to face his own mortality and write about it. And in that regard, Maurice Sendak, the award-winning children's book author and illustrator, said the mission of a writer is to "tell the truth as best you can."

This book travels my road again in three parts. I start where I began, with my boyhood and education in India and my decision to go to America. I then recount the highs and lows of my years at Rohm and Haas, including the pitched battle at the end to conclude the company's purchase by Dow Chemical. The third section deals with life after Rohm and Haas, offering first some hard-won lessons about life in the boardroom, then, fittingly, returning to my family, and finally sharing reflections on what influenced my life. Such reflections are best curated by time and experience.

I have thought with much more passion since leaving Rohm and Haas, and in much starker relief since my episode with prostate cancer, about how I have lived my life. Ultimately, what is important? What provided me with the greatest happiness and fulfillment? Did I make the right decisions and take the right paths? Am I on the right path now?

Working with colleagues James Allworth and Karen Dillon, Clayton Christensen, a leading expert on management, innovation, and growth, who has waged his own battle with cancer and other serious health issues, asked some of the same questions in his much-admired and insightful book, *How Will You Measure Your Life?* (2012). I hope that this book can similarly establish with the reader, as the probing and persistent interviewer Mike Wallace once called it, a "chemistry of confidentiality."

PART I

From India to America

1

A Boy's Life in Northern India

"The voice of parents is the voice of gods, for to their children they are heaven's lieutenants."— Shakespeare

I grew up in Uttar Pradesh in northern India, the most populous state in the country, with more than 215 million people. If Utter Pradesh stood on its own, it would be the world's fifth most-populous nation. It shares a border with Nepal and is the birthplace of Hinduism and home to many Buddhist shrines. It is also one of the poorest states on the subcontinent, and if you come from there you are considered a second-class citizen. Nonetheless, eight of India's 14 prime ministers did come from there, the highest of any Indian state. And when economists and politicians talk of India's "demographic dividend"—the millions of young people flowing into the work force each year—it is Uttar Pradesh that is the source of much of that bounty. In my time, I was part of that dividend.

I was born in 1945, two years before India won its independence from Britain, in Muzaffarnagar, about 80 miles northeast of Delhi in the extreme western end of the state. Muzaffarnagar is an industrial and agricultural center and a transportation hub for much of northern India. It is located near the Yamuna and Ganges Rivers, and many canals flow through the district, providing irrigation for the area's rich and fertile land, some of the best in India.

My father was a civil engineer, which meant our family was middle class, perhaps even upper-middle class. Much of his work involved building and running the myriad canals and hydroelectric power stations in the area. We moved around frequently, living in half a dozen cities before I left home, all in Uttar Pradesh.

The first house I remember was in Bareilly, a center for the manufacture of furniture and the trading of cereal, cotton, and sugar. We had a big house, built for a British family, and I can still draw the shape of its rooms in my mind's eye. We rented half of the residence, and the other half was rented by one of my father's colleagues. There were eight of us in three bedrooms: my mother, Rukmini Sahai, my father, Phool Prakash, and the six children they had in the space of seven years. I was the next to oldest. I had an older sister, Pramila; a younger brother, Arvind; and three younger sisters, Sujata, Aparna, and Indu, the baby of the family. We lived there for seven years, from 1951 to 1957, from when I was 6 years old until I was 12, six little kids running around in a big house.

My first vivid memory is of my mother's bringing Indu home from the hospital in 1951. Somehow, the arrival of this newest baby, who turned out to be the last, made me realize that I was just one of a number of siblings. I also remember my father's traveling a lot for his work. Actually, he was away most of the time, coming home for a week and leaving again for three.

This schedule was hard on my mother, almost comically so. I remember one of my sisters getting sick. My father was away, so my mother had to round everyone up and take us all by public transportation to the doctor. When we got to the doctor's office, she counted just five children. She had mistakenly left the ailing sister at home.

It was a busy household, but a happy one. Growing up in India means growing up with a lot of people around you—friends, family, and strangers. I probably have 85 first cousins. It's the way everyone is brought up. My mother was one of five children, and my father came from a family of ten (nine boys and one girl). His family was economically and socially well-off and he excelled at school. He had a privileged life compared with the others in my extended family. But he also believed in a life of honesty and hard work.

Even though he was away most of the time, my father was the biggest figure in our family life. When he was home, he would make sure that the eight of us sat around the table and ate together, and he set the standard for much of our behavior, defining the values we should live by. But we were really raised by our mother. It was she who instilled the values of education and well-roundedness and the importance of friends and family—the warp and woof that goes into how we live our daily lives. She had an enormous influence on all of us. In a sense, my parents complemented each other.

My Father

When my brother and I got older, my father would take us with him on some of his long work trips, usually on horseback. We got to see what he was doing, how he interacted with his colleagues, and how he handled work issues. So I got to know him very well, although at a distance, because he was so reserved. He was a role model to me, the embodiment of a man of principle, and I had a huge amount of respect for him and how he acted.

For instance, my father never gave in to the temptation to take bribes, as some of his colleagues did. He paid a price of sorts, because the families of those men had much more money than we had. In those days, many who worked in government service and dealt with contractors, especially on high-ticket projects like building dams, canals, bridges, or power stations where huge sums of money were involved, would take a piece of the contract for themselves. But my father would not. I knew all this because most of our social life revolved around his peers, superiors, and subordinates and their families. It was very easy to see how some of them lived compared with how we lived. My father had to be very frugal, we had to live within our means, but a number of his colleagues could be much more generous with their families. I could see the difference when I was just seven or eight. People even talked about it—who was on the take and who wasn't. My father didn't discuss it with us, but we knew where he stood.

My Mother

My mother was one of five children. Her father was also an engineer. Her mother was totally illiterate, yet my mother was given a fine education. I'm not sure what the rationale was, but she was the only one who pursued serious studies in her family. She went to a boarding school at an early age and remained there until she married my father when she was 19, a path almost unheard of for an Indian woman at that time. And she later went to college, which was even rarer. None of her brothers or her sister went beyond high school.

She had a special bond with her father. A story my mother told me was that during breaks from boarding school, she would travel to where her father worked. Since there was no other means of transportation, she would ride a camel or an elephant from the nearest bus or train station to the work site. Her father used to send a female servant along with a male one to make sure that she was safe while she traveled those final six or seven miles to be with him.

That continued when she met my father, who must have seen something very special in her. It may have been her motivation and focus. She poured everything into her studies and what it took to complete them. And that carried through to how she brought us up. She said that education was the most important thing that she and my father could give us. She knew how important education had been to her development and the role it played in my father's family. And she saw how her own siblings had been limited in their lives and careers by the shortcomings in their schooling. Her faith in education was tied up in her determination as a young girl to be independent. This fierce independence lasted her whole life and was passed down to us. We had no choice but to take that gift.

I remember one time in the early 1960s, my family was split in half, living 200 miles apart. My brother, older sister, and I had been sent to live with an aunt in the city of Aligarh, where the three of us attended Aligarh Muslim University for a year. The three younger girls stayed with my parents, who were then living in a small town that couldn't offer the older children the right education.

My mother decided that the youngest, Indu, should join us for the holidays. She was nine or ten at the time. My mother put her, all by herself, on a train to the bus station where she took the bus to the city where we lived and then rode in a rickshaw to our house. My mother had absolutely no fear in sending my little sister by herself on all of those public conveyances with total strangers. This is shocking to me. I later asked my mother what made her do this, and she just shrugged and said she had no idea; she just knew that my sister would be fine. That's the way it was for my mother—my sister "would be fine." The lesson for me was my mother's insistence that we value our independence above all else.

Independence was entwined with education in her mind, and both passions were behind our daily after-school ritual. Beginning when I was in grammar school in the early 1950s and extending to when we were all in school together, we would come home each day from class, have a snack, and then take our assigned seats at the dinner table (we had each scratched our name on the back of a chair). My mother would sit at the head of the table and ask each of us to open our school bag. She would tell us to take out our homework and anything else that was in the bag. She did this to see if there was anything there that didn't belong to us. And occasionally, there would be a new pen or pencil, or an eraser, and she would ask, "Where did this come from?" We would usually make up some story that we found it in the school or it was lying on the ground. Then she would ask, "Why did you put it into your bag? Tomorrow, you put it back exactly where you found it. This is not yours." Part of her definition of independence was being free to do the right thing.

An Arranged Marriage

My parents' marriage was arranged, as most marriages in India were when I was growing up—and as mine was. The process was that people of a similar social and economic strata would learn that you had a daughter, and they would announce that they had a son. Then some intermediary would say, "We should see if we can arrange a marriage." It was a practice that essentially made the wife the lesser partner in the marriage. Most of the time, the wife did not have any real independence, and if the marriage was an unhappy one, she couldn't return to her parents unless the situation was quite dire. Once a family married off a daughter, she belonged to the other family. She belonged to her husband. Her parents, in a way, dissolved all of their responsibility.

Because they were bound by a life contract, most couples realized that they needed to go into the marriage with a commitment to make it work. Some worked out better than others, of course. The husband was usually the linchpin who brought in the money and supported the family. If he failed at that task, or just wanted to make life difficult for his spouse, the wife had very little recourse. If it wasn't a good marriage, they would have to suffer through it.

Fortunately, my parents had a very good, solid marriage. Neither one was particularly expressive emotionally, however. Other families in our immediate circle gave big hugs to each other and talked in a very public way about how much they loved and cared for one another. My parents did not show their affection outwardly to each other. I never heard them argue, but neither did I ever see them hug and kiss or even touch one another. Maybe they thought that wasn't the proper way to act in front of children or family. But to me it did not mean that they didn't care for or love each other. Their way of expressing affection may have been somewhat detached and formal, but it was no less real. They worked as true partners in raising us, and we understood the deep respect and feeling they had for each other. (I, too, am not a touchy-feely person or a big hugger. I sometimes wish I were, especially with my wife and daughters, but I have to show my affection in other ways. The pull to mimic my parents' behavior never quite goes away!)

Since my father was gone so much, my mother took on other roles in addition to raising six children. She took care of all the finances. While my father brought home the money, my mother paid all the bills and kept the house running. It was a clear division of labor that worked very well, but it was very unusual in an Indian household in those days. My father also relied entirely on my mother for their social life, and they had a very active one, even with the six of us underfoot.

But how much time did they have to be alone with each other? Apart from the end of the day, when all the kids were asleep, or in the morning before we woke up, I'm not sure. There was no telephone and no email then, so the only way of communicating was face to face. They clearly had a great understanding between them in terms of respect and responsibility. They got along well, and I don't recall their ever raising their voices to each other.

My father did have a temper, although he was usually able to mask it when we were around. In his early teen years, I was told, his temper would sometimes get the best of him, causing quite a scene at home. As an adult, he was much more in control of himself, but occasionally his anger would flare up over work. When he got angry in his office or at home, everyone could hear it. But he never directed his wrath at my mother or at us.

Still, I recall one time in my teens when my parents went through a rough patch and there was tension between them. I don't know for certain what it was about, but I have an idea. My father was in his 40s, and there were guests in the house, and I think there was some misunderstanding between my mother and father over the attention he was either getting from, or giving to, another woman. My father was a very handsome man— 6-feet tall and fair-skinned. My mother, perhaps, was jealous. Whatever it was from, the tension lasted for three or four months until they worked it out. And yet, before, during, and after this period, we never saw them fight or argue. It was just one of those things. It wasn't something we could ask about, nor was it something that my mother or father would talk about. But I learned that all marriages have bumps in the road at some point, some serious and some very surmountable, as my parents' tiff was.

My Father's Illness

Their marriage—and our whole family—was tested in a far more serious way when I was nine. My father had been away on a project site, as he had been so many times. But when he came home this time, he looked very disoriented. He walked in and nearly collapsed. He couldn't speak and seemed to be almost paralyzed. He was only 35, and we had no idea what was wrong.

The medical facility he needed was nearly 100 miles away. It took a while before the doctors there could make a diagnosis: it was encephalitis. My mother had to stay close to him in case he needed her, his condition was so dire. But she couldn't just leave the family behind—my youngest sister, Indu, was then just 2 years old and the oldest, Pramila, was only 10. So my mother did what she felt she had to. She sent five of us to live with uncles and aunts for what turned out to be nine months. She took Indu with her, and essentially moved into the hospital to look after my father.

He nearly died. This had a traumatic effect on me, and I suddenly had a looming fear that we would become poor and homeless. But my mother was resourceful, and because we had always lived within our means, we made it through. To live frugally was the rule that each of us learned from our mother, and one that I still live by, even with the substantial means that I have long had. My mother not only nursed my father back to health, but she kept the family intact. She saved all of us.

Encephalitis is an insidious disease. In my father's case, the cure took nine months, but the recovery probably took three to four years. He was not himself all during that time. In fact, he never really came back fully. He looked perfectly normal, but for the first two or three years after returning to work he didn't have the same memory or energy he had before. He was very good at hiding this, but in private he suffered from depression, perhaps because he saw himself diminished by his disease and unable to care for his family in the way he once did. The after-effects lingered until he died suddenly at the age of 59 in 1978.

Because of my mother, we made it through all of this as a family. She was an incredibly resilient and strong woman—stronger than all the rest of us put together.

Two Boys on a Bike

Because of their added income from bribes, some of my father's colleagues were able to put their children in very expensive boarding schools. My parents made it clear to us that they didn't have the resources to send all six children to those schools, and they didn't think it fair to send just the two boys. So we all wound up in public schools. My brother and I got lucky, though, since my parents found a really good public school for us when we were living in Kanpur, a big industrial city in central Uttar Pradesh. The school was six miles from our house, however, and Arvind and I had to ride back and forth each day on my bike. I was in the 7th grade, and Arvind was in the 6th, and we rode the bike through the middle of the city. We were lucky that the traffic usually wasn't too bad, but we still had to navigate those roads and cars with both of us perched on just one bike. Arvind and I left home on my bike at 7 a.m. and didn't get back until 5 or 6 at night. We did a few chores and then did our homework. Dangers aside, it was worth it. That school, Bishambhar Nath Sanatan

Dharam Inter College, (BNSD), a middle school and high school, gave me structure and purpose.

Much of my later confidence came from my years at BNSD, which had established a reputation as one of the top public schools in Uttar Pradesh. The teachers there prepared us for the statewide exam that was the basis for college admission. About 250,000 students took the exam each year, and eight to ten students from BNSD would regularly rank among the top 25 statewide.

To consistently maintain that level of success, the school employed a system to identify and support the best students. Each grade in the school had about 1,000 pupils who were divided into 20 sections and tested regularly. Based on those scores, the top 50 students in each class were eventually assigned to a special section where they were given extra work and instructed by the best teachers. You can imagine the competitive spirit in the top 50—all the pressure from their families along with the self-motivation to prove that you were as good as the other students and perhaps better. It was an incredibly powerful experience.

That kind of academic rigor set the foundation for my studies; it boosted my confidence immensely, starting from when I was 12. BNSD taught me the importance of structure. As I mentioned, Arvind and I did chores and homework when we got home. I also studied with the fellow who scored number one in our class. Every other day, we would go to each other's house and work together. He was a great partner, and I was lucky to be able to study with him. (We still keep in touch, by the way. He lives in Chicago and is doing well.) I worked very hard at BNSD to become one of its best students. By the time I was 16, I was good enough to get into the Indian Institute of Technology (IIT), India's equivalent of MIT or Caltech, to pursue my engineering degree in Mumbai. I was extremely proud of that accomplishment and thought if I worked hard, I could compete with anybody. When it came time to take the statewide exam, I placed sixth out of 250,000.

I was proud to be among the top students. But my being there was really the result of a combination of things. First, the strong family support that I mentioned previously. And I'm not talking about having a mother who was a "Tiger Mom" or a "Tiger Father" dad. They weren't. We were a well-rounded and, I think, happy family. Second, we didn't have distractions that might have put our focus on something else, such as working after school or during the summers, but our parents encouraged us to work hard in school as well as play sports and socialize. We had plenty of opportunity to play and participate in athletics because we had 4-5 acres of grounds with huge gardens. We had our own cricket field and badminton court outdoors, and all of my friends used to come to our home after school. So when I look back, there was a natural competitive spirit facilitated both by our parents' focus on education and our ability to engage in healthy sports. But clearly the first indication of how well that was paying off for me came in the state exams and then later at IIT before coming to the U.S.

At any rate, when I was 15 years old I was ready to leave home. This was partly what independence meant to me—not being emotionally attached to my sisters, to my brother, or to my parents to any great degree. From that perspective, I was perfectly fine, set to be on my own. In a way, I had internalized the lessons of my parents and certainly my mother, who ingrained in us her own "declaration of independence." This was the year before I went to IIT, in 1961-62, when it was just the three of us—my older sister, my brother, and I—living with an aunt. It was an interesting experience, this second time our family was divided. My father was working in a smaller town and my three younger sisters went with my parents to the little town of Jhansi. We three older ones went to live in Aligarh, famous for its Aligarh Muslim University, where I went to school prior to IIT. Aligarh is also the seat of many nationalist movements as well as the hometown of a few Bollywood artists. It is a rich and culturally diverse city and also the birthplace and home of my wife, Kamla, who lived there all her life until she and I were married.

Aligarh taught me many things, as did attending the university where 95 percent of the students and 95 percent of the faculty were Muslim. There was a major communal riot the year I was there. As a result, the University was closed down for about two months. That was one of the strangest experiences of my young life—feeling like a minority in my own country. India, as people know, is a primarily Hindu country, and here I was, a Hindu minority living in a Muslim pocket of India.

The whole experience in Aligarh made me think about religious and cultural differences and how life can play out when people of two different faiths and cultures, such as Hindus and Muslims, are living together. How does each feel about the other? What reinforces these feelings? What else is going on? Certainly the Muslims have to feel pretty isolated in India overall, even though they make up more than 12 percent of the population today. There are 150 million Muslims in India, making it the second-largest Muslim country in the world, after Indonesia. So it's interesting how and what you learn about all the minorities when you spend some time actually being one—how each feels, how different psyches work, asking whether each can come to understand and respect the others. Living in Aligarh did not influence me negatively. Rather, it made me appreciate how one feels at being isolated, a lesson that had a lasting impact on me.

Equality, Up to a Point

In many respects, my parents were very liberal and forward thinking. They taught us that girls had the same right to everything that boys did. In the Indian culture, and this is true for other Asians as well, sons are put on a higher pedestal than daughters are. There are families who will even say the boys should get better food and other creature comforts than the girls, so you often have enormous inequality at the family level. In families with some means, Indian boys would get whatever they wanted in terms of toys, education, food, clothing—everything really. This favoritism, in my opinion, has had insidious effects on the larger culture, leading to sometimes degrading, violent, and criminal treatment of women, both in public and in private, with even the worst behavior often going unpunished.

My parents had a very different view. For them, their children were their children—it didn't matter whether they were girls or boys. We each had an equal claim to their affection and their resources. That wasn't true for many families then, nor is it now.

My father set down great goals for my brother Arvind and me. He wanted one of us to become a mechanical engineer because he was a civil engineer and he believed mechanical engineering was going to be the next big thing in India. I got the nod for that. And Arvind was tapped to join the most prestigious profession in the country, to be a high-level civil servant in the Indian Administrative Services. My father and my mother set us both on the road to achieving those goals. (Arvind, as it turned out, had other ideas and joined the navy before starting a career in business later in life.)

My parents treated my four sisters exactly the same way as they treated the two of us boys—but with one very large exception. My four sisters were all very bright, talented, and ambitious. Yet despite her own upbringing and education, my mother decreed that none of them was to become a doctor or engineer. Instead, she said, they all had to be married before they were 20. At the time my mother's edict was announced, there was great pain in the family, and to this day, I am baffled by her decision, so inconsistent was it with everything else she taught us. It seemed to be rooted in her acceptance of the limits of a woman's place in Indian society and in a larger sense of her belief in tradition. She wasn't opposed, per se, to a woman's having a professional career. But if a woman did that first, my mother seemed to be saying, she would be well past 20 by the time she finished her education and launched her career. Then she would marry late and would no doubt have much stronger opinions and less ability to adjust if there were contrary views from her spouse. My mother was, after all, a product of her world and upbringing, and this had debilitating consequences on my sisters in different ways, especially on Pramila and Sujata, who rebelled. They kept asking, "Why can't we pursue our studies? All of our classmates are less smart with lower grades, and they're going to go into medicine." Medicine was a big deal for a woman in India, although it was less prestigious than engineering and civil administration. But my mother put her foot down. My father didn't weigh in on my mother's decision in front of us, as he didn't on most issues within the family or in our social circles. Maybe he argued with her privately. In front of us, though, the two of them were always of one mind.

"Seeing the Girl"

My mother's decision caused Pramila, who is just one year older than I am, to have one of the hardest roads to travel. She was very intelligent, but she was average looking, as I am. When she turned 17, as part of the arranged marriage process, families with a son who might be a possible partner started to visit our house to meet her. It was called "seeing the girl," or *pennu kannal* in Hindu. The families, including the son, would sit in the living room, and my sister would be on view as if she were a family jewel being appraised and either purchased or politely declined. This appraisal and rejection process probably happened eight or nine times before a husband was found for her. During each visit, siblings from both families would sneak behind a curtain and watch, as I did on several occasions, a fact Pramila was painfully aware of. I could see how degrading it was, and I never forgot it.

Looking back, I know that Pramila was hardly ready for marriage at 17. Yes, eventually she got married, and happily so for almost 50 years, but the experience affected everyone in the family, including my brother and me. When my turn came, and I was 22 and ready to start graduate school in the United States, my parents said I wouldn't be allowed to leave without getting married first. I told them (as did my brother) that I didn't want to go through what our older sister went through, so my brother and I made a deal with my parents. We each agreed to an arranged marriage, but we wouldn't participate in the "browse and buy" process. If they wanted us to get married, then they could choose the girl. We'd accept their choice and move on with our lives. And that's what we did, both of us.

Pramila endured this cultural practice with all its attendant religious and historical trappings, got married as my mother had wished, and eventually went on to graduate first in her class for her master's degree and then to earn her Ph.D. My parents were more understanding by the time Aparna and Indu, the third and fourth daughters, approached marriage age. But it was still hard for my second sister, Sujata. She had a very difficult adjustment to her marriage at first. She and her husband grew happier as time went on and they became closer.

In a reflection of how emotionally formal we are, I've never asked my sisters how hurt they were by all of this and if they still have any big regrets. They seem to be well-adjusted and they seem to be happy. But it was not an easy road for them.

I couldn't escape from my sisters' experiences and the impact they had on me as a brother and as a man. But I certainly don't want to portray my mother as someone who was stiff or wooden about her opinions in general. She was a very well-rounded person, and she wanted the best for us. Education was part of it. Independence was part of it. Responsibility was part of it. Those things were incredibly important to her and less so the external demonstration of affection. To her, substance always trumped the façade. But on the issue of marriage, she simply couldn't or wouldn't budge.

The Role and Importance of Higher Education in India

In those days, you either went to school or you didn't go to school. It's different now, but in those days for many Indians, primary school was the only education they received. Education is still an unmet national need and one of the reasons my generation, as well as students today, want to study abroad. There are not enough fine schools in India and certainly not enough schools so that every Indian can get an education. When Nandan Nilekani, founder of Infosys Technologies, Ltd. and chairman of the Unique Identification Authority of India (UIDAI) talks about the potential of India in his wonderful book, *Imagining India* (2008), he puts education at the top of the to-do list. I agree. America had then and still has the finest colleges and universities in the world. In many ways, it was against the odds that a middle class Indian would be able to go to a fine Indian university and then on to America for graduate study.

For a typical Indian farming family or a blue-collar worker, the path would be primary school and then joining the workforce. The relatively few who were able to continue their educations widened their opportunities considerably. There was an education hierarchy. The smartest people went into engineering or Indian administrative service. The second-best might go into medicine, followed by law and the other professions. But engineering was at the top of the pyramid, the most prestigious, with administrative or civil service and medicine just below. I knew that, of course, and set my sights on engineering at IIT, and I was lucky to have a very generous mentor by the name of Prof. K.P.K. Nair, who went on to become Dean Emeritus at the University of New Brunswick business school in Canada.

IIT was established by the Indian Parliament in 1961 to serve as a training ground for skilled professionals. Five separate campuses were initially established, each with individual autonomy but linked by a common mission and a joint entrance exam followed by a highly rigorous curriculum. One out of 50 students who take the exam is admitted. For all five schools, approximately 100,000 are vying for 2,000 seats, so it is a highly selective process. Consequently, almost everyone takes special training in preparation for the test, because getting in is the opportunity of a lifetime. I felt a great sense of exhilaration when I was accepted. Very few students are not appreciative of that honor and privilege. I should note that within just the last few years, the Indian Parliament has established nine new IIT campuses, including one for information technology, allowing continued training in engineering, math, science, and information technology. They are now among the finest universities in the world.

When the IIT schools first opened in the early 1960s, each IIT school had a sister school in another country with which they collaborated. For example, the one in Chennai, India collaborated with a university in West Germany; the one in Delhi with a British university; and the one in Kanpur had an American collaboration. The one that I went to in Mumbai had a Russian collaboration. So a lot of our textbooks were in Russian. Each IIT was in a different section of the country because the Indian subcontinent is so big, but each student had to pass the same entrance exam, and selection was based solely on merit. It didn't matter if you were well off, or had a family member who had attended IIT, or made a huge school donation. You got in because of your own merit.

The second piece of my IIT experience was that I was now alone and on my own for the first time in my life. And as I said, IIT drew students from all over the country, so I was thrown into a vast melting pot of different people who were coming from all over India, and I had to learn to understand, adapt to, and get along with these diverse students. India is not a land of one language. There are multiple languages and multiple religious belief systems. To give you an idea of how different the languages in India are, I cannot read a word and I cannot speak a word of most of the 20-plus distinctly different languages that Indians speak. Each has its own pronunciations and alphabet, and they are very different. The only commonalities were the English language, which all Indian students learn when they start school, and our shared status as IIT students. Other than English, most IIT students spoke a little Hindi.

Attending IIT was my first immersion into a multicultural world—a world that makes India one of the most diverse nations in the world. I think that IIT taught me how to mingle, survive, grow, and form bonds later on with people from all over the world. Later, when Kamla and I and our daughters moved from the U.S. to England and then to France, I think it gave me the ability not to be intimidated and not to feel isolated just because I was different or living in an unfamiliar environment.

I don't mean to say I thought the IIT experience was easy. I saw and experienced hierarchical social structure and experienced cliques. As a young man from Uttar Pradesh I was not considered an elite student or someone of privilege. Many of these students came from the big cities in the southern and western part of India. I don't think there's a direct correlation with the U.S., but it would be akin to someone from the rural South's going to MIT, Harvard, or Stanford and being around students from elite northeastern prep schools in New England or New York. I was a kid from the less-than-prosperous northwest state that bordered Nepal, and the big city boys came from Mumbai and Delhi where they went to very elite private schools. So it was really a class-conscious place from that standpoint, not unlike other universities that drew students from diverse backgrounds, schools, and geography. The big-city students associated with each other and rather looked down on others. The trick was not to be intimidated by them but instead to get to know them, become friends, and hang out when circumstances allowed. That's a very fascinating experience. You get to see what makes them tick, and that's useful, both in getting to know them and later in life when you met the same types.

And finally, I would say my IIT experience really confirmed that I could compete with the best. It gave me confidence. Most of us, when we entered there, were at the top of our class or the top 5 percent in high school or college. Not long after our arrival, it became painfully obvious that everyone else in our class was amongst the best of *their* classes, so somebody had to end up in the bottom of the class at IIT. And I didn't want it to be me! The total student body at our IIT campus was about 1500, with about 300 in our class, not large by any means. And, sadly, the pressure got to some. We had one or two suicides due to the extraordinary expectations of their families and of themselves that they were not able to meet.

I wasn't immune from pressure either, so I spent nearly all my time studying. This was a pretty isolated place, and there was not much of a social life other than once a month or so, when we'd go into Mumbai to see a movie. Plus, the climate of Mumbai was kind of bizarre; in the summer, it rained almost every day. There was hardly any outdoor activity one could do, so I studied. What it did was make me work pretty darned hard. But it paid off. I finished second in my class in mechanical engineering, and I was learning how to compete with the best. To do that, you have to give your best. And when I look back on those years at IIT and having to confront these highly educated, smart, and competitive students and doing well, I realize it gave me confidence, or at least the foundation for confidence, that I could return to and build on as I met and interacted with other people in my business and social life. Later, as I took on more responsibility at Rohm and Haas, I mingled with people who were also going up the ladder or who had achieved significant success in their careers. It would have been easy to shrink from any full-fledged or peer-to-peer relationship, but I didn't. I wasn't intimidated, thanks to IIT.

So what I took away from my childhood and early adulthood in India, and particularly from IIT, was understanding and appreciating the diversity that comes with life while developing the skills, resources, and character that have allowed me to face crises, improve my decision-making, and see untoward events in a manner that allows me to make good decisions and ultimately to be successful. This is not an individual achievement. It is a collaborative one, drawing on the skills, assets, and good judgment of others as well. Because even at IIT, there was an unspoken perception that some students were from "second tier" places or came from "second tier" schools. Well, I came from what was considered a second tier place and perhaps a so-called second tier school, but it was that perception, I think, that gave me the guts to boot-strap myself into my own place of confidence. And the lesson for me was the very strong belief that people start with stereotypes and biases, and pretty soon they have to come down to dealing with the individual. It takes a while, but we do. We all do. I know I did at IIT and later when I began to learn about how Americans really are. We start with the stereotype and move to the individual man or woman.

Summing Up Life Lessons from Home

I sometimes ask myself, why do we come to be the way we are? It's not just how we were brought up, because our genes and life experience play a role. But these cultural, biological, and experiential influences certainly give us "life pushes." My experience and upbringing have given me a couple of things that have allowed me to pursue life on my own terms. One is the sense of freedom to do what's right and not compromise. I've tried to be responsible, to be fair, to be objective, and not to disappoint others. These character traits go back to the value system that my mother and father gave us—*you* are responsible for your actions and your successes. And second, accepting failure is not an option. You've got to keep trying. It doesn't mean you don't ever fail or you don't learn from failure, but from a very early age, I had a very clear idea about how I was to be measured and how important it was not to let people, or myself, down. That value system has given me a benchmark and a bar to guide my actions.

One of our most important family values was respect for those less fortunate. In India it is very easy to pre-judge someone on the basis of their class or caste. In our home, however, we were taught to be respectful of everyone, regardless of whether he or she was the janitor, domestic help, or somebody who was in a different economic stratum. When I see someone being emotionally abused, whether personally or professionally, it infuriates me, perhaps because I come from a culture where it is still not uncommon to see such treatment of others. When I was growing up in India, people in the lower job ranks or economic strata were treated like human detritus. It was disgraceful. I abhor the fact that people who are doing everyday jobs to make life convenient for other, more fortunate people, are sometimes patronized by their supervisors. I cringe when I see it. So my parents' view of basic human respect as a core value was something really unique. I don't know where my parents got it or how the two of them came to it, but they passed it along to us, and we did the same with our children.

High expectations among Indian families is a key trait. And what I am referring to is the concept of *implied* expectations. Each one of my family who grew up in India was expected by implication to do better than the sibling who preceded him or her, and I think much of what we all did was set by our parents' example, how hard they worked. We knew who the achievers were, but it wasn't as though if you didn't do well in your semester you were grounded or forced to study harder. We watched our siblings: I mentioned my older sister's challenges and the career she carved out for herself. She worked hard, so I worked hard. I worked hard, so my brother worked hard and succeeded in his own way, and so on. The other thing our parents gave us was frequent examples of their peers' kids who were doing well and vice versa. Indian parents love to brag to their friends about their children's accomplishments. It was no different in our family at home.

The underlying drivers of this inherent expectation trait were 1) hard work; 2) honesty; and 3) not worrying about the consequences. Our parents' basic belief was that things will fall into place if you adopt those three ideals. Indians' parenting style is often compared with the Koreans and Chinese, whose parenting style was made famous by Amy Chua's book, *Battle Hymn of the Tiger Mother* (2011), about how she constantly drove her two Chinese daughters to shine academically and professionally. That may be the extreme, but Indians, especially the middle class families I grew up with, know that the only ticket to having a decent life is academic excellence. So they place an enormous amount of emphasis on kids' doing well in school. And yes, many would pound on the table and make sure their children were working X hours a day, doing all kinds of extracurricular activities, special projects, and lots of AP courses. It's probably not as intense as in some Asian cultures, but I would say that the first generation Indians in America probably had the same upbringing. Hence, most of the engineers who came here wanted their kids to be doctors because that was a more lucrative profession. Pressure was something I felt growing up but tried to moderate as a parent with my two daughters.

But what I seem also to have received from my mother, and my father, is a reluctance to express affection, as I mentioned earlier. It has been a costly omission, and one that I still struggle with. It has prevented me from having a closer relationship with my siblings and is something I am still working on as I try to be a better husband, parent, and now grandfather.

I was saddled with a couple of inhibiting complexes, as well. My brother was a lot taller than I was, had a fairer complexion, and was much better looking. I also had a lot of facial hair that grew quickly, and so I started shaving early, making me look much older than I was. These things put a brake on my behavior in terms of how I thought of myself, at least socially, and how I might appear to the opposite sex. I overcame most of these feelings eventually, but they clearly shaped my adolescence and self-image.

When I look back at my childhood, it is my parents who stand out and whom I miss the most. They were indeed God's lieutenants to me—and I am attached to them now perhaps more than I was then. I never wanted to let them down and I have both of them in my heart to this day.

My Brother and Sisters and What They Became

I don't ever remember being sick as a child or my brother or sisters being unhealthy for any reason, at least not while they were growing up. My adult brother, however, suffers from diabetes and has had several heart attacks, one that almost killed him. Despite these health setbacks, even today he remains positive in his outlook, almost incredibly so. He's my hero in a way and someone who was in my thoughts when I went through my own bout with prostate cancer a few years ago. He has my mother's resilience.

I'll tell you why.

I mentioned that in my father's plans, my brother was anointed to be a high level administrator. A year after I entered IIT, my brother was ready for college. My parents said in order for him to prepare for the competitive exam, he should go to Mayo Hostel at Allahabad University because it has the best record of getting its students selected. Arvind had other ideas.

The problem was that my brother Arvind liked the "good life." He was probably smarter than I was, but he started smoking in his teens, partying at school, and after one year at Allahabad, he was flunking his subjects, even before he got to the competitive exam. My mother was furious. She yanked him out of school and had him enter engineering school so he could study mechanical engineering. But just before he was to finish, a navy recruiter came by offering a position in the Indian navy. Part of the deal meant getting a significant stipend, just like ROTC. This had great appeal for young Arvind, and he jumped at it without letting my parents know.

It worked out well, all things considered, but not immediately. Arvind happened to be a lover of good food, let his weight get the best of him, continued smoking, and then had a massive heart attack in his 30s. But Arvind wasn't finished with either life, risk-taking, or shocks. About two years later, he turned his life around. He left the navy because his career kind of stalled, but while he was there, he got his MBA from a good school in Mumbai, started a machine shop, and then moved on to working for a company making bicycle parts. During that time, he traveled all over the world—China, Taiwan, Mexico, U.S., Europe—representing other manufacturers in India, despite his heart problem and even a stroke. Arvind was both a risk-taker and a survivor.

Arvind also taught at a graduate business school for a couple of years. While there, he was shattered by the experience of two burglars breaking into his house, threatening him at gunpoint, and taking all his valuables. He then moved and for six years became an administrator at a boarding school, managing about 1,000 students between the ages of 8-18. He's now retired, living with his wife in a spacious apartment, and enjoying life. When I look at him and his life, I can only think of the path not taken and Arvind's resilience, despite all the risks and pitfalls he endured. He's a happy man. Even with his multiple careers and myriad health issues, he never stopped doing what he wanted. He's a very tough and spirited guy, much more so than I. I think he gets it from my mother. But my sisters have it, too. All of them. Though each bowed to my mother's wishes and married early, they later on continued their educations.

I described the life-changing experience my sister Pramila went through by abiding by my mother's directive that she be married by age 20 and the humiliation I felt her endure each time a boy came over to "see the girl." Not only did she feel acute embarrassment, but also she had to delay and ultimately sacrifice her first love—medicine. Pramila's youthful plight, as I mentioned, has had a profound effect on my own life and the belief I have held ever afterward that people should be treated with the respect they deserve. My sister ultimately prevailed, after much soul-searching and because of her resiliency, but she is not a physician, a dream that she always had along with the personal skills to have made it come true. Pramila earned a Ph.D. in botany and has accomplished a great deal despite my mother's mandate. She became a professor at a major agricultural university. Now in retirement, she still teaches and has started a bio-agro business. She was and is a brilliant woman, but she paid a very high price for not being a man, including giving up her dream of becoming a medical doctor.

Indu got her master's degree in physics, but she also has a career as an artist and, interestingly, a chicken farmer for the last 15 years. Indu is probably one of the most cheerful persons I know. When Indu grew up, she married a man who, like my brother, also joined the Indian navy, so his career has meant he was away for long stretches of time. That left Indu to raise the family and to maintain family relationships, as well as tend to her business. Indu's life has had a lot of similarities to my mother's—a husband who was away a lot and being the disciplinarian of the family. So as she was raising her two children, she called on many of the traits that she had seen in my mother. Her husband is retired now and home, but Indu has thrived in and maintained the independence gleaned from her childhood and family life, becoming another of the Guptas who had multiple careers. Resiliency takes many forms.

Sujata was a science teacher with a master's degree in education and the sciences. She was diagnosed with diabetes when she was in her 20s and, despite her health issues, remains incredibly positive and resilient—a trait, perhaps, she got from her mother.

Aparna is an IT expert who worked all of her career with the state of Michigan, and still lives there. She has faced a major setback. Just five years ago in 2010, she lost her 24-year-old son in a car accident. As devastating as losing a child is, she persevered. She is moving on with her life and trying not to let the death of her son push her off the tracks. I think that resiliency in the face of adversity really comes from our parents—dealing with what's in front of you as it comes and moving on. Aparna shares this trait.

So we are all partly the products of our environment—how we are raised, the interactions we have with our friends, our parents, our siblings, our teachers, and the observations we make of how our world works and our place in it. I believe it is those experiences that become the strands in our own unique biographical fabric and, depending on talent, luck, and the fortitude that we have within ourselves, they allow us to achieve the goals and aspirations we set for ourselves. But family, I think, is the wellspring of much of what we become in later life and molds the early impressions that comprise the little voices that point us in one direction or tell us to beware of another, all combining to form the foundation of later life, underlying the meaning of Wordsworth's observation that "the child is father to the man." It certainly was true in my own life.

2

THE PULL OF AMERICA AND THE LURE OF THE AMERICAN DREAM

"All our dreams can come true—if we have the courage to pursue them."
—Walt Disney, entrepreneur, animator, and dreamer

At IIT I started to form a life plan, at least a general outline. Coming to America to study had always been one of my missions, and that probably goes back to even my early teen years. Now whether this desire developed because of Hollywood movies or it came from all the famous universities we heard about—MIT, Harvard, others —I don't know. I just knew I wanted to come to America. It may sound odd to an American, but remember, I saw America from another world, another civilization, another culture, and the contrasts I saw had a huge impact on me and what I thought that meant for everything else, including my own future. A telling anecdote is that going back to the early 1960s, the U.S. mail carrier delivered letters driving a car, or at least many of them did in suburban and rural areas, as they still do. In India there were engineers who worked their whole lives and couldn't afford a car. So to me as a young Indian boy or young man, this perception of prosperity had a huge influence, not to mention other things I saw watching American movies about what life was like, or at least what was portrayed as American life.

Then there was the lure of a fine education, because historically in India, education was *the* credential Indians needed in order to help bridge the gap with the English colonizers. It was the Indians' ticket out of a humdrum life and into a life affording great opportunity and advancement. So MIT, Stanford, Berkeley—the marquee universities to which Indians aspired, especially if you went to IIT—were viewed as tickets to a better life, the places where those who graduated at the top at IIT got scholarships.

And that was part of the fascination of going to IIT as opposed to other schools that were closer to my home. There, I was in India's own melting pot—a European past, Hindu and Muslim religions that lived side by side but saw the world differently, and an intensively competitive generation of young men my age who wanted to get ahead and be proud for themselves, their families, and their country. I was no different in that way except that I wanted to come to America because of its great promise, what it stood for, and the fact that it could offer that promise to anyone—to me—regardless of where I was born, who my parents were, or the color of my skin, which was brown. In fact, I remember writing in my notebook when I was 17 and 18 years old that I would get an M.S. and Ph.D. from America, and then become an assistant and associate professor at IIT.

That was the life I had dreamed. That's what I wanted. I didn't come from a family that owned or worked in a business. I came from a family of professionals—my father and my maternal grandfather were both engineers. Business was foreign to me.

These were the driving forces in my life—a middle class family, who had worked themselves up by earning professional degrees and positions, instilled in their children that same drive to get the best education they could and, through independence and hard work, make the most of themselves and in turn their own children. And America was for us, for me, and for millions of other Indians, the place where that could best happen.

The Decision Not to Be an Engineer

I knew I was going to finish my engineering degree at IIT, but I didn't know if I wanted to become an engineer. When I was about 18 years old, I was two years into engineering school while studying mechanical engineering. My first summer job after that second year was at a steel plant in eastern India. The temperature was 110 degrees. I was assigned to a blast furnace where I guess the temperature was 130 degrees. I was a student trainee, learning about how operations are, just being out there and walking around and talking to people, writing my reports, and I knew this wasn't my thing. It didn't get me particularly excited about being in manufacturing, or about being a mechanical engineer. I didn't see it as what I wanted to do or aspire to. So I gravitated towards operations research/industrial engineering, which is what brought me to Cornell. I had no idea what I wanted to be. I just knew that I didn't want to be mechanical engineer. But the decision not to be a mechanical engineer was most certainly borne of my field experience in the scorching eastern Indian summer.

What guided me towards operations research and industrial engineering was a professor I had at IIT. He was one of the few professors there who had published in the *American Journal of Operations Research and Industrial Engineering*, a very prestigious journal. Whichever graduate student was assigned to him was either the top one or two student in the class and would end up writing a paper with him for the *American Journal*. It was now the spring of 1967, my final year at IIT. I don't know the history precisely, but a few years earlier, there had been two or three students from IIT Mumbai who went to Cornell to get their master's in Operations Research and Industrial Engineering and then went on to get their Ph.Ds. I guess the head of the department at Cornell, Professor Bob Bechoffer, liked the quality of these students so much that he offered the top two or three from IIT, depending on the funding available, a scholarship to come to Cornell with a view that some of them might quit after the master's degree and others would go on to earn their Ph.Ds. As an academic, he wanted people to earn their doctorates. That was his mission and one very typical of grad school professors. Operations research was an emerging field. I thought if I wanted to do a Ph.D., then I had a pathway into Cornell. It would be my ticket to getting a Ph.D. in a subject I liked and an opportunity to come back to teach that subject in India. I finished second in my class of 60 in mechanical engineering and along with one other classmate was offered Cornell admission and a fellowship. But something unexpected happened. We were supposed to

28

come to Cornell in the fall of 1967, a couple of months after graduation, but for whatever reason—Cornell ran out of funding or they offered too many grants or fellowships to students, I don't know—both of us received a letter asking us if they could defer our start date to the spring of 1968 instead of the fall of 1967.

The deferment was a bit of a disappointment, but it was kind of a Hobson's choice for me. My parents didn't have the money to finance even one semester of my education. They said they had to borrow money to buy my ticket to the U.S. and could not do more. Cornell said I could come if I could fund myself, but I couldn't. So I just deferred matriculation. I now had no job and six months to kill. My professor at IIT knew about this and invited me to come to IIT and be his teaching assistant. I thought that would be better than just twiddling my thumbs, and it was. It turned out to be a great experience and a management lesson at the same time.

I lived in the staff quarters, which made it possible to get to know a lot of the faculty who had taught me. My former professor assigned me to teach the same class that I had taken before graduation. That meant that all of the younger guys who had been my *friends* when I was a student were now my *students*, and they didn't let me forget it. Since they knew my personal traits and were basically my age, they would sit in the back of the room and kind of giggle and make faces. That was a distraction, but I survived and even enjoyed it. Academically, it turned out well because I was fresh out of school, so I knew my stuff. But I learned a lesson in dealing with students who were my friends as well as my peers. It's very difficult to be both, and it's better to err on the side of professionalism rather than friendship. As students, they were there to learn, and as a teacher, I was there to teach. I couldn't blur the lines.

When the time came to start at Cornell in late January 1968, I was ready. What I didn't realize was what lay ahead of me.

$8.00 and a Bride

One challenge for emigrating Indians was India's currency law. Indians were allowed to take only $8.00 of foreign exchange out of the country, so I had to arrange that with the Reserve Bank of India. I also had to get a visa to enter the United States. And I needed a passport. So in December 1967, during the semester break, I was visiting my family to get my passport, my visa, and my eight U.S. dollars. I remember in the middle of one afternoon, my mother received a phone call from a family acquaintance who said, "We understand Raj is at home. We would like you to consider our daughter, Kamla, for Raj to marry."

Wow. I had only two days left before going back to Mumbai and my teaching job. Picture this: I'm out on the lawn. The sun is out. The weather's beautiful. I'm a 22-year-old kid on a holiday break. And my mother asks if I'm ready to get married. "No," I said, but I will do whatever she thinks is right, I tell her. "What should we say?" she asks. I ask myself, "Yeah, right, what do I say—their obedient son?" So my mother called back and she said, "Yes, my son will come for a visit." Kamla's parents lived about 100 miles away. And Kamla's father said, "Come tomorrow and we will have a little ring ceremony."

By the way, my mother had not even met my future wife, although my sister had. I had seen her picture, but she had not seen mine, even though Kamla's older sister and my sisters were neighbors and friends in a city completely different from where I was living. And so they had gotten together to meet Kamla with the possibility of my marriage to Kamla in mind, I'm told. It's complicated, I know. Anyway, the family agreed, and the following day when we went to her house, I gave Kamla an engagement ring.

I was very shy. Kamla probably thought I was too shy. We had the ring ceremony. We had a little dinner and my parents and I returned home. Everything was the same except that I was now engaged. A ring ceremony is not like an American engagement party or wedding. It's very informal and understated, unlike an Indian wedding which is very festive, extravagant, and hugely attended. I don't even think all of my sisters other than the ones who were staying at home were there for the engagement ceremony. There were her parents, her immediate family, some of my family, some extended family in the same city, altogether probably some 40-50 people, which is not a lot of people by Indian standards.

I still intended to go to the States and finish my master's degree and I thought I would then come back and get married. It was now the end of December or early January. I had to go back and finish my teaching, unwind my affairs in Mumbai, and get ready to fly to the U.S. on January 28 to start at Cornell, so I returned to IIT. I don't know what exactly happened between my parents and her parents, but they decided that I should get married before I left for Cornell. This was a time when there was no internet or cell phones, and long distance calls in India took days to connect, even from my parents' to Mumbai. They later claimed they had tried to reach me to tell me that I was getting married, but when I boarded the train on January 21, I had no clue. I knew only that I was going back home for the last time.

It was something like a 30-hour train ride from Mumbai to Delhi, where there are two stations, the old Delhi station and the new Delhi station. The trains stop at both stations. So I did what I would typically do and that was to get off at the first station, get on the bus, and travel to my parents' house 40 miles away.

Meanwhile, my family knew I was coming that day, so they had planned the wedding for that same day. They gathered all my sisters and everybody else, and they drove to the second station where, of course, they didn't find me. So they were in a little bit of a panic. They decided that there was nothing else for them to do but to go the town where Kamla's parents lived and see what would happen. This was over 47 years ago, mind you, and I remember it as though it were yesterday. Anyway, I did my usual thing and came to my parents' home. We had a guard and a housekeeper, and they looked at me as if I were a ghost. They had no idea I was coming, as they thought my parents would pick me up and we would go to the wedding that night. They told me what was going to happen that evening. So the first thing I did was take a shower, try to get my wits about me, and try to relax. Then I took the four-hour bus ride and arrived at Kamla's home at 5 o'clock, the time the ceremony was scheduled to start. Kamla's father was in even more of a panic than my parents or I were. But the ceremony was beautiful, and we were married. Four days later I was on my way to the U.S. to start my graduate studies and a new life. My wife came to New York six months later.

On the day I left for the U.S., the whole big extended family on both sides came to the airport. I don't know how many people, maybe 100, came to say goodbye. It was my first time ever on a plane. I flew from Delhi to Paris and after a couple of hours' layover at Charles De Gaulle, then on to JFK followed by a flight on Mohawk Airlines to Ithaca, NY, home of Cornell. I had a couple of suits, a few shirts, and my precious $8.00. I was supposed to be met at the Ithaca airport by my roommate, but he was not there because my flight had been delayed, so I had to take a cab to campus. The cab fare was $5.00! So I arrived with practically no money, but I had arrived safely to start my new life in America.

My wife and I had made a promise to each other that we would write a letter every day before she came. We did that just to get to know each other. This must sound strange to an American, but it's the way for many Indians who have arranged marriages. They may even be living in the same house, but they still need to get to know each other, literally. So for those first seven months, I would write Kamla about what I was doing, what school was like, what Ithaca was like (It was cold!), and what it was like having a roommate for the first time in my life and having to share an apartment with another person. When I say Ithaca was cold, it wasn't just cold, it was frigid. Upstate New York in the winter looks and feels desolate. The weather, when it isn't snowing, is oftentimes gray, and people scurry quickly in and out of their dorms to go to class or the library, and on weekends they try to have a little bit of social life. Like many of my fellow grad students, I was figuring out the study management part of my life and thinking about a summer job.

My first semester was pretty stressful because I was finding out that operations research, my major, was more challenging than I imagined. It was more abstract math and statistics than I had thought it would be. It was not that I couldn't cope with it, but it wasn't something that really excited me. I was a more practical person. Being away from home for the first time, I was also very uncertain about my future. I felt a need to be with my new wife, and we made arrangements that she would join me by the fall. And I was anxious about not having financial resources, so I needed a summer job to make some money, especially since I would have a wife to support when she arrived. So I was dealing with a general level of uncertainty that involved living in a totally different culture and by myself. Luckily, I had a great roommate, an Indian who had gone to IIT three years before me, who was very understanding. He even taught me how to cook. And he had a little VW bug that we drove to visit some

Indian friends of his, so that made a difference in my not feeling so cooped up and isolated.

But I did make some decisions that first semester. I knew I wasn't cut out to become an operations research expert. My heart wasn't in it. I would finish my master's degree, but I wouldn't go on for the Ph.D. I was glad I was there at Cornell, though, because I wanted to be the U.S. I wanted to be in a good university; I never doubted that. I just had to figure out what the next step was going to be. Meanwhile, I was interviewing for summer jobs on campus. And actually, as it turned out, I was able to land a job in New York City with St. Regis Paper Company, because my roommate had worked there and helped me through the interview process, which is made more difficult for Indian students on a student visa. I got the offer in April just before the start of summer. The job paid $600.00 a month, which was generous in those days. Then I had to find a place to live.

I had a friend who had just started his job with IBM and had been living with a roommate in New York and said I could live with the roommate. So I lived in the Bronx for three months with my friend's roommate, and it worked out fine. He introduced me to some of his friends, and the combination of working and saving allowed me to accumulate a nice nest egg of about $1000, which was a big deal then. Every day I went to work and came back to the apartment. That's all I did.

Meanwhile, Kamla had been going through her own travails. In April, while I was finishing my first semester and trying to get a summer job, Kamla's 46-year-old father died of a heart attack. Kamla and her eight brothers and sisters were suddenly without their father, and I couldn't even attend the funeral. I had no money to go to India and back to the U.S., but I knew how difficult it was for Kamla and her family. Then a few short months later, she left her family and came to a totally new country, new culture, new language to be with her new husband, a man she barely knew—a guy who felt he was in the wrong program and didn't know what he wanted to do with his life at that point. Talk about uncertainty. I was hardly a man with a plan.

Life in Upstate New York

If I felt culturally isolated, I can only imagine how Kamla must have felt. I met her at JFK airport, and I cooked our first dinner in my little New York apartment. Then the following day, a friend and his wife drove us from the Bronx to Cornell in Ithaca where we moved into a two-room apartment with a small bedroom, living room, bathroom, and tiny kitchenette. It was a big, big shock for Kamla, that's for sure. Welcome to America.

Kamla spoke practically no English, and she was very shy. She had lived in the same house in the same town all her life, so in Ithaca, a small town with a very big university on the outskirts, she had to find her way. This was fine until the weather turned cold, and Kamla was forced to deal with upstate New York's ice and snow. Not an easy transition for a woman who was from half a world away, and a hot world at that. It was even more unnerving for her when she tripped and fell on the ice several times. She must have felt as though she had moved to the North Pole—short days, cold nights, and snow everywhere. Not surprisingly, she cried a lot. It was not an easy life for her. We had a grocery store about half a mile from our apartment, and the only way we could get our groceries was to take the trolley from the apartment to the grocery store and back. That was our weekly shopping ritual on $8-$10 a week.

Yet, we were happy. Neither Kamla nor I ever thought of it as a hardship. We knew we didn't have much, but we also knew that we were going to live on whatever we had. And it wasn't going to be forever, we knew that. Soon after, two things happened. First, Kamla got a job as an Avon Lady. It wasn't a big success, but it was a job, and she learned English, a little bit about the ways of America, and certainly a little bit about the cosmetics business. The other event was that Kamla got pregnant, which meant that she couldn't keep working. It wasn't worth the risk, we said.

As for me, I was going along in my studies, doing maybe B+ work. That was a change for me because all my life I had been someone who placed at the top of his class. But for the first time in my life, I really couldn't get excited about my studies. I worked hard, mind you, and I knew I was going to finish my master's degree because I didn't want to let other people down. Not letting people down is a leitmotif in my life. I came to America to do this degree and now I was going to do it, but even so, I triggered a worry response that lasted for a very long time. It started with worrying about my and our security, having a new wife, and being in school at the time the baby was coming. And I had no health insurance since I was between being a student and starting a new job. I knew all the money I had saved from my summer job would have to go toward Kamla's childbirth. That was a precious $1,000, and 1969 wasn't the best time for looking for permanent jobs. Plus, I had only a student visa, not a permanent visa, so I needed a sponsor. In those days to get a permanent visa, you had to have a job and somebody to sponsor you. Neither was in ample supply.

I interviewed on campus with Xerox, Kodak, IBM, Burroughs, Scott Paper, and St. Regis Paper. In 1968 I ended up with five offers, really astounding in a way—an Indian getting job offers right out of grad school—one from IBM in Endicott, NY; from Burroughs in Detroit; Kodak in Rochester, NY; St. Regis in New York City, where I had worked in the summer; and Scott Paper in Philadelphia. This all happened three to four weeks before graduation. The positions were all in Operations Research/Computer Science because that was what my degree was in. Salary ranges were all between $12,000-$13,000 a year, but they were in different locations, and that affected my decision. I wanted a warmer climate than Ithaca's. My refusal of their offer didn't sit well with IBM, which, in Endicott, NY, was the computer titan that sold the System/360 series. They were highly offended by being refused by anybody. They made a barrage of phone calls to me, even sending questionnaires asking why I refused IBM's offer. Burroughs was the same way. It was hard for me to say no, but Kodak was more understanding, as was St. Regis.

I chose Scott Paper in Philadelphia for two reasons. First because Kamla was expecting and my uncle, my father's younger brother, was a professor at Villanova University, just outside Philadelphia. And second, Philadelphia's climate was a lot milder than Michigan's or upstate New York's or Manhattan's for that matter. Anyway, Philadelphia was the southern-most location. The big attraction for me to Scott Paper was that a new baby was coming and someone in the family was nearby. And, don't laugh—I didn't know how to drive a car! I always took a train, subway, or bus in America, or someone drove us. I did get my driver's license a few weeks before leaving Cornell. I could not afford the expense of driving lessons, but a friend of mine who had a car became my teacher.

My Career Begins: Scott Paper Company

We packed up our meager belongings, rented a car, and landed in Bryn Mawr, Pennsylvania, a suburb of Philadelphia, at my uncle's house. By that time, we had selected an apartment, as Scott Paper had flown Kamla and me to Philadelphia to do a house search. We had found an apartment in Ridley Park, west of Philadelphia and not far from Scott's headquarters in Chester, PA. I was on my way, I felt. I had a lot to be thankful for: I had learned a lot, I wasn't in debt, as were a lot of grad students after their schooling, and I had a good job and a loving wife. We stayed with my uncle for 2-3 days until we moved into the apartment and got busy with the usual things—buying new furniture, buying a car, and settling in. We bought everything on installment because the $1,000 I had in the bank was destined for Kamla and Amita, our first daughter. I was becoming an American in a hurry—I was buying on credit. I remember shopping at Levitt's furniture and for our first car, a 1969 Ford Falcon, bare bones with no air conditioning.

I commuted the five miles from our apartment to my job in Operations Research. We did a lot of production planning and scheduling as well as financial modeling. It was an exciting position, but more exciting was the birth of Amita Gupta on August 27, 1969, in Taylor Hospital in Ridley Park, PA. My life had changed dramatically—new baby, new job, and new location. In a way, the rush of all these new changes prepared us for our later life of living abroad and moving from place to place in different parts of the world.

It's interesting how our lives challenge us in different ways. For me, this was all something that seemed familiar in a way because my father was a civil engineer and we had moved every couple of years. I had lived in different houses, attended different schools, and then gone to college farther away before coming to the U.S. Kamla, on the other hand, had lived her first 19 years in the same house in a big family compound where everything was always the same, a stable environment for her. But, despite the difficulties of adjusting to life as the spouse of a graduate student, I think she was adaptable from the beginning, which was surprising to me then. If anything, she thrived on the challenges. She adjusted to life in the U.S. She learned English, she learned to drive, and she made new friends, at first Indian couples with young children like we had, and then others as our circle of acquaintances widened. Both of us, of course, were sometimes aware of living the "double life" as Indians and Americans.

Perhaps six months after starting at Scott, I decided I needed to complete my MBA if I was serious about a business career. I had gotten into financial modeling, working for the director of planning and strategy, Phil Lippincott, who later became Scott's CEO. Here again I was lucky. Phil became my mentor. As early as 1969 Phil was touting the advantages of computer modeling. He used to say: "We should be using computers to do financial simulation within the business, scheduling, production, marketing, and research." I also worked for a colleague named Ashok Bakhru who was Indian and who came from the same background as I did. He had been four years ahead of me at IIT, had gone to Cornell in the same program as I, and had worked for Western Electric for a few years, then Celanese Corporation, before joining Scott Paper as an Operations Research Manager. I was one of five people who reported to him, and we developed a friendship that has lasted over 45 years.

I followed up my plan to get an MBA by enrolling at Drexel University in Philadelphia. Kamla, for her part, enrolled in adult education and attended school one or two nights a week, as well, to learn accounting, bookkeeping, and English. We were a busy family with a newborn and lots of homework. Kamla and I had a very distinct division of responsibility from the beginning, and really right up till now. She basically ran the household, from managing all the everyday details to paying the bills. Even today she keeps our social calendar, communicates with our daughters, and manages the myriad responsibilities of running a home and the family network. Without her, I wouldn't have a clue. My responsibility was/is to work hard and provide the means of our support.

Time to Move — Already

Shortly after I arrived at Scott Paper I began to see storm clouds on the horizon. Scott's dominance and competitive advantage in paper goods and products was fast being lost to the likes of Kimberly-Clark (with better towels and tissues that were fast eating away at Scott's market) and Proctor & Gamble (with its iconic and vintage "please-don't-squeeze-the Charmin" ad as well as Pampers baby diapers). Because I was in strategic planning, I was able to see better or more vividly than others that Scott was going through significant turmoil. All of a sudden, this company that had had the world to its own with Scotties, Scott towels, Scott wipes, and other household staples, started to scramble. I was the new kid on the block, and so I became nervous. At that time, I thought, I would have been the first to be asked to leave, so I began to think about what I should do. Part of my consideration was the fear. Part of it was the insecurity. And part of it was my new family—I had a two-year-old baby. While there was no actual indication that my job was in jeopardy, I felt at risk. I needed to know or at least perceive that I had job security in order for me to perform at my best. I believed that security gave me independence, so it was a big deal. Never in my life did I want to be dependent on somebody and have to ask for help. It was something that harkened back to my own family values and what I saw happen when my father got sick.

Living within our means was a mantra in our family. So during my moments of uncertainty at Scott, I became concerned and thought I should make a move to a more secure company and employment, and I applied for and won an entry-level position at Rohm and Haas, a specialty chemicals company headquartered in Philadelphia. Over time, my anxious mindset paid its dividends, because my career move allowed me to make choices that were balanced and right choices instead of choices based in fear. As I grew older, job security helped me to be much more independent and objective in my thinking and in my relationships, certainly as I moved up in my new corporate world.

But the Scott experience was not without its importance in my development, and when I think of my three or four real character-building experiences, I think about Phil Lippincott, former chairman and CEO of Scott Paper. When I was at Scott, Phil was a rising executive, and one from whom I learned a great deal. That was an impressionable period for me, very early in my career, my first job in America. Back in the early 1970s Phil was Director of Strategic Planning, not even a line role. And he was a very young man, mid-30s at that time, I think. I was really lucky to have exposure to somebody like him. In those days he was still a senior middle manager, but frankly you could see in the way he presented himself, the way he thought about issues, the way he communicated up and down the organization, that he was destined for bigger places. What struck me was the way he interacted with others, how he communicated with colleagues, how he presented himself, how he impacted others and was able to have an impact on the company at an early age.

The example that comes to mind was the time that Procter and Gamble bought Charmin. When Kimberly-Clark and Proctor and Gamble launched new baby diapers (Pampers), Scott Paper, who had been king of the hill, I would say, was lost. It had been an enormously successful company, but all of a sudden it saw goliaths coming into the business with product innovation and resources and shelf space control that Scott did not have.

Phil was the calming voice in those days. He didn't panic. He thought beyond the immediate, about things that Scott should do such as altering its portfolio by pruning poorly performing products, investing in the four-or-so brands that sold well, and working on quality. To me, he was the voice of reason in what I would say was a chaotic period in Scott's history. One of the things I learned from Phil was to remain calm under stress and pressure. He was unique in that he really had a sense of not getting bound up in the immediate crisis but thinking beyond that, and then he also had the ability to articulate and communicate and convince others that thinking beyond represented the path forward. Crisis always comes to the CEO. It's the ones who are ready for it and can see beyond it who keep their companies viable.

Phil's calm demeanor was not lost on his superiors, so when he presented to the senior management and the board, he knew he had the ears of the CEO, and because of that, his peers also listened to him. He had an enormous impact without having authority.

I think the second thing which was salient about the Scott experience was another boss, Ashok Bakrhu. He came in as my boss with a very similar track as mine, five years at IIT and two years at Cornell. I would say in retrospect, he probably had a lot of influence and people perceived it. What I took from Ashok was that people with his background—my background—can move up in this culture. He continued to do very well and rose to be Scott's CFO. He had a superb intuition about things and how they work, and he experienced more of corporate America in very senior positions than I did before becoming CEO of Rohm and Haas. He was, in a very informal way, a kind of counselor to me, a relationship that came about because we would play tennis together every couple of weeks and have dinner occasionally. Conversation always centered around his experiences, my experiences, what works, how to react in contentious situations, and how to get things done. He had, without being explicitly so designated, become a mentor in the sense of being somebody to whom I could relate, who had experience and success in this environment and was willing to share his experiences. I acknowledge that I have often said one needs to be mentored by those in the mainstream of the culture one is working in. That is true. One needs both, in fact. One is the touchstone of the other, in my experience. The point is not to bind yourself with others who are just like yourself, but be diverse in your relationships, including those with both mentors and protégés.

This raises another important issue—having a life plan or life goal. I had had one that changed when I enrolled at Cornell and didn't find operations research exciting and decided instead to pursue a career in business. My next plan was, "I will get a job, earn a certain amount of money, and then we'll go back to India." But that changed as well. Kamla and I fell in love with America and with our own American dream for what it could mean for us and our new family.

And—and this is important—I never built my career or conducted my career with the idea that I wanted to be a CEO. Many of my peers and colleagues did, and I don't fault them for it. But I didn't. I didn't have a life plan in that sense. What guided my career was the process of taking advantages of the opportunities that came my way, observing the shortcomings or lessons where either I failed or others did and understanding why, and building on the relationships and positive experiences I had in order to gain more opportunity—for myself, yes, but more specifically for the company, because I knew if the company was successful, I would be successful. That's how I conducted my career, and it goes back to my family's values, including those of my father, who never took a bribe, my mother, who made us empty out our school bags each day after school to keep us honest and independent, and the professionalism and hard work my father exhibited as a civil engineer.

And, I was indebted to Scott's Phil Lippincott and Ashok Bakrhu, who had knowingly and unknowingly served as my first mentors in America. My decision to accept the position at Rohm and Haas was made by a Raj much better prepared to meet the future. And it was the right decision.

PART II

My Career at Rohm and Haas

3

On the Way to CEO

"What you want in a mentor is someone who truly cares for you and who will look after your interests and not just their own. When you do come across the right person to mentor you, start by showing them that the time they spend with you is worthwhile."
—Vivek Wadwha, technology entrepreneur and academic

Game Changers and Lessons Learned

The Fibers Business Disaster of 1975

One of the first major game changers I encountered at Rohm and Haas was already developing by the time I joined the company.

In the 1960s, Rohm and Haas had been the primary producer of Plexiglas® as well as offering a successful and highly profitable product portfolio consisting of coatings, paper, leather, textile, and agricultural chemicals. The expansion into fibers was motivated by the fear that one of the large chemical companies would challenge the company's so-called "acrylic backbone" and erode its profitability and viability by competitive onslaughts in the Plexiglas® and acrylic emulsion markets where Rohm and Haas was a recognized global leader. So Vince Gregory, the CEO at the time, embarked on a diversification strategy into what he believed was the highly profitable business of synthetic polyester fibers. This was a market that DuPont, ICI, Hoechst, Celanese, and Monsanto dominated but that

Rohm and Haas believed it could enter profitably and successfully, even in a crowded field, through its time-tested approach of adding high value to a product and gaining market share and niche status. Customers had always been glad to pay the extra price for the higher-value-added component.

The key players, along with Vince Gregory, the chairman and CEO whose responsibility it was to guide the organization into markets with significant growth potential for the company, were Larry Wilson, the CFO at the time, and Jack Doyle, then head of the fibers business. Larry and Jack were very balanced men, but more importantly, they produced a calming effect that allowed Vince Gregory to function in a way that guided the company between the shoals that could have sunk us. And the leadership quality that Vince Gregory brought was his capacity to listen to wise counsel—to Wilson and Doyle in particular. I know this because I saw them in action.

Fibers was a different kind of business for Rohm and Haas. It was highly dependent on oil because synthetic fibers are petrochemical-based and in addition, it was not a market segment in which we had a lot of experience, so we didn't know the chemistry as well as the market leaders did. And finally, it included consumers we neither knew nor had done a lot of research on—the women's apparel market—so there were a lot of unknowns. Still, the company believed it could carve out a successful niche and bolster an already profitable product portfolio. So fibers, along with a new health division, were launched in the early 1960s at great cost, burdening the newly-public company with its first-ever significant debt.

The perfect storm began in 1974 when the price of oil quadrupled almost overnight to $8.00 a barrel from $2.00. Second, Rohm and Haas's model of adding value and charging premium prices backfired. The new synthetic fiber that was supposed to give fabrics added stretch without altering their appearance cost 20 percent to 30 percent more than the spandex and Lycra consumers had come to love. And third, women and the women's wear market were abandoning girdles and other undergarments that were a major market for stretch fabrics in the late 1960s and early 1970s. So from 1974 to 1975 we went from having a record year to near disaster. We had had big plans in '74. Now we went from proclaiming "We are going to do this, and we are going to do that" to reporting our first loss as a public company in 1975. Demand for Rohm and Haas fibers just disappeared totally.

When we realized that the fibers business was in deep trouble, hemorrhaging money and market share almost overnight because of the rising price of oil and the competitive pressures of the aforementioned leaders in that business, we knew we had to exit as fast as we could. We went on weeklong trips to make a deal to sell our fibers division to Monsanto in St. Louis, and then to Chevron in San Francisco because we thought Chevron was considering a better offer. We had invested $200 million in the fibers business and were looking at a $65 million offer from Monsanto and hoping we could do better with Chevron. Chevron, it turned out, had no interest in buying the business, so we flew back to St. Louis to accept the Monsanto offer. Meanwhile, Monsanto had discovered that we were shopping the business, so they had reduced their offering price by 20 percent by the time we came back. I was able to witness all these machinations in trying to unburden a bad business, or a business we shouldn't have been in to start with.

I knew all this would have a lasting impact on me personally because it nearly sank the company (we were only an $800 million revenue company to begin with back then, and health and fibers was a significant chunk of that). In addition, the uncertainty inherent in all business acquisitions or ventures involves a risk that would be repeated time and again, no matter where I went, or, more importantly, if I were going to be a in position at Rohm and Haas to be making similar decisions some day.

Lessons from the Fibers Crisis

The "perfect storm" scenario in which our fibers market disappeared almost overnight taught me that sometimes there are going to be instances where an event, through no fault, cause, or response on your part, could basically sink the company. It would be like the Titanic—the iceberg that was never seen, that didn't appear on any navigation maps—or a storm that came out of nowhere. Yet its catastrophic potential was as great or greater than anything the company might have done or allowed to happen to injure itself. I learned that you can't control everything no matter how good your planning might be or how smart you think you are, that the unexpected happens, and that you have to react to it. And excuses don't make it go away. You can't say it wasn't your fault or that everyone else is having the same problem or there's nothing you can do. You have to guide your own ship and keep your passengers safe.

If you are a leader in the marketplace who thinks you know it all, you will make decisions that can have untoward consequences for the company or worse, lead to bet-the-farm consequences, and this is what the decision to enter the fibers business really did for us. Then when the worst happens, sometimes leaders under stress isolate themselves as opposed to becoming more inclusive, and I think when you are in crisis mode, it's extremely important to be inclusive and listen to different perspectives. While walking the tightrope that the fibers business became, Vince Gregory was a listener, trusting that his key personnel had ideas to contribute. In this situation, on one hand, you want to be perceived as being in charge, so you want to be decisive, but on the other, you don't want to be running off with a plan that isn't well thought out, rational, or inclusive. You have good people around you because you trust their judgment, so you owe it to them, to the company, and to yourself to listen to their counsel. In the end, of course, you have to decide and live with your decision. That's why life lessons, as well as character, are so important. In our case, Vince listened to the wise counsel offered to him and we survived.

But each crisis is different. A scandal that hits the company has to be dealt with immediately and without undue hesitation. A reputation issue has to be dealt with from the standpoint of recognizing the issue, accepting blame or the consequences, apologizing, taking corrective action, and then mapping out a strategy to stakeholders that commits the company to doing the right thing going forward. Other crises, such as a huge market downturn or collapse of prices, need a version of that and then a clear plan to move forward—whether it be divestiture, reorganizing the business, changing market focus, or combining with another company to achieve some synergy not available before. A large part of the success is in how well the CEO manages his or her own decision-making, including uncertainty and even ambiguity as to the eventual outcome.

These were lessons top management learned, as well, from the Fibers Division crisis. From the period 1977 on, the company re-built itself.

When the crisis subsided, we did a lot of rationalization of capacities and keeping costs in mind, and we became profitable again. We focused on our RONA, the return on net assets. We needed metrics we could use and that would give us a way of calculating and keeping us on track. All of a sudden, in the wake of a near-death experience, the value of return on capital was a lever by which we could see our way forward in a way that made financial and strategic sense. We were becoming a global company in need of more sophisticated planning and financial systems, and in that realm, the cash flow sheet was king. No more could it be just growth, growth, growth. Growth had to be managed; growth had to be profitable; growth had to be smart.

We asked Fred Shaffer, former CFO of Rohm and Haas, to share his recollections of the fibers crisis. His remarks appear in the shaded text, below.

The Burning Platform

Fred Shaffer, former CFO:

Raj learned a lot from the fibers crisis. It became almost a burning platform for him, in terms of what he saw: how Vince reacted, what Larry brought to the process, and the lesson of maintaining steadfastness of purpose, and clarity of vision, when it would have been easy to run in all directions. It had been a perfect storm of what I believe was a bad business decision to start with, because we had no product knowledge, and a macroeconomic event that had a domino effect. When the oil crisis hit in the early to mid-1970s and the bottom dropped out of the nylon textile business, a business that basically DuPont invented and that we knew nothing about, we were on course for a Titanic-type scenario.

I've learned that what makes a project work and what doesn't can be boiled down to three factors: 1) knowledge of the market; 2) knowledge of the product; and 3) knowledge of the process. When you know all three, you'll probably do better than you expected; if you know two of the three, you have some chance; when you know one of the three, you have no chance. When you don't know any of the three, you're absolutely dead. Rohm and Haas was in category three. We knew nothing about the market or the product. And it showed.

> After trying to use our polymer technology for a rubberized textile that was quickly pushed aside by the introduction of Lycra and spandex, Rohm and Haas turned to denier nylon and then denier polyester, two forms of tougher material that had a broad range of applications. A plant was built in North Carolina that ended up costing over twice as much to construct as the original estimate, and by the time it was up and running the price of textile denier nylon had dropped from $2 a pound to $1. The company kept pouring money into the business hoping to resuscitate it but, aside from a few good quarters, the failures and losses continued to mount until the oil crisis hit and the company was forced to sell the plant it had built and the business and market to Monsanto in 1977. It was like pouring gasoline on a raging fire. The write-down and operating loss in fibers, which totaled $58.8 million, exceeded earnings of all the company's other divisions by $11.8 million, causing Rohm and Haas to report its first operating loss in history.
>
> Raj closely watched the event and absorbed its lessons. It burned into his mind the need for equanimity in the face of crisis and never betting the ranch on one thing or putting so much investment capital into a technology or business Rohm and Haas didn't know. While he was always open to new and innovative technology that promised growth and profits, he moved carefully and prudently. He used the lessons of the fiber crisis when he faced the setbacks of the Morton acquisition and the tough times that followed.
>
> And the other lesson he learned is the importance of cash. Cash is king in a crisis. Raj never wanted Rohm and Haas to run out of cash or even be close.

The CME Tragedy

Another game-changing event that I witnessed early in my career was the tragedy involving bis-CME and CME, two components used in the making of ion exchange resins, tiny plasticized pellets that were used to purify water by chemically removing impurities. What was not known to the company as we developed the ion exchange manufacturing process was that one of the reactants, bis-CME (di-chloromethylated ether) was a lung carcinogen. Workers who made this product inhaled the compound and later developed oat cell lung cancer—a debilitating and deadly cancer.

The deaths of over 70 employees at our Philadelphia plant beginning in the 1970s paralyzed the company. Nothing like this had ever happened before and, quite candidly, the company did not act quickly enough, in my opinion. Mr. Otto Haas had always put Rohm and Haas employees first, and when this tragedy happened, the family, the company, and our employees were devastated. The *Philadelphia Inquirer* article that first chronicled the tragedy in "54 Who Died" on October 26, 1975, became required reading by the director of public relations, John McKeogh, for whom the event became *the* teaching moment for the company, as it did for the Haas family and others, including myself.

Lessons from the CME Tragedy

Once the cause/effect of the worker fatalities was clearly delineated and a process put in place for sealing the system, treating affected employees, and dealing with their families, the company vowed never again to put its workers in such a health-risking situation. As part of that effort, our Employee Health & Safety (EH&S) Department initiated vigilance and scope on a scale that led the industry. From that point forward, worker health surveillance, regular epidemiological studies and a host of other safeguards, precautions, and health and safety regulations were instituted by a staff headed by Dr. Phil Lewis, an occupational health physician and expert in public health, and Ph.D. epidemiologist, Dr. Arvind Carpenter, brought in from the National Institutes of Health, as well as other physicians and industrial hygienists. We learned not only about health and safety but also about the importance of knowing what we don't know, preventive health safeguards, employee surveillance, process safety, and finally, crisis communications.

In a situation like CME, what you say, how you say it, and when you say it become very important, not just to the media, but to all your stakeholders. It's a delicate balance, a sometimes elegant dance, a heart-to-heart talk, and a high-wire act all at the same time. It's not something you can just delegate to someone else, but at the same time, the CEO can't micromanage the process. It comes down to, in my opinion, trust in your advisors, your employees, customers, the media, and most importantly, confidence in yourself and your instincts. That includes having crisis communications and risk management training and precautions as part of your company's preparedness. The best crisis management is preventive management, but when that isn't good enough, honesty, transparency, rapid response, and caring are the antidote to bad news or a crisis. The slow tick-tock of some companies that seek to hide behind bureaucracy and artfully worded PR statements delude themselves and the public that they are truth-telling or honest. It is better to err on the side of openness and transparency than secrecy and obfuscation.

Long before the crisis occurs, any CEO or student of business needs to make plans regarding:

- How do you react under the stress of managing in a crisis when some of the statements of the press are going to be incomplete, under-reported, wrong, slated against you, or personally hurtful? The media isn't your PR Department.
- What are you going to say to your employees and when?
- Who is going to be talking to your customers?
- How do you communicate with the families and reach out to them in ways appropriate to their needs and feelings?
- How are you going to do all this when you're not even sure of what caused the event or what else may yet happen?

Every stakeholder has a right to know what is happening and what you are doing about it, but you don't want to scare people unnecessarily.

I don't have a cookbook answer to these questions and issues. But I would say, first, be a human being. React as someone who is what you are expected to be: a law-abiding corporate citizen, a good corporate neighbor, concerned about your employees, customers, community, and the environment, and one who accepts the obligations of operating safely and responsibly to your shareholders. If you start from there, my sense is you'll wind up in a good place. Those who think media training is the answer should be disabused of that idea as a silver bullet. People can tell who the executives are who have been media trained, and while I am a proponent of knowing how to deal with the media, particularly in view of the 24/7 news cycle, and the fact that social media is changing the playing field of media and the dialogue among companies, their customers, and the public, it is not enough to think there are clever responses to tough questions or recipes for disaster control or antidotes for abusive actions. In the end, there are only good, humane practices.

Personally, I would say that the CEO needs to do several things when a crisis befalls a company. He or she needs to state the facts as they are known, calmly and forthrightly, and outline the plan forward to address the issue(s). Hoping the situation blows over can be not only costly to your ability to maintain control over the story, but also hugely damaging to your company's reputation. You can always say you don't have all the information, but you can't stonewall and hope the information doesn't get revealed, because it will. I am reminded of the comment by Rupert Murdoch following his testimony to Parliament at the Leveson Inquiry in 2012 about the phone hacking scandal that enveloped The News Corporation: "Failure to maintain ethical standards can be immensely expensive." He was speaking of both finance and reputation. These events can turn into an almost Shakespearean tragedy when a company makes an error in judgment.

The Importance of Mentoring

I offer a remark I made on my 25th anniversary with Rohm and Haas. We had a lunch in the corporate dining room, and I told the attendees, many of whom gave me help and advice along the way, "The best thing about this organization from my perspective is that when I started here, I felt like I didn't belong anywhere. You made me feel like I belong everywhere." An American wouldn't make a statement like that to an American audience. That goes to the heart of the matter here—both personally and professionally—Rohm and Haas made a huge difference in how I developed professionally over the course of 39 years and how I saw my adopted country over an even longer period.

Even though I was a mechanical engineer with an MBA and did not have specific training in finance or chemical engineering, I was always treated like I belonged there and more importantly never felt discriminated against or ignored when opportunities arose that fit my aptitude or expertise. It could have gone the other way but it didn't, and that's what I meant that day at my luncheon. It's something that is so much a part of how Rohm and Haas was, and it had a huge impact on my life and my family's. In many ways, it is hard to separate work experience and successes from the people who really made an impact. I had 17 bosses and 13 jobs at Rohm and Haas, and they all taught me something. Sometimes I lose sight of the fact that one does not have to travel a straight road to one's destination. There was no single role model I had to figure out how to fit into business.

A lot of my jobs were opportunities created either for me or by me. Each gave me the opportunity to work for very different characters on very different assignments. Each in its own way provided an experience that taught me to learn how to build relationships and earn the confidence of very, very different people. I say to people just starting out, "Don't think you need to know where you want to go or how you're going to get there. You need to learn from everyone you meet and to take every opportunity as something that gives you another clue or insight as to what you want to accomplish or achieve in your life." I always focused on the nature of the jobs I received, and the kinds of people with whom I interacted. They all left an indelible impression. Some were good, and some didn't really fit. But they all told me something of what I needed to know or would experience later. That was an asset in my own development and one I implore others, including Indian students, to internalize.

Mentor Fred Shaffer

I'll mention one individual in particular—Fred Shaffer—the man who recruited me to Rohm and Haas and who was my first boss. I was hired as a financial analyst, responsible for the analysis of the capital budget, preparing schedules for the board meetings, etc. First bosses are very important. It's like the old adage, "you don't get a second chance to make a first impression." First bosses are the first impression of the company and can be lasting ones. Good bosses tend to breed good employees and vice versa.

When I look back to those first years, I think there are two or three things about Fred which really stayed with me. One was his work ethic. I mean, this man worked every Saturday and Sunday. He didn't brook incompetency or sub-standard work. Occasionally he would get irritated when something didn't go right or someone didn't give him the right information he was asking for, but he was generally a pretty level-headed person. He had very high standards and was extremely bright. He was a history major at Duke, attended seminary at Yale and then went to Wharton because he wanted a career in business and finance. Talk about the spiritual and the temporal—this man knew both sides.

For some reason or other, and maybe he did this with many people, Fred took a strong interest in me. He not only recruited me, but also he gave me an extraordinary amount of freedom to learn and grow in what started as really an entry-level finance job.

Fred, as comptroller, was responsible for preparing all of the financial materials for the board meetings. As anyone knows, getting ready for a board meeting is like an army fort's getting ready for a visit from the commanding general. In addition, Rohm and Haas was largely family owned, and that meant F. Otto Haas, Jr., the founder's son, and to a lesser extent his younger brother, would be clambering all around. Fred, and I have no idea why to this day, allowed me direct access to the preparation process, sometimes even allowing me to be his substitute. This gave me—at the age of 25-26 and in my first job at the company—invaluable exposure to Rohm and Haas's highest executive ranks. Then he brought me to the attention of Larry Wilson, who was then the CFO. So my rapid moves through my first three bosses—the cash manager, a man by the name of George Wills, Fred Shaffer, and Larry Wilson, who was then treasurer, later CFO, and eventually CEO—were because of the incredible opportunities given to me, first by Fred Shaffer, and later by the others. They didn't put me in a corner or in a box.

Mentor Vince Gregory

I never believed in just accepting the status quo. A lot of times, you go into a job and you just want to do it the same way it's been done before, and there is no reason for it to be changed. Every position I've been in, however, I was always looking to see what we could do better. One was econometrics. Econometrics was big in the 1970s and 1980s when Wharton Econometrics was in its heyday. We would see what economic models could tell us about how to price our products, how to tie in commodity prices and supply chain management, economic forecasting, even product planning.

What we were able to do really got CFO Larry Wilson's attention and stimulated a lot of useful conversations and planning—first around the lunch table and then later at meetings, trying to apply the models to our business. These conversations, in turn, created new opportunities for me as we started to think about the company's longer-term plan, looking out five to six years, rather than just quarter by quarter. Thirty years ago, long-term planning was only beginning to take shape in companies. Quarteritis, sometimes referred to as quarterly capitalism, or short-termism, was the syndrome of the day, beginning in 1970 when the SEC forced public companies to report earnings on a quarterly basis, something that has grown into a "beat or miss" mentality, unfortunately, ever since and is, in my view, anathema to sustainable growth and the pressure on a CEO to produce.

But to his credit, CEO Vince Gregory had implemented strategic planning as part of the Rohm and Haas business plan in 1974, just three years after taking the helm and thus becoming the first non-Haas CEO since the company's founding in 1908. Vince believed his job was to think where this company should be heading. When Larry Wilson called me one day and said Vince would like to have lunch with me, I was flabbergasted. Vince Gregory was a larger-than-life kind of person. He could be intimidating, despite his compact size. Not only was he a graduate of both Princeton and Harvard Business School, but also he earned both his bachelor's degree and MBA in the same year. All this after having served as a fighter pilot during World War II. Talk about a high achiever! Not surprisingly, I was pretty nervous about the invitation. I went into

Vince's office and he said, without any small talk, "I want you to work for me." Then he told me to think about the offer and we'd figure out what the job would entail. When he saw my dumbfounded look, he said, "We've seen what you've done, and I really want to create a long-term vision plan for this company, and I want you to help me with that."

My job entailed helping him create that vision for what the company would look like in 1980, what I believe was the first-ever, 5-year plan at Rohm and Haas. A lot of my work was going out and asking people, who were running the business around the world and who had no idea who I was, about their growth assumptions, their forecasts, and the business outlook. The culmination of that was a big meeting in the Seaview Country Club near Atlantic City, New Jersey. There were about 300 senior managers from all over the world, the company's management in effect, and Vince asked me to present the plan.

Talk about being stressed out and not sleeping, worrying about standing before 300 of the company's top people in 1974! That was really being put to the test. They called me the voodoo guy. Small wonder I was going through panic attacks at home in the middle of the night and had gained so much weight. But I think that Seaview presentation was an important event in my career. It allowed me access, exposure, and to see and be involved with strategic planning. It was the first time a long-term plan had been offered at Rohm and Haas, something that I came to learn had to be part and parcel of executive management's obligation to the board and its shareholders, in addition to the rank and file of employees who steered the company on a day-to-day basis. Can you imagine a cruise ship or tanker not knowing where it wants to go? Similarly, where the company was going and how it is going to get there should be the first thing on any CEO's mind, for it will certainly be so on the minds of its board and investors. And if you don't have strategic vision, how can you can lead, inspire, and motivate your employees to deliver on their goals? This is what Vince Gregory taught me.

Vince Gregory was more than a mentor to me, he was a friend in the sense that he was willing to tell me things and give me advice that few others did or maybe felt they could. Here's a quick story to illustrate what I mean.

When the CFO of Rohm and Haas, Fred Shaffer, sent me to the U.K. to be the finance director in 1978, I was very reluctant to go. My life history up to that point had been quite successful. I knew I was reasonably intelligent and worked hard. My grades and academic achievements had always been high. But I always thought there were other elements at work in terms of how I thought of myself, perhaps based on the fact that I was an outsider, an Indian, who was trying to make it in America. That was a subconscious factor in how I went about my work and perhaps even my relationships at work. But I was fearful about going to the U.K., a nation which had ruled India in one form or another for 300 years, from the time Queen Elizabeth issued a charter to the East India Company in 1600, to the time when it became a British colony in the 19th century, to the time India finally became independent in 1947.

Quite frankly, I knew that if I turned down the assignment it would be a disappointment to those who were trying to help me in my career and to have me get more experience. Vince knew this and sat me down one day and said: "Raj, I think you have a good heart. You're a good person and a very competent professional. I know you have a lot on your mind and you're very worried about this assignment. I think you'll be fine. But give yourself six months. And if for some reason, it doesn't feel right, just give me a phone call and we'll bring you back." This assurance about giving the European assignment six months and knowing that I had a fallback that wasn't going to derail my career, or worse, put my family in jeopardy or in a hostile environment, was something that was of inestimable value to me. Vince had spoken from his experience of living in England with his English wife. He knew what the U.K. was like, and he could relate to what I had been feeling and fearing. His words quelled my fears but unfortunately did not put an end to the siege of anxiety episodes I had been experiencing for a while.

4

ANXIETY AND THE HIGH BAR OF
SELF-IMPOSED EXPECTATIONS

"The only way out is through."
—Robert Frost, poet

Defeating the Demon of Anxiety Attacks

The attacks first started with the Seaview experience. Barely three years into my tenure at the company, I was being showcased in front of the entire company leadership, and I didn't want to let them down. There was a lot to do, and I would say, "Oh, my God, how am I going to do it?" In those days, it wasn't that you could be at home and do your work. All of the equipment and the mainframe computers and calculators were in the office, and there were no PCs or smartphones. I used to have to go to the office between 4 and 5 a.m., just to make sure I got my work done and that it met the expectations of my superiors.

My weight had become a problem—I had ballooned to 192 pounds, far too much for a man of 5' 7" in height—and when I would worry, I would get heart palpitations, my hands and feet would perspire, and my blood pressure would skyrocket. I would be in a state of panic, and more times than I care to remember, Kamla would drag me to the hospital emergency room at odd hours of the night. They would give me some medicine, and I would calm down and then go home until the next episode. I knew I had to do something, so I started playing squash and lost the weight as starters in my self-care routine. It wasn't that hard to do because I had been physically active for most of my life. But the attacks continued.

Kamla was a real soul mate. I don't know what I would have done without her. By then we had two daughters. Amita was 5-years old and Vanita was just a year old, and Kamla would load both of them into the car and take me to the hospital. But the cause of the anxiety was not just Kamla and the girls. It was, I always thought, something else. So I knew I had to get to the bottom of this or I would be shackled by these attacks all my life.

I knew the attacks must be self-imposed, and I figured the initial cause was the pressure of work. My boss at Rohm and Haas set pretty high standards. I used to go to work almost every Saturday and work very late on the weekdays to show my superiors that they had good reason to put their faith in me and that I could live up to their expectations. It is hard to recall exactly what I was feeling at the time. It certainly wasn't pressure in the sense that I feared losing my job, but I must have internalized my superior's high expectations and the heavy demands they made on me to meet them, as well as the pressure I put on myself.

I also worried about what would happen to my family if something dire happened to me. We were in a foreign country with no immediate family, with no strong network of friends or financial security. It was nothing like the average American starting out might have, I thought. I took out life insurance. Still I asked myself what else could be causing this extreme reaction. I knew I wasn't the only guy in the world who had a young family, was just starting a job, and didn't have a big family network to take care of his family if something happened. So I went back into my own family history to see if there might be some answers there, and I glimpsed some insights.

Even as a nine-year-old, I had recognized the severe implications and grave possibilities related to my father's encephalitis. And I understood the impact this had on my mother, who, in order to care for him, even had to put her five older children in the care of aunts and uncles, while she stayed with my father and baby sister in the hospital. I realized that my fear of what might happen, of what she would or might have to do, and of what effect this might have on my father and our family had never really left me. The symptoms just did not become overt until I started shouldering the responsibilities of an adult, being a husband and father, knowing that if something bad happened to me, they would be in the same position my mother had been in.

Other events occurred. When I was in the U.S. during the fibers crisis in 1974-75, I felt the world was on my shoulders. I was the low man on the totem pole, trying to prove myself. Although I certainly didn't have the pressure these men at the top did, still I would go into panic modes at home.

Then in 1978 I got my first oversees assignment, to London, and the very first week we were in England, I had the same symptoms in the hotel room. Kamla took me to the emergency room just as before.

Several specific events seemed to trigger the attacks I experienced in London. Some events were due to my immediate superior in London, whose home was near where we were staying in the London suburb of Croydon. Every couple of weeks he would say, "Raj, I'm going to come down and spend Friday afternoon with you and then go home." As finance director for the U.K. company that Rohm and Haas owned that wasn't doing too well, I was anxious. It was another new and challenging job and another new culture, as well. I became paranoid whenever he would call and announce he was coming. I wouldn't sleep, thinking that I had to prepare for his visit. My obsessing about it would then trigger the symptoms, and then the attacks would start.

Finally I saw a doctor who put me on valium. By this time, I had resumed an active lifestyle and was down to about 170 lbs. One day I was watching a show on the BBC about the negative side effects of valium on health. I had been taking valium to calm my nerves, which most people did in my situation at that time, but the side effects were significant. I had noticed some balance problems, fatigue, and even mild depression. I knew valium was not a permanent solution, and so I just stopped taking any medication. I went cold turkey. And then for 20 years, I took no medication whatsoever. And what's more I haven't had another panic or anxiety attack.

What got me through it was perhaps another family trait, the emotional resilience that my mother instilled in us from the very beginning and that has allowed me to weather other emotional storms in my life.

In some ways, I haven't changed. Even today, if I have something on my mind, I'll wake up at 2 or 3 in the morning. But I don't have any of those debilitating panicky symptoms anymore because I know that like my mother, I am going to stay calm, I'm going to pace myself, and I'm going to get whatever it is done.

Early Rites of Passage and Lessons Learned: The U.K. and France

Another issue that triggered fear occurred in London during my first stint in the U.K. in 1978/79. Those were dark days in Britain—big strikes and riots—the whole country was being shut down. Electricity was sometimes shut off. Unemployment in manufacturing was in the double digits. There was resentment against immigrants, particularly South Asian and Caribbean immigrants, by a group of people called skinheads, white youths with shaved heads who were very, very angry. In 1979, in the west London neighborhood of Southall, riots were particularly vicious.

The incident that involved my family happened also to be coincident with my father's passing away quite suddenly in December 1978 with no prior symptoms or significant health issues other than the encephalitis years before. He was only 59 years old. Soon after his death, my mother came to visit for a few months. On one of their outings my mother, Kamla, and Vanita, who was 4, went to a nearby McDonald's restaurant, and the three of them were sitting in the corner when in came a group of skinheads. They started menacing my mother, Kamla, and Vanita because they were Indian, throwing food and shouting, "Go home, Paki!" It scared the living daylights out of Vanita. It was one of the first times, if not the very first time that she had encountered anything like this. They quickly gathered their things and left. Later Kamla and Vanita had to drop off my mother at the airport where there were again shouts of "Go home, Paki."

That particular experience for Vanita had a lasting impact. It came to play a significant role in how she viewed what's wrong, what's right, what's fair, and what's not fair about how people should be treated in public and in society, especially minorities. Over the years, it was probably compounded when she lived in France and saw the same kind of treatment of Muslims from Morocco and Algeria. She has made fighting for social justice her life's mission, and I can see the roots of her life's quest and profession sprouting from the incident in London. While I wasn't there and was only told what happened, I felt the sting and helplessness almost as much, perhaps particularly because I wasn't with them. It really did have an effect on me in the context of what discrimination can do to people of different races, color, and cultures.

My own example occurred in the U.K., as well, at work, when I was the finance director. While not violent or menacing, it was still hurtful. As in most offices, there was a water cooler. In our case, it was a 5-gallon water bottle that sat on a stand upside down, from which you fill your cup by pressing a lever. About a month after I started the job, I walked into my office after being out most of the day at a meeting. There was a note sitting on my chair that said, "We have decided it's your turn to fill this bottle." I recognized the handwriting. It was from one of the junior people who worked in the accounting department. I still vividly remember that note and that handwriting. I didn't sleep that night because the message so consumed me. I knew the note writer came in early, so I got in early the next day and told him to come into my office and close the door. "Here, I see this note," I said. "I have only one question. Did my predecessor, who was a white American, do the same?" He answered, "No." I said, "OK, then why did you expect me to do it?" He didn't have an answer. I couldn't figure out whether it was just a prank or he was trying to test me and my mettle, so I said, "You have a choice. Obviously, my predecessor did not do it, so I am not going to do it. If you don't like it, you can walk out of here, and I will never see you again. Or you can apologize and we'll move on." He apologized and stayed on, and might still be there for all I know. But I never held any grudge against him after that.

By the way, from that day on, my reputation in that company really took a different tone. They knew not to fool with me, that I was a straight shooter, and wouldn't buckle under pressure or intimidation. I wanted to send the message that I had a responsible position, and that I wasn't to be taken for granted. To me, it was a test, a test of whether this Indian guy is the real boss here. I had come there from America, was highly paid, at least compared to a British salary, and yet they wanted to test me. It had a profound impact on me, to be honest, and ultimately in a good way, because I think it gave me the confidence to be much more assertive in my life rather than just to crumble under any expectation. It was a kind of rite of passage, too, something you can't study for, prep for, or learn about from your teachers or colleagues. It was my own life lesson to endure and learn from, the best and most beneficial kind, in my judgment

In retrospect, the water cooler incident was a very tricky situation. But in all honesty, there were a few tricky situations in my career. If the skinhead and water cooler incidents were my social rites of passage, the Duolite acquisition and my position there comprised my career rite of passage.

One of the company's big challenges in Europe lay in expanding our ion exchange resins business when the company acquired Duolite International, a French-based subsidiary of the Diamond Shamrock Corporation that made ion exchange resins. The Duolite transaction was complicated for a number of reasons, starting with its business sense, meaning it had to make sense for the company and we had to overcome any regulatory issues associated with it. Not only was Duolite a competitor with Rohm and Haas's Amberlite ion exchange resins product, but also there was an intense rivalry between the two companies. They were arch enemies in fact. And the rivalry was deeply ingrained in both organizations. They hated each other. It resembled Coke vs. Pepsi, and it was very visceral in our organization—at the salesman level and all the way up the hierarchy. The senior leadership at Duolite put forth all kinds of obstacles to the acquisition—writing letters to the European Union Commission, the French Antitrust Authority, and the U.K. Antitrust Authority, trying to block us. But the bottom line was that both the financial and marketing justification made the acquisition highly desirable. With Duolite, Rohm and Haas would have an 80-90 percent market share and all that that meant to growth. My superiors knew all about the potential positives, and they expected me to make the acquisition successful.

There was no honeymoon in this marriage. The very first month after the acquisition in 1984, Duolite employees announced that they didn't want to be a part of the Rohm and Haas Company. When two or three of their senior leaders left and took away all the company files and customer data and put them in a competitor's hands, we had a problem.

Duolite was my first real job running a business, and my office was only a few yards from the cafeteria. I used to be really afraid to go get a cup of coffee or go for lunch. Afraid, not for my physical well being, but of just what I was going to see, because people stared at me and sometimes put negative comments, largely racial, on the notice board; once or twice that had happened, not about me personally, but negative comments about Indians. I didn't make a big show of responding other than in the several instances wherein I had to fire two or three people who were causing disruption in the workplace and instigating these comments, one of whom, by the way, was the HR director, which was totally unacceptable to me. I made some tough calls with my senior people. They clearly did not want to be part of the new Duolite and were playing games to make it as uncomfortable for me as possible.

Looking back, these experiences made me a stronger person. While aware of being different, I learned to believe in myself and developed the courage always to do the right thing. I was able to put a team in place that I trusted, and financial performance from the acquisition showed strong improvement. This gave me the confidence to deal with difficult challenges, make tough choices, and rely on my instincts.

5

The Best Lessons and Advice are Based on Negatives

"Failure is simply the opportunity to begin again, this time more intelligently."
—Henry Ford, American industrialist

Uncertainty and crisis management go hand in hand. Both raised their heads multiple times throughout my career, including but certainly not limited to the fibers business that almost sank the company a few years after I arrived at Rohm and Haas. I saw the effects crisis had on senior management, watching them really come unglued at times, showing incredible brittleness, realizing that the company that was coming up on its seventh decade was at risk of going under. As I mentioned, I had a front row seat in how decisions are made, and, when they are made under crisis conditions, how a whole other layer of leadership is exposed—both good and bad.

The first lesson was that crises create unusual behaviors in people whose all-too-human fragility and lack of self-confidence is exposed because they're under incredible pressure. Second, decision-making in a crisis is much more apt to become irrational or even non-rational due to the pressures of time and unfolding events, not to mention the criticism of the media and others who may never have criticized your management decisions before, making you feel under siege both personally and professionally. The lesson for me initially was the importance of remaining calm so as to be more thoughtful and focused—no knee-jerk decisions just to appear to be in control. Hurried decisions are the recipe for more untoward events to follow.

The high water mark of personal courage in crisis, in my opinion, was New York Mayor Giuliani's response to 9/11. Both the man and the city showed incredible leadership, calm, and control in the face of incalculable loss and destruction. Despite the unmitigated tragedy in the loss of over 2900 lives, including the very nature of the tragedy—planes crashing into huge skyscrapers and the carnage that resulted—Giuliani patiently, powerfully, and prudently led his city forward, despite what must have been as harrowing a time for him as it was for the country. The courage, support, and empathy he evidenced throughout are almost unimaginable in a person in that situation, with the world's eyes and ears trained on his every word and action. Unquestionably, he shepherded the largest city in America and one of the greatest cities in the world through its darkest moment.

While such catastrophes don't often strike individual businesses on that scale (9/11 affected countless businesses both personally and macro-economically, as well as the nation as a whole.), they can on the micro level, at least they did at Rohm and Haas where I witnessed the other side of crisis—when executives became very fragile. We made certain decisions that were not-well- thought-out, spur-of-the-moment decisions made for the sake of expediency.

So I think the fibers business crisis in 1975-76, discussed previously, was a pretty important experience for me to keep in perspective. A lot of short-term decisions such as "cut this; cut that" get made when you are in crisis mode.

Closing a Plant No One Wanted to Close

Another event happened on my watch in Europe in 1979 when I was sent for the first time in a strictly business role. This involved the re-evaluation of our European manufacturing footprint and business plan. What it turned out to entail was the closing or downsizing of plants, reorganizing, and cutting jobs. That is never a task that a manager wants to do but sometimes must.

To take advantage of the explosion in demand for paint emulsions, in the early 1970s we built, to great fanfare, Teesside, a plant on the north British coast. Its purpose was to synthesize acrylates, the basis for paint emulsions, in a new way, and to make one of the building blocks for emulsions, methacrylate monomers. The technology was brand new to us and several years went by before the plant could even out its capacity. It was costing us millions and not adding anything to our business. As newly appointed strategic planning director for Europe, it was my job to recommend on the future of Teesside as well as other problems that were hurting our European operations.

Let me explain some of the factors that I considered. Otherwise, it might appear that closing plants is an exercise in obliteration, like launching a missile from a remote-controlled drone from 10,000 feet, or a crossing-out exercise that an accountant many miles and floors away from the human beings involved might do with a keystroke without seeing or sympathizing with the people and families he is affecting.

The cost of energy in the U.K. in the late 1970s and early '80s was very high, and it was likely to remain high. The pound sterling had become the petro-currency because of oil and bioproduction. Costs could never be nailed down. They could quickly go from $2.40 to the pound down to $1.25 to the pound and the whole economics of production would change. And the market for the product was continental Europe, not the U.K. These were really overarching factors that would not change with time or be mitigated with tinkering around the edges. In the case of Teesside, it was the wrong location, the wrong cost structure, and an uncompetitive plant. On top of that, it did not operate well. It didn't matter what we did, how good we got, or the passage of time, it was not going to be viable. These were the factors that drove the decision—factors that had to be first identified, and then weighed.

And then there were the people issues to consider—the 250 employees involved. We had to consider what would be done for them. But I think the biggest challenge in this one was convincing the European management, the U.K., and even some of the folks in Philadelphia, who sort of knew in their guts what we had to do, and that was to close the plant. Teesside presented the challenge of stepping away from the emotional factors of history, individuals, and politics and being analytical, objective, and persistent. This wasn't my job, by the way. I was finance director of the U.K. company. I didn't have line responsibility, but I had an obligation here. I saw this. This is what I did all my life—spot something which I think is a better opportunity and start thinking about it, talking about it, and making a case for it.

The problem with Teesside was that no one had really confronted the facts and let them lead to where they needed to go. They said instead, "Well, Teesside had a bad production month; they had very high costs. Another week or month of good production and everybody will be behind us." That wasn't solving anything. That was wishful thinking. It wasn't facing the facts and thinking honestly where they may lead you. The challenge of management in these situations is to digest uncomfortable truths about a situation and to make an honest analysis of the facts. The bottom line for Teesside was that it was never going to be operationally profitable. Our costs were never going to be competitive. Teesside's continued operational overhead was forcing us to be in markets where we didn't belong, instead of building the long-term business for Rohm and Haas in Europe. So when you did the analytics and ran all the scenarios, it didn't matter what happened or how favorable the market or currency got, Teesside could not be viable. It all came down to the fact that everything had to be perfect for the plant to be profitable, and that's just not reality. So my recommendation was to close Teesside and import the building block chemical we needed from our Houston plant where the economics were very favorable.

This recommendation was doubly hard for me, because it wasn't my job to make the decision, and it was the first time that I had been put in a decision-influencing position. Up until then there had been a lot of analyses, presentations, projections, but not accountability for decisions. But as I said, my position as Rohm and Haas U.K. Finance Director came with a high level of functional responsibility. It was up to me to understand the challenges the plant presented and to step up, push hard, say we needed to do something, and present the case as to why. And Teesside was my first big issue. It preceded my second U.K. challenge which was making a case for substantial reduction of our footprint at our Jarrow, U.K. plant for similar reasons—both difficult but necessary decisions. These actions were not popular with my European colleagues, the local government officials, or even with my colleagues in Philadelphia. But once we got through with it, everyone saw the logic of it and stopped worrying about it.

The Teesside and Jarrow Lessons

So, the restructuring of Rohm and Haas U.K. was my primary contribution in my first two years in Europe. I came to see that as a tough, necessary, and even a lightly courageous act because no one throws bouquets at someone who closes plants, even though it may be required for the viability of the business or enterprise. When I was CEO I always gauged my direct reports in terms of what they were willing to do to get to a potentially thorny and ego-bruising decision. There were several who could step up and do what was necessary and several who could not.

I think having to make these tough calls gave me confidence and it gave me a lot of credibility. Before that, as I say, I suffered from the perception that while I may have been a very smart financial person, very good in analytics, I didn't really have the experience or maybe even the guts to make a tough decision. So this was really the first time I had to get corporate, regional, and country management all together on the same page for a really difficult, not to mention politically sensitive, decision that needed to be made. So I had to muster all the executive skills I had. It was really a case of persuasion without authority.

But I did have enormous support from several people, including the fellow who replaced Larry Wilson in Europe when Larry went back to take on greater responsibilities in Philadelphia—a man named Alan Levantin. People generally gave Alan less credit than he deserved. His forte was sales—in particular polymers and resins—and he was a high-potential executive, but people thought he was an intellectual lightweight, and his being American was held against him. They thought he was put in Europe to be a figurehead. I never did. I thought of him as an incredibly personable guy, very empowering, and an extremely good listener. To me, in many ways, he was as responsible as I was for the transformation of Europe from being a regional and isolated outpost to making Europe a real contributor to the Rohm and Haas Company, an achievement that lasted until Asia began to emerge as the great new market for the world.

Alan was the one I could talk to. As time went on and our relationship developed, I knew I could use him as a sounding board, count on him to listen to what I had to say, and to give me advice. He had a knack for seeing good ideas. When he saw something in what I was saying or wanted to do that maybe hadn't occurred to him or that might be difficult to implement, he never discouraged me. In the cases of Teesside and Jarrow, he heard me out, listened to my analysis, and agreed that we had to do something. He provided me with a political umbrella and served as my cover when I was trying to make the case to the other senior people in Europe. He would say something like, "I have some ideas about something, why don't we just get together. Come over to my office."

He was, on reflection, instrumental in allowing me to bring up new ideas and get his support. He would never stand up and be directive or dictate what had to happen. He would listen to everybody, and he would give me an opportunity to explain my logic; and if somebody contradicted or interrupted me while in the middle of something I was saying, he would say, "Hear him out."

And here is my point about Alan. He taught me that sometimes in business you run into people who may not have a great analytical understanding of business, but they have good instincts—good instincts about business, about people, about customers, about a lot of the soft things that go into a business decision. They could make the case for something their gut was telling them was right.

And the second thing I learned from Alan was the ability to say, "This is what we need to do in light of the facts that have been laid out." That's what he did with me, and that's a lesson I learned executives have to do. They have to evaluate the facts and then they have to decide. They can get input, but they must, in the end, make a forceful decision. Alan could do that, and it led to the transformation of Europe. Once the European leadership team saw that we could make a decision on the two plants in the U.K. that needed change, they could see that others needed change as well. They said, "OK, let's move on to other issues needing change—fragmented plants in other countries, making ion exchange resins in four plants in Europe instead of maybe two that would serve us just as well"—to the point where it created a whole new job for me, Strategic Planning Director for Europe. So, Alan taught me many lessons, including the one that said, "Don't believe everything you hear about someone; see for yourself."

My next assignment was to look for growth through acquisitions. This involved looking at the entire company in terms of growth and at the same time asking: "What should we do in Europe?" So really I had two tasks, serving the management in Philadelphia and serving with Al in Europe. I was kind of a free-wheeler. I had no job description. I was just there trying to grow Europe. We looked at some acquisition opportunities like the plant in Scotland in Grangemouth and a new investment in Jarrow.

I was learning that jobs had two very important components—analysis and politics. I had to understand the industrial landscape, talk to consultants, think–about areas where we could get acquisitions and growth, and consider the politics of whatever we decided to do—how to sell it inside and how to integrate the acquisition.

Borg Warner—
An Example of Seizing Technological Innovation

I learned yet another set of personal management behaviors in my new role of looking for new growth in Europe, when we were able to realize a dream we had of acquiring a PVC modifier plant. Because of our focused strategy and vigilance, we saw an opportunity when in 1981 Borg-Warner offered us their plant in Grangemouth, Scotland that manufactured a line of methacrylate-butadiene-styrene-type PVC modifiers, made in a process different from what we did at our other plants. We realized that Borg Warner's process eliminated the contamination issues we were having and would allow us to make products for more profitable PVC markets, such as transparent bottles, the market we wanted to be in. The Borg-Warner technology had been developed by a Japanese company, Kureha Chemical Industry Company, and so we entered into a joint research agreement with Kureha in order to stay on top of the technology. We extended that partnership to make those modifiers at our Louisville plant in the U.S. for the domestic market.

In the meantime, I was dealing with the power of personality in business and the importance of navigating it. The head of Europe was Basil Vassiliou, who took over after Alan Levantin went back to the U.S. Basil did not mince words. He had strong opinions and could be belligerent to the point of intimidating people. This did not endear him to his peers because he was perceived as very political and motivated in terms of glorifying himself. But he was highly respected for his intellect and persistence and the fact that he had built a bond with Larry Wilson when Larry was CFO and Vince was CEO, so he was a force to be reckoned with. People knew that he had influence, so you didn't want to cross him. Not very many did.

Basil had very strong opinions about people but deep inside he was a very warm and caring person. So Basil's was a personality I had to take into account and constantly try to appeal to in terms of what drove his opinions. I recognized that he cared about the company and what was best for it. You just didn't want to go toe-to-toe with him politically.

The other personality I was dealing with at the time, almost an opposite, was Larry Wilson's. Larry was one of the least political persons I have ever met in my life. He was one of the best listeners I know and was probably one of the best executives I have seen who was able to connect the dots. But he was also very hard to draw out. He almost rarely expressed something with great conviction.

I don't think Larry liked confrontation. But I learned something very interesting. If you asked him a direct question, he'd answer you. And what's more, you'd better be prepared for the answer, because if he said it, it was cast in concrete. So if there were consequences you didn't want to absorb or take or accept, then the wise person would avoid asking Larry for his opinion. If you had the courage to ask, he had the courage to tell you exactly what he thought. I admired him tremendously for that. There's a management strength there that I never forgot, and that strength was in knowing that sometimes less is more.

And the upside to Larry's approach is that if you wanted or needed the guidance, you got it. In several situations where I was wrestling with a decision, I asked Larry what his opinion was and he gave it to me. That gave me clarity. He taught me something about corporate communications, and that is that you don't communicate only when you want to exchange good or encouraging news or opinions. You communicate to inform or be informed, enlighten or be enlightened, ask or answer, elicit or placate, or provide or take direction. When people are by nature not communicative in that way, their reports have to accept part of the responsibility themselves for dealing with it. Another lesson he taught me was not speaking ill of people. He didn't engage in gossip, and he didn't encourage it among his direct reports. It wouldn't have served any purpose, in his mind.

I tried to internalize that habit as well. I learned that I could be effective or exert influence by treating people with respect both to their faces and behind their backs. I listened, but I didn't engage in gossip. I wasn't brought up that way and people like Larry showed me you didn't have to do it to advance or show leadership. He didn't engage in *ad hominem* discussions in his personal or professional life. He actually de-politicized the organization in that way, and I tried to learn from him.

Putting all my European experiences together, I would say that the Duolite experience was a baptism of fire for me. As I said in the previous chapter, it was a very important acquisition for the company—its largest acquisition until then—but it possessed a leadership team I could not trust, a culture that was new and different from the one I had known, and on top of all this, it was my first "business" experience. Expectations were high, and I did not want to disappoint my superiors. The confidence came after I resorted to what my instincts told me: communicate candidly and frequently, make the necessary personnel changes to get alignment with strategy, set clear goals and milestones to implement that strategy, and monitor progress very closely.

Teesside taught me the lesson of calling it like it is, despite the toes that I had to step on. Letting it linger would have helped no one. Borg Warner taught me the importance of adding value where it was real and could be leveraged across the company. I later took that mindset when we looked at Asia.

But at this point in my career, we were able to show tremendous progress in a couple of years. We had a motivated team, and it gave me confidence in my leadership skills. Thankfully, my personal and professional growth was also noticed by higher-ups in the organization, but more importantly I had learned to listen and observe others, and that was a trait I would never abandon. It would serve me well later, personally, as well in my career.

Building Emotional Competence
through Management Development

In a twist of the saying, "Desperate times call for desperate measures," I would say desperate times call for *different leaders*. Larry Wilson, chairman and CEO in 1987, realized that, in the wake of Michael Porter's *The Competitive Advantage,* published in 1985, and other business scholars looking at forces that could re-shape business strategy and competitiveness, Rohm and Haas leaders had to start thinking differently. He directed his head of HR at the time, a man named Mark Feck, to lead an initiative designed to develop holistic thinkers at the company. Larry wanted advice about first, the kind of leaders this company needed as it entered a new era of strategic competitiveness, and second, how we would go about developing them. What Larry wanted were "new" leaders for all of Rohm and Haas's businesses and people. He wanted a leadership cadre that would allow us to become bigger, more diversified, and more global. We needed more people, he said, who had both general management skills and functional skills, which had been a hallmark of the Rohm and Haas executive up to that point. He wanted people who were smart and not only able to recognize talent in others, but also able to see and use the wisdom of everyone in the organization. He wanted them to tap the knowledge and expertise of everyone in the organization, including our customers, our communities, our supply chain, and our shareholders. In other words, he wanted a team of executives who reflected the collective judgment of all of Rohm and Haas's stakeholders.

Mark contacted a well-regarded industrial psychologist and executive consultant named Karol Wasylyshyn, who had made a name for herself as someone who brought many perspectives to her practice in addition to executive coaching, a field she almost invented and continues to lead through her workshops, lectures, teaching, and writing. She saw successful leadership as a quality that blended innate business acuity with emotional intelligence or competence, as she prefers to call it.

The Washylyshyn-Feck program began in 1987. I was in the second group of four or five executives. It was a totally unique process, especially so within the context of the company then. At the time, performance management at Rohm and Haas was almost nonexistent—you came to work and you did your job. As time passed, some people were promoted, the only indication of performance management, and often, people didn't know *why* they got promoted. So it was a very mysterious process, and the pervasive belief was that who you knew was more important than what you did. If you did your job, you got a bonus and a thank you at the end of the year. Hardly anybody was fired.

Karol's "inside-out" approach was guided by four principles: 1) a holistic development model; 2) trust grounded in confidentiality; 3) the power of psychological insight; and 4) the conveyance of executive wisdom to the executive team and the organization, something that resonated deeply with me. Furthermore, her program was peer-guided and included executive spouses as well. Leadership, in Karol's view and experience, was not something practiced just at work. Having input from those who lived with them at home was as important as having a 360-degree view and input from those who worked directly with the executives. The effective leader is also an "affective" leader, knowing the limits and contours of his or her emotions as well being able to listen and respond appropriately to others. One has to observe oneself as well as others to be a complete and competent leader.

Dr. Wasylyshyn showed us the need to see the valuable combination of both emotional as well as technical competencies when developing our leaders and choosing those most well equipped to help the company move forward and convey that same leadership brand throughout the organization. These traits and behaviors included what you might expect management consultants to stress: market awareness, customer-centricity, strategic focus, global perspective, and the qualities associated with the pursuit of profitable growth. But she also brought to our leadership team the awareness of and focus on the executive as a high-functioning human being, in whom personal credibility, business acumen, persuasiveness, interpersonal effectiveness, and people management skills were part and parcel of the leader's make-up. This was groundbreaking work in the 1980s and 1990s.

In addition to fostering emotional competence in business, she helped us identify key leadership behaviors, such as courage, emotional fortitude, enterprise thinking, pragmatic optimism, steel-trap accountability, truth-telling, and being tough on talent. Her battery of psychometric tests for assessing these behaviors and values was both quantitative and qualitative so that the program was far more than a check-the-box or gloss-over as some management consulting programs end up being. You couldn't duck weaknesses and you couldn't overplay strengths.

And you were told the truth by your peers and your family, so you couldn't run and you couldn't hide if you volunteered for the program. But like any other program, you got out of it what you put into it. Each generation of leaders who went through the program was mapped in terms of their own development, and the aggregate scores and results were compared over time to see if the company had improved its leadership quotient. Just as a reputation for product quality can be improved by quality control and assurance over time, company leadership can be distilled and improved, if it is subjected to rigorous scrutiny and nurturing. Both are critical for companies to go from good to great.

Some large chemical companies are still run in a traditional top-down way that clusters mature expertise at the top in a system that over-estimates their ability, over-weights their level of knowledge, and breeds over-confidence in their ability and skills in making complex decisions. This disrupts and, in some cases, prevents the cross-fertilization of good ideas and organizational wisdom, thus creating a silo culture. Manufacturing becomes totally controlled by the engineers and scientists; sales and marketing is run by MBAs; and finance is focused on Wall Street and quarteritis. Very few by themselves have full grasp of running an entire business long term, or even more importantly, a company where sustainable growth and value are generated.

The other element of the Feck-Wasylyshyn leadership program that I think was critical was the peer-review concept. This ongoing program would be conducted by leaders in the company, not by professors and outside consultants. It would be the CEO and COO and the senior management team who would spend two, three, or four days with a group of 15 or 20 executives around the world. Why is this important? Because almost everybody in the top 150-200 would receive real training on how to be a general manager, how to be independent, and how to bond emotionally, in addition to taking on more profit-and-loss responsibility. It would continue to encourage future leaders to rely on each other as well as themselves in enlisting good ideas, innovative approaches, and respect for decentralized expertise, as well as independent thinking. There would be no information or decision cascade with executives being pushed "get on board." Thus, the current leadership would become invested in those who followed, learning interactively, setting the tone for what is expected, and charting each executive's development path.

Mark and Karol worked very hard in parallel to make this program as holistic as possible, operating according to the underlying principle that successful people are not successful among just their peers, they're comfortable and successful as human beings, leading what positive psychologist Marty Seligman calls "the flourishing life" in his book, *Flourish: A Visionary New Understanding of Happiness and Well-being* (2011). They know who they are and the elements of their personality that make them behave the way they do, as well as what they want to achieve and why. Knowing these things, they are in a better position to change what they want to change and strengthen what they're good or gifted at, as well as conveying and facilitating that wisdom and process to others.

The Feck-Wasylyshyn program asked, "How can we recognize leadership potential in others so as to strengthen the company bond with them and help them develop to their best ability?" Talent retention is based on talent recognition, so it makes sense to know what you're looking for as well as to recognize it when you see it. You're not trying to find the smartest person to run your company, you're trying to find smart people who respect one another's ideas and collective decision-making ability, who will allow the company to make the best decisions over time.

Larry Wilson's mandate and the resulting leadership initiative really ignited change. It was the first time we had ever received 360-degree feedback. And all the people who were selected into the program were people who obviously had good track records. This program wasn't just about whether people met the numbers or whether they worked well with other people. For example, the program asked and measured as best it could: How did these employees think? Did they know their own strengths and weaknesses? Were they given meaningful examples? How did they engage with other people? Were they given behavioral goals? Did they act on the follow-up? Did they sustain their progress? All of that and more.

For my 360 evaluation, Karol talked to 8-10 people who obviously knew me very well, including some of my direct reports, some of my peers, and some of my bosses, previous bosses, and higher-ups.

And the profile of me that emerged was frankly shocking—shocking in two dimensions. One hurt me in particular. Some people thought I had a personal agenda that I was pushing and that this was demonstrated in the way I expressed myself. And second, I was very critical of others, they said. They gave examples. One was in meetings. They said I would sit and listen and not express my opinion and then late in the discussion or afterward, when the decision had already been made, I would offer contrary views that would have altered the discussion and perhaps the ultimate decision. They said this behavior was confusing and, to some, suggested some other motive at work. Fundamentally, they said I was a very smart, analytical person who really had some great ideas and had done some wonderful things, but they weren't sure that I could lead a large organization.

When I asked for more detail, they said that I seemed very focused on climbing the corporate ladder and was a self-promoter in order to advance my prospects and visibility with senior management. Furthermore, they said that when I gave my opinion on an issue to someone, that person took it as criticizing him so that I would look better. They believed I managed up. They pointed to my three or four yearly visits back to the U.S. when I was in Europe. They said I went out of my way to carve out meetings with Vince, the CEO, and Larry, then EVP, and Fred Shaffer, the CFO and my mentor, in order to advance my prospects, keep contact, and stay in the limelight. It was true that whenever I came back to the U.S. I would visit these executives, but my peers believed I was doing it just to get attention, brown-nosing, as they say.

This feedback came as both a shock and a surprise, because I had no idea my actions were being perceived in this way. Managing up or self-ingratiation was not what motivated my actions. I believed these to be empty strategies that some people adopted in order to make up for a lack of innate competence or demonstrated ability. That's not the way I thought of myself. I thought of these senior people as my teachers and mentors. I would ask for maybe 10-15 minutes of their time, but I never used that opportunity to talk about where I was going next or my career outlook. Truth to tell, I took the 360-feedback hard, and it took me a while to overcome that criticism.

Empathic Leadership

As time went on, Dr. Wasylyshyn spent more time with me discussing the feedback. This included debriefings with two or three colleagues whose comments and observations were considered most significant, including my direct boss and one or two others who wanted to be part of the process as well as serve as personal resources or mentors, if we needed to consult. Importantly, in the Wasylyshyn plan, you had to give permission for these colleagues to participate, especially if they saw you regressing back to behaviors you indicated you wanted to change. In this regard, they would serve as counselors, because you had a plan for what you wanted to do with the feedback you got, and you shared that and talked about it with your circle of peers or bosses, so they were key.

Karol also included spouses, if you wanted your spouse to be part of it. It certainly wasn't required, but it provided a holistic approach to each individual, an element I thought was critical. I asked Kamla to participate because I thought it was important to her, to me, and to the company. I learned a lot about myself through Kamla's view of me that I wouldn't have been able to discern by myself. Karol spent three to five hours with Kamla to gain a sense of her relationship with me and our daughters—the theory being that people change when they get to work, change in the sense that they take on a different role, the work role. This was not an "aha moment," but learning the specific details and examples of how people perceived me *was* a transformative moment for me. The person you think you are may not be the person your wife and family think you are, especially when you are traveling a lot or are stressed at work and the strain ultimately affects the family. So after Karol's one-on-one with Kamla, the three of us sat down and Karol walked us through what she heard. Very enlightening.

What I learned happened as a result of the sensitizing process that accompanies all of these conversations and feedback sessions. And this was a particularly traumatic period in Kamla's and my life because we were going through the recognition that our older daughter was gay. So it was a stressful period for me personally as well as professionally, and I needed to be able to connect the different strands or components of my life in a way that made sense to me and that recognized the importance of the individuals and their lives (and choices) who were my family.

The "Raj before" and the "Raj after" were in fact much different. I saw positive changes that I liked. The process sensitized me to how people felt about issues and about me personally. Once I recognized how I was perceived, I allowed the realization to sink in over time, to let myself evolve with that information. I don't think I always did it consciously, but I held in the back of my mind where I wanted to go and be.

I changed my tone of questioning people, how I gave feedback, how I asked about different scenarios or consequences of a decision, and when I chose to weigh in with a conclusion and then decision. I learned self-assurance. Part of this came from personal experience, part of it from the executive coaching process offered me at Rohm and Haas, and part of it from my reflections on my own up-bringing and what my parents had taught me. We are always navigating our behavior and our life path, and certainly I am no different. We are the children of our parents not only when we are growing up in their midst, but throughout our lives.

Bottom line: without Karol's guidance, interventions, thoughtful feedback, peer review, and the help of my wife and mentors, I would not have arrived where I did. Not just a slim chance. Zero chance. I'm clear about that. Karol was a forerunner of today's executive coach. She brought the field to where it is today. This kind of holistic process, wherein you hear really candid assessments of yourself from people above you, alongside you, and who report to you, coupled with perceptions of the people you love and who have an intimate connection with you, has the potential to help you truly become aware of yourself from the outside in. Then you can leverage that feedback in being more impactful in larger settings or bigger arenas, especially when you need to state your position and close the dialogue. It made me become a better executive, a better decision maker and, frankly, a better person. I would recommend to others that even absent a life or career coach, they seek out a mentor who will give them unvarnished observations. They're worth their weight in gold.

Jarring Advice I Never Forgot

Another interesting story about someone else's view of me is a conversation I had with one of our executives, Basil Vassiliou. Born in

Greece and partly educated in the U.S., Basil was a senior vice president at Rohm and Haas and a Ph.D. chemist by training, who was heading up Europe for the company. This was in 1992-93 near the end of my 15-years' stint in Europe. I was getting ready to go back to the U.S. to take on an even greater responsibility, heading up the company's Asia-Pacific region. Basil called me into his office one day and said he wanted to talk with me. I said fine.

We made some small talk at first and then Basil got quiet and said, "I want to share with you two observations, Raj, both of which I believe strongly and both of which I think are important for your development. First, I tell you that you have tremendous instincts," he said, which I was pleased to hear. "And the second observation is that people seem to think that you have this compelling need to justify your opinions by marshaling an overwhelming amount of facts and figures. The way you communicate at times gives an impression that perhaps you have another personal agenda that you are not sharing with them," Basil said. "I tell you these things for two reasons. First, I think you are a tremendously gifted executive with great potential, and second, I care about your progress and development, and this trait or perception," he said, "could hurt your progress as well as personal development."

So Basil proceeded to tell me, or to suggest to me, that I needed to be clearer about what is leading me to the decisions without the apparent array of numbers in order to justify them. "People know you have experience and demonstrated credibility. You have judgment. And you have facts behind your decisions. You don't have a compelling need of elaborating a lot about it," he told me. "They need to see Raj, the thoughtful, strategic business person, not Raj, the analyst. Not at the levels you are preparing for, at any rate."

What I took from that was that I needed to be comfortable with my own instincts and decisions and to be able to communicate them in a way that didn't have to rely on analysis alone with no perception of people's personal agendas. It was the first time anyone had ever said that to me, and it was advice I took to heart. Before, I had seen my path to greater opportunity as dependent on my ability to marshal facts and figures to get to a decision. Now I was being told they were getting in the way.

How did I react to this advice? First, I never forgot it, and second, I realized that in some ways it contradicted my education and early career. I was trained as an engineer who relied on thoughtful analysis and good numbers to get to the best decision or answer. It had worked when I started at Scott Paper and then as I rose quickly through different finance jobs at Rohm and Haas, and even, I thought, during my years in Europe restructuring our supply chain and our acquisition of the French ion exchange resins company. When I reflected on what Basil said to me, I tried to dig deeper as to what made me so reliant on numbers.

I had always been taught and believed that numbers are the bottom line of business. They show who is doing a good job and who is not making the grade. And I always aimed at not just making the grade but getting the best grades. So I thought numbers were the currency of business. And, when I was a newcomer to the U.S., I was also looking for a language that spoke compellingly in either India or America, and numbers satisfied that condition from a business as well as a cultural standpoint. No one could argue with the numbers, but they could argue with me. So numbers were my mask, my armor, in a way. And perhaps I was also overcoming some innate sense of intimidation, adopting an outsider's protective camouflage, so to speak. All this made me believe I had to justify myself at every turn when I offered an opinion, and because I had an almost photographic memory for numbers and I liked finance, it was a natural for me.

I think maybe what helped me most were the words of wisdom from Basil. These things mattered more: "You don't have to justify yourself all the time. Don't be critical of others. If you have a point of view, express it. You have good, sound judgment, good experience, and good track record." It became my mantra. I came to rely less and less on numbers and being analytical and instead began engaging people in a more up-front manner, asking for their input and then providing my own.

The other piece of advice Basil gave me that day was that I needed to be more forthright in expressing my opinion or thoughts in groups. "One-on-one," he said, "you have some very good thoughts, very good ideas, and very good suggestions. But when you are in a group of peers," he said, "you can be very reticent about expressing yourself." Basil's point of view was: "Raj, if you don't express your opinion, people won't know what you're thinking. In that sense, you're cheating yourself and you're cheating the company." Even though I would have put Basil on the far end of the spectrum as being too confident in expressing his opinions, I never forgot what he said to me that day and took it to heart.

When you are in a leadership position, people need to hear, at some point in time, where you stand. It was a fair assessment and I repeat it here because it is part of my own development and it is good advice for others who must balance the collaborative style with the CEO's role as ultimate decision-maker, especially perhaps the Indian man or woman whose culture has taught him or her that study and hard work are their own rewards. They are necessary but are not sufficient criteria for success. There is both a social and cultural component to decision-making, especially in the U.S., that requires camaraderie and social interaction. Clearly, each has a role in the process. Although you want to encourage and engage in an important dialogue or discussion, you have to, at some point, come to a conclusion, come to a decision, and that was Basil's point to me. It showed the need for social and cognitive balance. I pass it along because it was a life-changing conversation.

More Advice I Never Forgot—Being Myself in a White Man's World

This happened around the time I'd come back from working in England and I was being considered as a possible CEO candidate along with two other highly qualified Rohm and Haas executives, Mike Fitzpatrick and Chuck Tatum, in 1996. I'm sure we were all feeling a little anxious, and Vince Gregory, who had since retired but kept an office in the building, called me in and said, "Raj, you need to get over this syndrome of the white man at the top. You do not have to be deferential. You have to be respectful. But you are your own man and you should act that way."

My lesson from these conversations with Basil and Vince was that effective leaders are those who not only have the ability to understand the business and to articulate a vision for the company but also have the temperament to lead— leaders whose outward actions reflect an inward emotional intelligence or competence, who can touch others with their humanity, and can be authentic as human beings. Vince had demonstrated his effective leadership to me.

Neither of these conversations, by the way, contained earth-shattering revelations of anything I didn't know or maybe could have said to myself, but thence forward I realized that being a CEO and a trusted leader meant being an authentic person first, in addition to all the business acumen you try to accumulate and the political and statesmanlike demeanor you try to demonstrate over the years. As the Dalai Lama has been famously quoted, "Follow the R's: Respect for self, respect for others, and responsibility for all your actions." For me that advice encompasses one of the most important traits of a leader—the ability to relate to others as human beings with feelings, fears, hopes, and desires. S/he can be skilled in the technicalities and nuances of the business and think strategically, but if he or she doesn't have the basic requisites of compassion, empathy, and understanding for the other person, his or her leadership will lack authenticity as well as the requisite temperament that makes a great leader as well as excellent CEO.

I had become the sum total of my life's experiences: I was Indian; I was the son of a professional; I had a brother and sisters who were all extremely bright but in some ways straight-jacketed by some aspects of their culture. I had married a wonderful woman with whom I had two incredible daughters. I was proud to be who I was but always respectful of what others had given or showed me.

Now I had to learn to be myself in a white man's world.

The Hunt for Growth

No one knew the seriousness of the challenge we faced in 1999-2000—the post-acquisition of Morton International when everything started falling apart. Rohm and Haas had become a very different company by the late 1990s from what it was in the 1970s. It was flush with cash and had very little debt. This time, the challenge we were facing was the need to grow.

We had just sold the Plexiglas® acrylic plastics business. We had a joint venture with the oil additives business, but we didn't see ourselves in that sector for the long term. In short, we knew that we needed to change the complexion of the company if we were going to maximize the potential of our technology and our core strengths in specialty chemicals. So we asked what transactions would give us critical mass. We were looking to grow to somewhere between $6 billion and $7 billion in revenue, from our existing base of $3.5 billion.

Morton got on our radar and stayed there. Acquiring it would give us about $2.5 billion in additional revenue, most of what we needed to reach our goal. All of its businesses on the chemical side fit with our own or extended our reach. Whether it was formulated biocides, powder coatings, some electronic materials, or some adhesives, every one of them would give us some new platforms or supplement what we had. As for Morton Salt, which was essentially a stand-alone operation, we expected to sell it eventually since it did not fit into any of our product portfolios.

We had been considering another option—purchasing the $1.2 billion specialty business of Britain's Zeneca LLC, the British multinational pharmaceutical and specialty chemicals manufacturer, but that deal wouldn't have changed our critical mass nor would it have added substantially to our product portfolio.

So we settled on Morton. We knew we couldn't borrow all the money needed to close the deal, so we were thinking about a structure that would be one-third equity and two-thirds debt. That way, we could issue more shares and effectively reduce the ownership interest held by the Haas family charitable trusts, a plan the Haases were totally comfortable with.

We presented the case for the Morton acquisition at a board meeting in Florida in 1998, just a few months after my promotion to chairman and CEO was announced but before I actually took over. The board gathering followed numerous meetings with Morton's chairman and CEO, Jay Stewart, and its president and COO, Bill Johnston, in Chicago, Morton's base, and in Philadelphia, our home town. In February 1999, we made the official announcement of the Morton acquisition to great fanfare on Wall Street.

By the time the Morton deal closed in June 1999, we had also acquired LeaRonal, a specialty chemicals company, as well as full ownership of Rodel, worldwide leader in polishing technology for semiconductors, silicon wafers, and storage media substrates, which together provided another $400 million or so in revenue. So we were well on our way to creating a new Rohm and Haas. I had been in favor of all of these acquisitions as far as weighing the pros and cons. But in retrospect we took on too much. We didn't manage the Morton acquisition well and, as typically happens, Morton's businesses were not as strong as we thought because they were probably dressed up to be sold. That's the way it always is. So we should have gone into the deal with an open mind and more widely open eyes.

The Rationale for Morton

Conventional knowledge at Rohm and Haas was that the Morton acquisition was Larry Wilson's idea because he wanted to leave a legacy that took the company away from acrylics and into a new arena. Morton and the electronic materials acquisitions would serve as the newer and higher-potential platforms for growth. But to do this, the story went, Larry had to look the other way in terms of some of the due diligence because Morton just seemed the right deal to make, and that was that. Rohm and Haas people, it was said, sensed Larry's element of compromise and backed away from pointing out the red flags they saw that might have derailed the deal.

But the conventional knowledge is not my view. I worked very closely with Larry throughout the due diligence process. He certainly wanted to lead Rohm and Haas away from the things that were getting commoditized. He had already made that move with Plexiglas®. We knew we would have to sell our agricultural chemicals operation at some point, and we were just too small a player in oil additives to stay in that market for long. So all of these things were under way. Did we have to get into something else? Absolutely. And it wasn't just Larry who was saying so. All of us were in the same place and on board with Morton. Otherwise, we thought, we would have a shrinking company and an uncertain future. That said, though, there is no question, at least in retrospect, that we did not do enough homework to prove the case that buying Morton was indeed a compelling deal. To some extent, we just got carried away.

And that's the lesson that resonates not only with me but I would think for other students of M&A as well. You are making huge decisions, and in the heat of the moment you don't allow enough time and you don't put in enough thought to the hard questions, such as: Have we analyzed all the upsides and downsides? Are we aware of all the most critical liabilities? Can we truly integrate their businesses with ours? Will this acquisition add real value?

Looking back, I realize I should have had the judgment and the courage to say that we needed more time to do more homework. When we met in Florida, though, ostensibly to review and weigh the pending deal, people thought that the train had already left the station. But whatever the faults in our process, I never felt that Larry put aside the company's interests to pursue a personal agenda built around a dream of a legacy. His comments appear in the shaded text below.

"It Was Necessary"

Larry Wilson, former CEO:

Morton was a big acquisition for us and one that was very controversial. Everybody went through a lot in managing that acquisition and its integration into Rohm and Haas. Certain things we did very well and certain things not so well. But the reason we did it was simple: it was necessary. Leading up to that deal, we had done several other very important acquisitions in electronic materials and we had sold off bits and pieces of the company that weren't making money or weren't key to our future growth, all to make way for a major acquisition. By the late 1990s, we had restored profitability but we weren't growing, and if you continue down that path, there comes a point where you cannot shrink any further without destroying the core of the company. So we needed more size.

We did a list of every possible acquisition that could give us that growth or where there were divisions of companies we could acquire to accomplish our goal. Morton International was one of these. Two-thirds of the company was chemicals and a third was salt, one of theleading salt companies in the world. We had no relationships with the salt business itself, but Morton Salt was, along with Cargill, one of the largest salt producers in North America, and extremely profitable. So even though it didn't relate to any part of Rohm and Haas, it was competitive as a stand-alone business. So that was not a drawback.

> As for the two-thirds that were chemicals, there were some very easy fits without overlap, all the way from the biocides business to the polymers business. You could see that by fitting the two companies together you could take out cost and spread overhead over the larger entity and it was a way to restore the volume that we had cut out by the divestitures of some of our businesses.
>
> For our larger purpose of jump-starting growth, Morton Salt, even though it was not a chemical business, made sense for us. Morton really understood the salt business, was a major player in both road and food salt sectors, and provided a predictable cash flow. It was very low-tech, requiring very little R&D investment. The seasonality even made sense for us. It paid for the winter and our agricultural business paid for the summer. It was the opinion of the various due diligence teams that Morton's salt business and its other businesses complemented our own portfolio. We saw the Morton acquisition as not only a good thing, but as necessary.

So everything seemed great with our rather hastily arranged marriage, formally announced in February 1999. But it was a short honeymoon. In 2000, with the dot-com collapse, it all started to unravel.

And now I was at the helm.

6

Being CEO:
A Cauldron of Change

"A corporation is a living organism; it has to continue to shed its skin. Methods have to change. Focus has to change. Values have to change. The sum total of those changes is transformation."
—Andy Grove, entrepreneur and co-founder of Intel Corp.

The timing was fitting: on the weekend of July 4, 1998, I was told that I would be the next chairman and chief executive officer of the Rohm and Haas Company.

Founded nearly a century before in Germany, Rohm and Haas had settled in Philadelphia in 1909, making its name as a chemical manufacturer of Plexiglas® and other acrylic products. A Fortune 500 company with its headquarters on Independence Mall, it was closing out the 20ᵗʰ century on an acquisition binge, determined to diversify and become the global powerhouse in specialty chemicals. Now, on this most American of holidays, it was turning to me, an immigrant from India, to lead it into the new millennium.

I was to be only the third CEO to come from outside the ranks of the founding Haas family, and the first to have been born outside the United States. But if I was different in background from my predecessors, I was also a home-grown product. I had joined the company just two years out of graduate school, and I never left. I started in the finance department, early on became special assistant to then-CEO Vince Gregory, spent 15 years in Europe reorganizing manufacturing operations and restructuring businesses, and for the next five years oversaw the development of the company's new beachheads in Asia and its fledgling electronic materials business before being named to the six-member chairman's committee and then to the board.

By the time I formally took over as chairman and chief executive in late 1999, I had spent 28 years at the company. I was as ready as I could be to take on the challenge of leading Rohm and Haas into what promised to be a very different future. As much as I had looked forward to this moment, I couldn't help but feel nervous once it arrived. Would I be up to the task? Had I fully known just how different and difficult the company's future was going to be, and how close we would come to utter disaster in my first few years in office, I'm sure that my answer to that question would have been, "No—no one is up to the task, certainly not me." But fortunately, we don't know what the future will bring, and so we don't bolt and run. And once that future arrives, if it is a dark and brutal one, it is too late to flee, and we have no choice but to stand and deal with it.

A circumstance in my case was the fact that the Haas family controlled 30 percent of the stock, so while we were publicly owned and operated, the Haas family had strong influence on the company. John Haas, the sole surviving son of the founder, never intruded into the operations of the company other than from the standpoint of the family's and board's appropriate governance and social responsibilities. That is a problem for some family-controlled company CEOs but not in my case. I invested a lot of time getting to know all the members of the Haas family—including the third and fourth generations. I met with them three or four times a year and we often traveled together to company sites and locations to meet our global team and see our operations. I encouraged them, as well, to meet with the board independent of me and to have an independent financial advisor, which they did.

We were now a new Rohm and Haas—an amalgam of several entities that included Morton chemicals and Morton salt, LeaRonal, Rodel, and Shipley, the last three to occupy the foundation of what we called our Electronic Materials space. We had acquired multiple new management teams, a variety of cultures, a dizzying mass of complexity, and a frightening amount of debt. We were many companies without the benefit of being a unified one, and we simply had too many independent business units. That's my judgment now. Then, I saw it as a puzzle to be figured out, a challenge to manage.

So we rolled up our sleeves. I put Pierre Brondeau, who had started in our research department, in charge of electronic materials. Pierre was given the overall responsibility to integrate Shipley and LeaRonal. We initially ran Rodel as an independent company, almost a stand-alone.

Morton was slightly different. Bill Johnston, its veteran president and COO, was still on the scene in Chicago, and I had given my deputy, Mike Fitzpatrick, the responsibility to work with him to bring Morton into the fold. We left some of Morton's businesses as stand-alones—salt, of course, and also powder coatings. And we moved to integrate electronic materials as well as biocides, the very small emulsion and adhesives business, and all the other Morton chemical operations into Rohm and Haas.

Mike was in charge of managing the synergy, and he did so with the help of A.T. Kearney, the global management consulting firm. In fairly short order, we recognized $120 million in savings from procurement changes, office reductions, plant closures, and supply chain efficiencies. We had a pretty-well-laid-out master plan. It was an exciting time for all of us, similar to getting married, starting out fresh, and not being sure what was on the horizon. We had grown dramatically in sales, product mix, market reach, and number of employees in the space of just a year, and our stock price was going up, too.

But I was taking charge of a company that was literally in pieces. We had just spent $4.9 billion to acquire Morton. And we had paid $400 million over time to gain control of Rodel, Inc., another $400 million to buy LeaRonal, Inc. We had gone, in little more than the blink of an eye, from being mostly in acrylics, with major interests in agricultural chemicals and oil additives, to becoming a key supplier for makers of computer chips, circuit boards, and other electronic products. We had nearly doubled in size in the last few months of 1998—growing from $3.5 billion in annual revenue to more than $6.5 billion and from 12,000 employees to close to 23,000.

But the new pieces had to be integrated into the old Rohm and Haas to make it all work. That included making sure that our investments in electronic materials, our big bet for the future, would gel with our already existing operation in that area, centered in the Shipley Company, a sector leader in which we had purchased a big stake several years before.

That was the main challenge facing me, I thought—to weld all these pieces together, overcoming the differences in corporate cultures and strategic agendas, while managing the mountain of debt, $3.5 billion, that we had taken on to get them. And I was prepared to do battle on that front, as daunting as that campaign promised to be. What transformed the battle into an all-out war were the challenges that took me by surprise, and that came in quick order, like ever-louder peals of thunder. The first came from a different kind of arranged marriage.

Rohm and Haas had a tradition of pairing its new CEOs with the executive who had finished second in the competition for the job. Vince Gregory, the first non-family member to become chief executive, had had Don Felley as his president. And Larry Wilson had teamed up with Jack Mulroney. These arranged marriages proved to be popular and practical. When it was my turn to become CEO, the board named Mike Fitzpatrick, who could just as easily have won the top job, as my No. 2. This marriage, unfortunately, proved to be counterproductive and rancorous. And it didn't stop there.

At a time when I most needed a strong and cohesive team, I also found myself with a new CFO who was brilliant at treasury matters and with investors but not particularly interested in operations, and many other of our high-level managers were having trouble finding their footing in our complicated new world. All this meant that instead of focusing on the critically important task of stitching together a new Rohm and Haas, I was mired more and more in efforts to patch the gaps in my own senior ranks.

Meanwhile, the storm clouds were gathering for what would be the dot-com collapse in early 2000, bringing with it a recession that flattened many of the assumptions on which we had made all those purchases. Suddenly, sales plummeted, not only in the electronics sector, but across the board, threatening the cash flow that we needed to service our debt.

And the final challenge wasn't really that surprising, since it had to do with my own shortcomings. Even after all those years at Rohm and Haas, I felt again, and on an important level, like a stranger in a strange land. Having spent so much of that time in postings in Europe, I didn't feel secure with either the founding family, who continued to own about a third of the company's stock, or with the board of directors. Although the directors had chosen me over Mike Fitzpatrick, I felt Mike had their ear in ways that I didn't. Some of these concerns were based in reality and some, perhaps most, grew out of the residue of my complicated, generally subconscious, feelings of being an outsider in a white man's world. Whatever the causes, the battle going on inside my head was hurting me as a chief executive, making me cautious and temporizing in some of my decisions, therefore putting Rohm and Haas further at risk.

Echoes of an Earlier Crisis

I was experiencing a kind of déjà vu. The company had tried to change direction once before, also with near-disastrous results with the fibers crisis a quarter of a century before I became CEO but one that still haunted me, which is why I reiterate its importance as I recount my tenure at the helm. I had known back then that the fibers crisis would have a lasting impact on me because the crisis nearly did us in and because it taught me that some business acquisitions or ventures had the potential to sink a company. I had needed to learn this because some day I might have the responsibility to steer Rohm and Haas through a terrible storm. And now I was in that storm.

With so many pressures being brought to bear, and so much at stake for my company and my career, I simply had to find ways to deal with all of these challenges and turn things around. It took more than four years of tough decisions, hard work, and some luck to put our house in order and get through the financial storm, not only in one unified piece but also positioned to grow again as the economy gained speed.

I certainly didn't accomplish all this on my own. The management team that I eventually put together gets much of the credit. And the advice I received from many other trusted colleagues—including my predecessor, Larry Wilson; the lead independent board member, Sandy Moose; and my first boss and mentor, Fred Shaffer, who stepped down as CFO in 1997— was simply indispensable. Together, we found the way through.

Outside Forces, Inside Turmoil

When the dot-com world started disintegrating in 2000, and with it the stock market and economy, it took a while to understand just how precarious our position was.

Some of the trouble began with currencies. The dollar was heading in the wrong direction, a trend that saw it decline 30-plus percent against the euro from 2000 to 2007. We were missing our projected revenue numbers and probably losing market share as well. It was hard for us to see integration savings. In fact, it was hard for us to see much of anything—we had more than 60 information systems spitting out data that we couldn't easily put together into a coherent picture, making the overall management of our sprawling new company a scattershot exercise at best. And, of course, the electronics business started to collapse. After making a record profit in 1999, by the time 2000 started, cracks were appearing in the wall. On top of that, the board was getting a bit nervous about events and our reaction to them. At one meeting, the leader of the agricultural chemicals business suggested we needed to divest ourselves of that unit and then made a recommendation justifying why we should keep it!

These and other missteps suggested we weren't paying attention to the right things. There were certainly a lot of things to worry about. Getting the culture right and realizing the potential synergies while fighting the headwinds of a faltering economy, unfavorable exchange rates, and the heavy burden of our debt made this a high-wire balancing act, something akin to Nik Wallenda's crossing Niagara Falls or the Grand Canyon. By the summer of 2000, things looked grim.

If we were going to prevail, we would have to stay calm, focused, and positive. I reached back to what I had learned during the fibers crisis in the mid-'70s, and that was to concentrate on three main areas. One was to manage for cash. The first commandment for business is never run out of cash. The second was to invest in the long term and not to compromise on essential spending. The company's seed corn is investment in technology, globalization, and information systems. Otherwise, we would just be postponing our demise. And the third essential mandate was to field the strongest and best-aligned team at the top. We knew that if we made a conscious decision to adhere to those principles, and if we got our strategy right, we would get to the future and it would be a successful one.

In some ways, creating the right team was the paramount need. That team needed to be cohesive, well informed, and able to communicate with all of our people. We could not generate growth and profitability if the nearly 23,000 people who were now under the much-bigger Rohm and Haas umbrella were puzzled by their mission. People need to hear about the goals and objectives that management has laid out and then be given the freedom, as well as the accountability, to act upon them. Employees can't intuit these things—they must have clear direction and purpose.

Once the deals closed on the new businesses, we began a leadership transformation from a Rohm and Haas-centric management team to an amalgam of 40 people that we initially called the Leadership Council. This group included the functional heads, the regional heads, and the business unit heads from around the world. It was a real blend of people, business backgrounds, and corporate cultures.

We had many all-stars in the group, and they were very talented and capable people. But they didn't function as a team, at least not a smooth-running one. A lot of what hit us in those early days came from outside macroeconomic forces, but much of the rest of our trouble could be traced to the "team"—all of these individuals working together for the first time—trying to do new things, to drive down costs, to hold on to the business, and to adapt to new colleagues and new products. And the results, to be charitable, were mixed.

One effort was to cross-fertilize the leadership across businesses. So we took some of the Rohm and Haas folks and made them head of some Morton businesses. We took some Morton folks and made them head of our businesses. In electronic materials, we moved some people from Shipley into LeaRonal and vice versa. One big dividend from this personnel shuffle was the emergence of a high-potential manager from Morton International, Jacques Croisetiere, who was tapped to run our struggling ion exchange resins business. He did what was required—closing or downsizing inefficient plants, re-configuring the product portfolio, and energizing leadership to the point that we put him into bigger and bigger roles.

Unfortunately, though, many other senior managers, who were very good leaders when things were in a growth mode, were not effective in dealing with a stressful external environment. That led to a combination of late and inaccurate information in their business forecasts and in their ability to deliver results. We were hearing more excuses about inability to solve the problems we were facing than suggested solutions, and this negative leadership trait highlighted the need to make even more changes.

Changing the Lineup

This proved to be my biggest challenge. In order to realize the tremendous potential offered to us and to make the corrections I needed in the businesses, I had to make sure that we had the right people aboard who could lead us through this down period. So I took stock of my senior team. I probably turned over half of them in the first two years alone. The entire process took a few years. It was not until 2003 that I hit my stride. That's far too long. To me, anything more than six months or a year is far too long, particularly in view of the way the world is operating today. If you don't have a team that you're aligned with and that you can fully trust to work together, it's very hard to get anything accomplished. I take as much responsibility for this long learning curve as anybody. I was inexperienced and uncertain in dealing with the board for the first time, so it took a while. Two observations emerge: 1) if a board appoints somebody, they ought to be very, very thoughtful whom they appoint; and 2) once appointed, he or she ought to have the freedom to put their team together relatively quickly and to hold them accountable for their performance against objectives.

At first, the only senior executive with real focus was Pierre Brondeau. He made sure that as leaders in the electronic materials business, we were evaluating which sites we needed and which had to be closed, who should be running the operating divisions, and the metrics that needed to be applied and met. During all my quarterly reviews with my senior team, Pierre was the singular exception in never offering an excuse as to why numbers weren't being met or insisting that nothing was his fault. This, along with his ability to see a business strategically and his calm, objective demeanor, stayed with me as time went on. Pierre motivated people and solved problems, without apologies and without waffling. But we had a new CFO who was proving to be a disappointment and who had left me in an embarrassing position with

Wall Street analysts early in my tenure. In addition, my arranged marriage with Mike Fitzpatrick was heading for the rocks.

Mike could well have been named CEO and chairman instead of me—he was a brilliant and highly capable executive with deep knowledge of our company. But as the runner-up, he became president and COO, and the two of us found ourselves bound together at the hip. We divvied up who would handle what. Mike got oversight of the polymer resins business, the integration and cost synergies relating to Morton, our supply chain, and the overhaul of IT. I made sure that he had a broad portfolio with real responsibility, the kind of challenging mandate befitting an executive of his caliber.

Unfortunately, not all arranged marriages are meant to be. For a brief time, it worked well. But ultimately Mike couldn't accept that the CEO's job wasn't his. Instead of functioning as true partners, as my two predecessors had done with their presidents, we became strained and at odds despite numerous attempts to find the right formula, I felt I had no choice about giving up on that marriage. Our difficulties were getting in the way of solving all the demoralizing problems that our company faced. With great reluctance, I had to let Mike go, and I took over the president's role. I eventually replaced our CFO, putting Jacques Croisetiere in his place after Jacques had done a tour running the European region and global Ion Exchange Resins business. Part of my reluctance to act sooner was my fear that the board would not back me. Fortunately, my fear about what would happen if I *didn't* act ultimately proved stronger. I simply had to get the team right.

Sandy Moose, board director, shares her recollections of this time period in the shaded text below.

Someone Wins, Someone Loses

Sandy Moose, lead independent director:
The choice of CEO came down to Raj and Mike, a chemist by training who had deep business and R&D experience, with extensive time growing businesses abroad. It was a decision that teeter-tottered for a long time because both of them were very strong and very capable executives. The key thing that we liked about Raj and why he ultimately got the job was his strategic perspective and ability to connect the dots.

But Mike had tremendous operating experience. He had been in virtually every aspect of Rohm and Haas's operations, including R&D, and played every role in every part of the world. Mike was a distinguished scientist in his own right and we rather liked that, too. And he had the confidence of the Haas family. They probably knew Mike better than they did Raj at that point because Raj had spent the bulk of his career overseas.

What it came down to in the end were the issues that the company had to grapple with and who could best address them. And for us, the key criterion was, who was the better strategic thinker? So it tipped to Raj. Otherwise, it was a dead heat.

Having said that, we felt Mike was terrific and didn't want to lose him. We thought about how well Vince Gregory had worked with Don Felley after Vince had been chosen as CEO instead of Don, and how that success had been repeated with Larry Wilson and his runner-up, Jack Mulroney. So when we chose Raj, we hoped that there had been enough role modeling done with the two prior CEOs that the same great partnership would happen again with Raj and Mike. I think Raj went into this trying to make it work, although he had concerns. I know that Mike had not taken the CEO decision well but that he, outwardly at least, said he wanted the new arrangement to be successful, and I think he did.

Because of the experiences I went through early in my career as a woman, I could identify with Raj in terms of the substance of his concerns about whether he was on solid ground with the board as well as how he felt emotionally, given that he had to navigate all kinds of barriers himself. He was born in India and was obviously raised differently from the old-line Philadelphians who filled the upper ranks at Rohm and Haas. (Larry was not from Philadelphia, but he had an Ivy League background and came from the South, and Jack Mulroney was a Philadelphian who had gone to Penn.) While I never detected any misgivings about Raj due to his being culturally or ethnically different from predecessor CEOs, I am sure Raj had some doubts along the way and wondered whether he would really be well-received as the CEO. And because Raj had spent so much of his career overseas, he didn't know the Haas family all that well and I think he was aware that the decision was a close one between him and Mike. He certainly knew that the board wanted to keep Mike on. So Raj was very uncertain about the confidence level that any of us had about him.

Truth be told, we were more confident in him than he thought we were. On the other hand, he wasn't being paranoid or crazy to worry about it. If that wasn't enough to keep him awake at night, not long after he was elected, we had a new CFO. The new CFO came from the outside and hadn't devoted sufficient time or effort to cultivate relationships and build trust with the business unit managers or even with Raj himself. Then, just 24 hours before the company was going to report its first-quarter results for 2000, Raj was suddenly informed by his new CFO that the results for the booming electronic materials had just disappeared and the company was going to miss its estimates by 20 percent. So the new CFO tells Raj and Raj calls me and says, "Holy mackerel" or words to that effect.

So here's the newly appointed chairman and CEO in one of his early conversations with the Street and he has to say he's missed his targets. That was a pretty devastating blow early on in his tenure and put him in a pretty lonely position at the top. I could understand why he felt the way he did. It seemed everyone was letting him down when he needed them most.

That was when I started to forge a relationship with Raj because he had no one to talk to at that point. He recognized that he was in a very difficult situation with a brand new senior management team that wasn't fully up to speed and people he did not know personally.

And then there was Mike. I don't know whether or not Mike took those initial missteps as an opportunity to start flexing his muscles. But what happened was that, over time, Mike just felt more and more embittered, that he deserved to be CEO, and that the board had made a mistake in selecting Raj. We were getting reports that he was running around and telling people how Raj was mismanaging the company, especially when results were disappointing. So the management question here is, what does the CEO do at that point? Does he have discussions with his No. 2 and say, "We have to resolve this"? Or does he try to work through it and hope it gets better? The former is the right choice. The latter is the default position Raj took and that seldom works out.

With Raj it took a long time to work out and I give Raj the benefit of the doubt. But in all candor, this is where Raj's vulnerabilities and insecurities came into play. I can't say I would have done anything differently had I been in his shoes because I know the situation and know how he felt. By that I mean he believed Mike had a lot of board support. And he knew and understood that the two previous CEOs had forged successful relationships with their No. 2. So I think he felt as though it was his responsibility to make that relationship work.

Consequently, he spent a lot of time with Mike, maybe an inordinate amount of time. And he tried several things. He asked Mike what he wanted to do at the company. He gave him big tasks to complete; he gave him businesses to oversee; he gave him the supply chain to revamp. He gave him all sorts of major roles and responsibilities. He asked Mike what he could do differently that would enhance the relationship. He got Mike involved and said, "You know, I am going to treat you as my partner. We'll make these decisions jointly." He did everything he could by way of talking it out.

And it would work well for a few months and then it would flare up again. Something would hit Mike's insecurities and then Mike would go off and do some things that Raj felt were undermining. Not necessarily undermining Raj per se, but undermining the company and its mission and objectives. But sometimes Mike undermined Raj directly, even in meetings. So then that led to even more candid conversations, but Raj isn't someone who likes confrontation, so the inevitable got put off.

Having those conversations was probably more difficult for Raj than it would be for someone like me — I am willing to be more confrontational or combative if I need to be. In any case, they ultimately would have another one of those "come to Jesus meetings" and being fairly candid about each other and what needed to be changed to make the relationship successful. Again, it would work for a while and then something would happen that set it off course and it would become crystal clear that what Mike really wanted was to be CEO and was jealous of Raj. I think it was at this point that they reached out to Karol Wasylyshyn, thecompany's external executive coach and counselor, before calling it quits.

Karol was important in this process because she had a relationship with Raj as well as with Mike. She was able to smooth out differences that worked for a while until they didn't. Raj kept me apprised of everything that he was doing. He didn't at first because he wanted to see how things progressed but then he finally said, "This is what I've done. You don't know this but these are things that have happened. This is where we are." So I said to Raj quite candidly, "Listen, you need to start telling the board and laying out what you're going to do. We hired you as the CEO, not Mike. You are spending way too much time on your management team. You've got a CFO that isn't working out, either. And you've got to get people in these positions that you feel comfortable with and can do the job. If that means parting ways with Mike, well, part ways with Mike." Those were strong words but Raj took them well.

After that, he started to tell the board and began to trust individual members. There was a lot on Raj's plate at that point. The acquisition of Morton wasn't going so well and we needed to build out our electronic materials platform and move at a faster pace.

So with all that in play and at risk, Raj finally went ahead and told Mike it wasn't working out and Mike left the company. Raj also parted company with the CFO. And he replaced the head of research. Bottom line: Raj did what he needed to do in order to get a a higher-functioning team and operation. When that was completed, the rest of Raj's CEO tenure went quite smoothly. People trusted him; they gave him information in advance; his confidence in Pierre manifested itself in Pierre's being able to show his abilities. A lot of good things happened.

The Management Lesson Post-Morton

If I were advising a CEO just starting his tenure facing a similar management situation—a company that had just gone through a huge acquisition and a management team that was inherited—I would offer advice in a couple of different areas. One, I think, is having a strong conviction about doing the right thing and the second is doing it even though it has costs, both personal and professional. That's easier said than done. Part of managing at the CEO level is having confidence in your own decisions and further that the decisions you make are accepted by your management team, even though some of them may not have initially come to the same conclusion you have. If the people you're dealing with are going to second-guess your decisions, whether it turns out they're the right decisions or not, your relationship with them has not fully evolved, and you have to make a change. Thinking that things will eventually resolve themselves is not a solution for two reasons. First, it is unlikely that things will resolve themselves on their own; and second, you are undermining yourself and your leadership—and ultimately the company's performance—if you fail to lead in both substantive and demonstrative ways. Why? Because you will not be able to set a clear direction and make your senior people accountable and responsible for setting and achieving the company's strategic goals and objectives. Clearly this is a daunting task for any CEO, particularly one coming into a new job, or in a company facing huge challenges. You simply have to do it.

The Legacy of the CME Incident

Another déjà vu incident that went to the core of what the company stood for involved an episode concerning employee health and safety that occurred on my watch in the early 2000s. We learned that a long-serving chemist at our research facility in Spring House, PA, had been diagnosed with brain cancer. That led our epidemiologist, Dr. Arvind Carpenter, to start looking back over the 40 or so years the facility was in operation to determine what the actual number of cases were in order to determine if there was a link between the employee's brain cancer and the Spring House research facility. Typically, an epidemiologist will first do what is called a cohort mortality study in evaluating the risk or impact of a disease or disorder in a particular population. If a higher number of cases is found than would be expected in the U.S. population as a whole, then a case-control study is done to determine specifically what may have caused that disease or disorder. Dr. Carpenter determined that there were 12 identified individuals diagnosed with brain cancer over the 40 years the site had been in operation.

Dr. Carpenter did a rough calculation and thought the 12 individual cases warranted the more detailed and precise analysis associated with the case-control study. This would enable the company, he said, to find a cause as quickly as possible as opposed to doing a cohort study that would have delayed the answer about cause or correlation by about three years. The company's driving priority was to learn quickly about and address any risks if any correlations with the brain cancers were found, so that's what we did. In addition, Dr. Carpenter recommended and formed an independent, outside group of industry experts in epidemiology and industrial hygiene to advise the Rohm and Haas study team.

After an 18-month exhaustive process looking at over 30 categories of chemicals that both the cases and controls were exposed to, the study team announced in January 2004 that it could not find a meaningful or significant correlation with any chemical compound or group of compounds at the research facility. This was both reassuring and troubling at the same time because although it revealed that no statistically significant epidemiological correlation could be established, it also meant that we didn't have an answer for the families of the employees who died of brain cancer, or the employees of Spring House. We were confident that the facility was safe and presented no undue risk to our employees—past or present—but we could not explain the brain cancers to the family members involved. Litigation ensued, and our motives were questioned, including those of the people who carried out the study. But in spite of the fact that we knew going into the study that we might find ourselves culpable in some way, we had done the right thing in order to know as best we could what happened. The Haas family in particular, as well as our board, all agreed we had to do the study if we suspected there might be something at our facility contributing to the cases and address it. And while none of the study team members could say or find what caused the more than average number of brain cancers, I can say we did everything we could to find out. And to their credit, Dow Chemical, who inherited the study and issue when they acquired us, did the same, repeating the study. Again, they found no correlation with the research facility and the cancer cases, a conclusion echoed in the litigation results as well. If we said that Spring

House was a safe place to work, we had to know that the science said that as well, if employees were going to trust us and the company's efforts to find out.

Springing into Action

At the beginning of 2000, I was losing sleep not only over our huge debt load and slipping operating performance but also over a pending write-off of $1 billion of goodwill, defined as the intangible assets a company pays when it purchases a another company or business over fair market value, that was mostly related to the Morton acquisition. I worried that we were in danger of losing credibility with our stockholders. I literally had just a few weeks before our earnings release to engage in quarterly reviews with each of the business leaders worldwide to understand our situation and what we could do to stem our earnings slide and get our businesses on track with better visibility in terms of their performance and outlook. That's when we decided we would have to sell the agricultural chemicals business. I knew what the business was worth, and I was pretty clear about the set of conditions we needed to settle on a price. We knew that we had to go about the sale quietly. We had connections with Sumitomo and we reached out to them because they had the desire to expand overseas. We agreed on a price of $950 million. However, the discussions with Sumitomo got very complicated and moved very slowly, with no certainty of a positive outcome.

Then, to be candid, we lucked out. Somehow Dow Chemical got wind of our intentions and made clear that it was interested and would act very quickly. Dow Agro Sciences is among the largest agricultural chemical manufacturers in the world and would clearly benefit from acquiring our business and patents. While we were going through an excruciating back-and-forth with the Japanese, Dow came in, and we put some numbers on the table. Dow offered $1 billion in a matter of just a few months and shortly thereafter the deal was completed and announced. For them, it was a very good deal. For us, it was a lifesaver. The money we received allowed us to pay off a big part of our debt, clean up the portfolio, and walk a little lighter. The sale basically took us out of crisis mode.

The lesson is that sometimes you need to sell the family jewels when they are no longer a strategic asset and they can do more for you in the form of cash than in the value they hold for sentimental reasons. With agricultural chemicals, we knew that growth had to come from massive research spending to pursue new, innovative molecules. Pesticides are a game-of-chance combination that only big research can provide, and without the ability to make that sort of commitment, we didn't see any payoff in the cards for us. Pesticides were coming under increasing regulatory and public scrutiny, making positive outcomes less certain. We just didn't have the R&D firepower to stay in that arena, nor did we have the critical mass. We were looking for high-growth potential with high profit margins, and agricultural chemicals wasn't part of that strategy.

We were active on other fronts, as well, and having some successes. We did a large amount of restructuring of the electronics business in the first two years to put it back on track, and by 2001 it started to take off.

But the Morton businesses faltered, except for salt. Some of the blame belonged to us—we didn't do a good enough job of integrating Morton into our management and business team structure. There was open criticism of Morton for everything from their safety standards and the quality of their plants to their operating culture. This open criticism was a mistake: a lot of Morton people left as a result, taking with them their energy, expertise, and institutional knowledge. But much of the problem came from the other side. We found that some of the Morton businesses had been so severely underinvested for such a long time that they couldn't be saved. Were it not for Morton Salt, which continued to be a cash cow, the acquisition would have been a full-blown disaster.

We continued to keep our focus on managing cash, honing our strategy, and investing in technology, globalization, and information systems. As the economy was starting to recover, we were able to fix our balance sheet and leadership team so that, from an investor and share price perspective, everything was responding very well. By 2004, the company had turned the corner.

When I look back to those first few years, it was a case of fixing what was broken, and there was a lot to fix. In 2000, things were so bad that we didn't pay any bonuses. Our safety record had slipped. Everything was going the wrong way. I would give talks to employees in the cafeteria, saying it is what it is and here is what we need to do and this is what I'm going to do to meet my own responsibilities.

From 1999, when I came into my job, until 2004, when we knew we had made it, our entire effort went into just getting back on track. It wasn't until 2005 that we could finally map out what was next. We had the right products and synergies. Things were finally falling our way.

And we also had the right people. Jacques Croisetiere had become CFO. We promoted a highly articulate and brilliant researcher named Alan Barton to head up polymers and our Asia initiative. And we continued to give Pierre Brondeau more and more opportunities to run the businesses. I finally had the team I needed to take the company where we wanted to go in the 21st century. What we were also now ready to take on, although I had no way of knowing it then, was the other macroeconomic crisis that bracketed my years as CEO—the looming Great Recession of 2008. But meanwhile, we continued the necessary task of examining our succession-planning process.

7

Planning for Succession and Then Acquisition

"The best laid plans of mice and men often go awry."
—Robert Burns, poet

From Crisis to Recruitment:
Predicting Success in the CEO Candidate

I am sometimes asked if I can tease out success potential in a person I am interviewing for a senior position or even CEO of a company. That's an important consideration, because you'd certainly rather know if that person has "the right stuff" before his or her coming on board than afterward when it's either too late or the parting of the ways would cause a significant distraction, not to mention expense, in the organization.

I think the traditional interview process is very much a beauty contest and doesn't really provide much of a glimpse into how a person is going to handle difficult management issues. You check references, you do due diligence, but in the end, it's really hard to predict how a person is going to perform, first because you can't predict what's going to happen and second, because people change. Their circumstances change; their whole mindset may change; they get distracted by things; they are less focused because of whatever else is happening out there. The challenges they are confronted with are very different from what their experience base has been. Any number of things can happen. And the interview table is not a confessional. So, because of these difficulties in properly forecasting people's future behavior, I suggest tapping the opinions of as many people you trust as you can, weigh them carefully, and then go with your instincts, go on what's in your gut.

And after you hire him or her? One thing I do differently today is to act sooner rather than later. On one occasion, where I was running a company separate from Rohm and Haas, I knew three months after we had hired a person that he wasn't the right person for the job. It didn't mean that he wasn't smart or accomplished—he just wasn't the right person. So we had to part ways. You have to make timely decisions in these cases. It's only fair to them and it's what you have to do for your organization. You want to give a person a chance, but you also want to be honest. And by the time it comes time to make your decision, they're often not surprised. "I guess you're going to ask me to leave," they say. It's a situation you certainly don't relish being in, but if you're facing that dilemma, you're really doing them a favor. If they're not the right person for the job, somebody has to pull the plug. And that's an unpleasant event but an important one for a leader to be able to do. It's certainly difficult for me, and it does not come naturally. And there are no algorithms that foretell candidate success, as far as I know, although there is a growing cottage industry in gamification in the recruiting and screening process, I'm told. But C-suite recruitment involves very complex dynamics—assessing social competence as much as, if not more than, cognitive business acumen.

With that said, as we learned from the Wasylyshyn program, there are some psychometric tests for leaders to consider in assessing predictive behavior, but of course, there are no guarantees. Much of an individual's success is determined not by what they bring to the table but by how they work with others in both the old and new environments. That is something you can't really observe, no matter how many interviews you put the candidate through. Even in one's own career, moving up the ladder is not about what you can do or what you have done. It's much more about how you engage others to be your partners so that they feel valued and encouraged to push their talent and fulfill their potential. That is how organizational knowledge and culture are deepened and instilled and leadership talent built, in my opinion. Those leaders who don't engage others will not add the level of value they could to the company or help it reach its full potential.

A turn-off to me are the candidates who always talk about what they did and what they achieved as if no one else was involved or mattered. That tells me that these are the egocentric leaders. They see the organization and its people in terms of themselves, in terms of their imprint, demeanor, or personality. That is a red flag for me. On the other hand, there are people who will come in and talk genuinely about what they were able to accomplish as a team and as an individual. They talk much more about what the organization accomplished and about the talented group of people around them that got the results than about themselves. That's a completely different emphasis from the candidate who can only talk about his or her own accomplishments. It's the difference between "I" and "we." I'd rather hire—as well as work for—the "we" leader.

In my own career, what gave me the greatest satisfaction were the people decisions I made. In retrospect, these decisions could have been considered bold at the time, but with the benefit of time and reflection they were the most important, because they were longer-lasting and had more impact on the organization than did making specific decisions regarding a business in the portfolio or a product addition. When I made a good decision and it turned out to be absolutely the right choice, it allowed me the biggest sense of accomplishment, especially when that person never thought he or she was being considered or when someone simply fulfilled their potential. Both are enormously gratifying, both personally and professionally.

One specific example that comes to mind occurred during the difficult time when we had to replace our CFO. We had come to the decision that we needed a different kind of CFO, one more operationally focused than someone who had expertise primarily in deal-making or acquisitions. The employee I had in mind worked in our European region and was in Canada at the time on vacation. My assistant called him to set up an appointment. "Absolutely," he said, "I'll change my flight." He appeared in my office a few days later and I said, "I want to talk to you about the possibility that I'm going to ask you to move back to the U.S. I've got some things for you in mind. I just want you to be prepared about this." He looked surprised and said, "OK, Raj, I trust you."

Two months later, all the pieces fell into place when he happened to be in the U.S. on business. That night I invited him and his wife to my house for dinner. We were in the living room, just him and me, and I said, "You're going to be in a new job. You're going to be our CFO." He was flabbergasted. He said, "Why would you even think about giving me this job?" I said, "Good question. And very easy to answer. These are the reasons: I see your energy; I see your drive; I see your experience in the past where you were the CFO of the division and demonstrated your analytical ability in turning around a troubled business and your ability to prioritize and focus on critical issues. That's why," I told him. "And more importantly," I said, "we need an operational CFO, a hands-on finance chief, not just a Wall Street kind of CFO, and you are our man. The board is very supportive, so what's your decision?" He accepted on the spot and he worked out even better than I imagined. So I think people selection and seeing their success is probably the most rewarding thing. While you don't always get them right, when you can look back and say "I got it right," you feel a special kind of satisfaction. That was Jacques Croisetiere.

Some people say that instincts are responsible for these kinds of successes—that there is something in your gut, as Jack Welch used to say, or in your unconscious mind, maybe, that pointed you in the right direction. I know this is a hot topic in business and decision-making right now, but I think these kinds of "instincts" are formed or honed over a long period of time as a result of accumulated experiences. In addition, you have to be able to connect the dots. Having experience means you have observed, were exposed to, suffered through, or even failed as a result of events or circumstances that have given you the ability to boil down situations so as to yield cautionary behavior, guidelines, or operational principles. Experience tinctured with reflection brings wisdom, and that's what you want in a leader. Experience yields many unique situations and outcomes. But overall, you learn somehow to connect them. So if you look at a new situation, you say it's similar to something that happened before, but there are other things that are going on here, and you ask yourself how they could play out.

So instinct, I would say, is the accumulation of experiences and your ability to see the big picture, where all the players are, and what's about to happen, what basketball aficionados used to say about what made Larry

Bird so great. It wasn't just his raw ability, it was a combination of qualities and skills—supreme vision, anticipation, coordination, endurance, skill, and confidence—that separated him from other gifted players and shooters. In business, you may not always be able to say exactly why or how you come to a specific decision, but everything you see and know tells you what's the right thing to do. Sometimes you consult your senior staff, sometimes a trusted third-party advisor, but in the end, you have to have the courage and confidence to be able to act on those instincts and be able to make a decision. You might call it instinct, but in my view it is almost accumulated judgment. Maybe it's the same thing.

CEO succession is taking on greater and greater importance as companies feel the growing weight and obligations of corporate governance, transparency, and effective management at the C-suite level. Rohm and Haas had always looked at the people inside the company to fill the top jobs, so we put leadership development at the core of the company. I was the company's fifth CEO since its founding in 1908, with the first being founder Otto Haas who had two sons, F. Otto, Jr. and John C. Haas. Both worked at the company, but F. Otto, Jr. was the one whom Otto groomed and whom he made president and CEO from his deathbed on December 31, 1959, after having founded and run the company for over 50 years.

F. Otto, Jr., in turn, ran the company for ten years until physicians told him in 1970 that his continued workload was putting undue strain on his heart. Shortly thereafter, following what was reportedly an informal survey of his top people along with his own instincts and discussions with the board, he elevated the 47-year-old Foreign Operations Manager, Vince Gregory, above his older and more senior colleagues, to the top spot.

Vince Gregory, in turn, after a nearly 20-year tenure that was credited as having put the company on sounder financial footing after the fibers crisis, implementing TQL management practices, and having a vision that included electronic chemicals to buffer the commodity-like transformation of acrylic sheet and paint emulsions, tapped his former Treasurer and CFO, Larry Wilson, in 1988. Wilson had helped guide Gregory and the company through its various management and M&A strategies and probably knew better than anyone else what the company needed to do as it entered the last decade of the 20th century in preparation for the 21st. The man who came in second in that selection became president and COO, a Philadelphia-born-and-raised chemical engineer named Jack Mulroney.

In my case, I was named chairman and CEO in 1999 with the man who came in second named president and COO, a New-Orleans-born-and-raised Ph.D. chemist, Mike Fitzpatrick who, like his predecessor, had worked his way up the ranks with greater and greater responsibilities and tests. I won't go into the details again about Mike's and my relationship, but I revisit them here because the selection process was both objective in terms of corralling the best people and also dysfunctional, in my opinion. It is akin to a presidential election where the winner becomes President of the United States and the person who comes in second becomes Vice President of the United States. Are both candidates qualified to lead the nation or the company? Yes, although they bring different talents and skills. But would they make a good team? Maybe. They did for Rohm and Haas under Larry Wilson and Jack Mulroney. Given my difficulties with Mike, when I managed the selection of my successor, I tried to change the final selection process.

The process of selecting the chairman and CEO in and of itself was clearly proved to be superior and contained all sorts of vetting opportunities and checks and balances by many different groups. The task of identifying, assessing, developing, and mobilizing recognized talent throughout the company was vested with the Corporate Leadership Development Committee, or CLDC for short. The questions the CLDC would ask were: Who is ready to lead the company or fill the senior slots in three to five years, and who has the potential beyond that? That process worked quite well, and I had no intention to change it.

As CEO, armed with the most current work product of the CLDC, I met twice a year with the board to give them an update about the talent and succession we saw for each of our senior management positions, typically one to three candidates for every one of the positions that reported to me. That included the president and COO, business unit leaders, the CFO, the General Counsel, the head of Public Affairs, Environmental Health & Safety, and Manufacturing. These candidates also included those who were being groomed as a potential successor to me.

We wanted to expose these leaders to the board so that the board, both collectively and individually, got to know them, and vice versa, so that the selection process could be as seamless as possible. I started this process soon after I was selected in 1999, because I didn't want there to be an emergency appointment if something untoward happened to me before my scheduled retirement. By the time I reached the age of 60 in 2005-2006, we had already identified several qualified people for each spot. We did this well in advance of my retirement because we wanted everyone to know whom we had in mind so that as we got closer to the time, potential candidates would be aligned with each other, the board, and the organization. Operating in this way, we believed we probably would not need more than six months of transition after the final selection was made. The two candidates we had chosen for chairman and CEO were the head of Europe and the electronic materials business: Pierre Brondeau, a chemist by training who had worked in research and had managed the intricacies of our fast-moving electronics business with skill and a facile, strategic mind able to think strategically and tactically simultaneously, a rare gift; and our CFO, Jacques Croisetiere, who came from Morton and showed tremendous energy and bias for action, delivering excellent results from our ion exchange resins business as well as several businesses that had come over from Morton, in addition to running Europe, and then conceiving several strategic initiatives as CFO.

By now it was three years before my scheduled retirement, and we had expanded the roles of both of them. And I think by the time we got to the middle of 2007, we were pretty much settled that our choice would be Pierre. To accomplish our goal, we planned to name Pierre as president and COO while I remained chairman and CEO. That would give us a smooth transition over a year so that by the middle of 2009, when I would leave, Pierre would be totally ready. That was basically the plan that we put in place and more or less agreed to.

The reader might wonder how Jacques took the news that it would be Pierre, since these kinds of choices go to the heart of the competitive instinct so well-developed in executives ascending the corporate ladder, choices that arguably define in large measure one's professional achievements. CEO is the brass ring in the corporate culture. The short answer is that I don't know how Jacques really felt about it, except that he continued to do his job as CFO and didn't appear to skip a beat in his enthusiasm, innovative ideas, or management skills. But I will say this about such situations, which

I have seen often. Highly qualified executives, many times, want to be CEO because they think that this is expected of them. They have often navigated shark-infested waters and come out on top or shown remarkable talent and leadership throughout their careers. I am not sure that deep inside they all want to have that responsibility. With Jacques it was hard to tell exactly what his thoughts were at the time or even since. He certainly had the "right stuff," but I'm not sure he really wanted it. And sometimes the difference in actually getting the job comes down to temperament rather than competence.

What would Jacques' role be post-succession? I would not ask Pierre to have him as his president and COO if that was not his wish. If it weren't, I would ask the board and Pierre to suggest a transition for Jacques and to choose a COO whom both saw as a possible successor to Pierre rather than someone who "came in second" in the selection process. I would also ask them to make a decision in a timely manner so each could get comfortable with the other.

I said to the board that whoever you decide to select as my replacement, he or she should not be saddled by their automatically anointing the number 2 candidate as COO, particularly given that these two people competed. I think it is exceedingly important for organizations to set a different expectation, so that the CEO has people he or she trusts, believes in, and who will take them forward instead of having to figure out the politics of how to get the person, who just lost out for the no. 1 slot, become part of the team he or she was not going to lead.

But as events turned out, we didn't have the luxury of crafting that challenge. What turned out wasn't knowable prior to late 2007.

In late autumn 2007, we had just returned from a big investor presentation to update stockholders on where we were with respect to our Vision 2010 strategic plan. I asked both Jacques and Pierre to come into my office. They had no idea what the meeting was about. I then gave them the astounding news that the Haas family had decided to divest itself of the company. I wanted them to hear it from me. I explained that Janet Haas, the wife of John Otto Haas (son of F. Otto Haas, Jr.), who was a physician in her own right and an influential member of the family, had come to me on November 9, 2007, and announced that the family's financial advisors had recommended they divest most or all of their ownership in the company. The Haas's charitable trusts and individual stock ownership accounted for approximately 30 percent of the outstanding shares, making them the largest single shareholder. I was shocked, not so much by the news itself, but by the timing of it.

Implicitly I had always assumed that as long as John Haas was alive, the Haas family and trust ownership of the company would remain intact. I had always counted and could rely on the Haas family's support. They knew I took into consideration the best interests of the organization and its values in whatever decision I made or direction the company took to maximize the value of its portfolio, competitive position, or marketplace approach. It had been a partnership in all ways.

The Collapse of the Prussian Shield: The End of an Independent Company

Quite simply, nobody thought the family would want to sell while John Haas was still around. Nor had John, from what he had told me. John had served as the family patriarch ever since his brother, F. Otto, Jr., passed away in 1994. When I was made chairman and CEO in 1999, John said that he would be spokesperson for the family and that he would fully support the decisions the board and I made. While at one time there were two Haas family members on the board—Tom, F. Otto Jr.'s son, and David, John's son—John, as sole surviving son of Otto Sr., had explained that he would represent both sides of the family and at the same time keep the families united and separate from company operations or decisions. He called his position "the Prussian shield."

The Prussian shield made sense for a number of reasons. While the family and its trusts represented the single largest shareholder of the company, they did not have super majority voting rights. This worked well for me as it did, I'm sure, for my predecessor, Larry Wilson. We certainly kept the family informed of our operations, meeting with them every quarter or taking them to our worldwide sites to see and meet our management and employees, but we did not go to them for decisions or permission to do what we needed to do to keep the company profitable, viable, and growing. Obviously the Prussian shield had now been breached, in the unofficial sense of a boundary between family and company interests. As I had not received any indications from the two family board members or from John about the changed view on the part of the family and its trusts, I had been rather stunned when Janet communicated their intent to me. As chairman and CEO of a publicly-traded company, however, I had to see her and the family as just one of the company's shareholders, a huge one for sure, but not the only one. So I told her that the company would respond appropriately to their request and that the board would be taking charge of this process.

Not surprisingly, both Pierre and Jacques were taken aback by the news, but they were both smart enough to read between the lines about the possible scenarios, i.e., that the company could be acquired. The most distraught and visibly shaken was Pierre for the obvious reason that CEO of *this* company was the job he aspired to.

Pierre and I continued the conversation that weekend over a cup of coffee at the Radnor Hotel on the Philadelphia Main Line, basically laying out the reality of the situation, determining that he would be part of the process, whatever it turned out to be, and assuring that confidentiality would be honored. I told only two other individuals—John McKeogh, my trusted PR advisor, and Bob Lonergan, our General Counsel—so five people in the company knew. I swore them all to secrecy.

Events took on their own speed and character between December 2007 and July 10, 2008, when we announced that Dow would acquire us.

Furious private negotiations for Rohm and Haas that principally involved DuPont, BASF, and Dow Chemical resulted in a hailstorm of discussions and negotiations between the Rohm and Haas board and their legal advisor (Wachtell, Lipton, Rosen & Katz), investment bankers (Goldman Sachs), and the Haas family and their legal (Cravath, Swain & Moore) and financial (Lazard) advisors. Throughout these months we left no details unattended and kept key stakeholders informed. I had been in on all the board calls, so I knew what was being discussed, and I kept my four confidante colleagues fully updated. I wanted as complete an engagement process as possible for all appropriate stakeholders, as much as the law allowed, and I wanted the board to fully discharge their fiduciary responsibility to the shareholders.

We had a number of discussions about succession during April 2008, as macroeconomic events were appearing to derail the deal with Dow, who had emerged as the buyer. Both Pierre and I had finally come to the conclusion that the best thing for Rohm and Haas, regardless of what happened, was to proceed with our plan and announce Pierre's appointment as president and COO. Doing so accomplished two things. We sent a signal to Wall Street that we were minding our own store and there was business as usual at Rohm and Haas; and we sent a signal to Dow that as president and COO, Pierre should be a leading player. And if for some reason he weren't, he would be in the position to leave the company as the former president and COO of Rohm and Haas. He obviously was my recommendation and the board's choice, so he was ready and able to take on the leadership mantle, regardless of what happened. And I wanted to help him. He was the best executive I had ever had the privilege to mentor. As for my own future, I was ready to move on to whatever that next chapter or opportunity might be, and this was made clear in the board's announcement on July 10th. The announcement capped for $78 a share, all cash, or a 74 percent premium over the share price closing on Wednesday, July 9, 2008, the day before the announcement, for a whopping $15.3 billion for the equity holders and at $18.8 billion in Enterprise Value (EV).

Cancer in the Face of a Corporate Acquisition and the Kabuki Dance that Followed

One does not choose if or when to have cancer. It chooses you and arrives with its own timetable. The choices that come after that are partly yours, partly medical science's, partly health care plan, partly physician advice, and partly luck. In my own case, I really had never been a sick person. So weighing anything like treatment options had to fit into something I already knew or could deal with; otherwise, I would go to pieces and not be able to handle it. I knew that in general I faced things as they came, so I tried to do the same thing when I was diagnosed with prostate cancer in August 2008. I told myself I would just deal with it and move on. I think whether it is relationships, or career, or something like cancer, you have to confront reality as it is, or at least your understanding of reality, so that's what I tried to do. I also knew I had to pay attention to my condition and that it could be serious. I planned, took actions, and mobilized all of my resources and contacts and came to a conclusion—I would have the prostate surgery. I don't like prolonging things, and one of the treatment regimens is waiting to see if it gets worse. Fortunately, mine was not in an advanced stage when I was diagnosed.

Now we fast forward from my diagnosis to September and October 2008. Dow and Rohm and Haas were moving full steam ahead in terms of the integration planning, the new organization structure, people assessment, and the optimism that surrounded Dow's initial decision to keep many Rohm and Haas people as well as place them in the majority of the important positions in the Rohm and Haas businesses coming over. Two concurrent events now occurred: one macroeconomic—the price of oil was rising, and the other organizational and legal—the two companies were working collaboratively to get the two filings done for both the U.S. and European approval for antitrust. The collaboration was all incredibly positive. It looked like the two companies would come together by the end of the year, so that by January 1, 2009 we would have a new organization in place, a new company.

But a couple of external events threw a monkey wrench into that collaboration. One was that the price of oil hit the roof. I mean, there was no end in sight. I think it peaked at $150 a barrel during that timeframe, dramatically increasing the cost of petrochemicals, the building blocks of the industry, for the downstream chemical companies. And then something even worse—the financial collapse that led to the economic downturn of a magnitude that nobody had seen or anticipated. Lehman Brothers was allowed to fail that September, and the combination of that plus the economic collapse of the housing market made the whole financial crisis a catastrophic event. Demand collapsed, costs were up, and clearly everybody's financial performance was going down the drain. And all of a sudden we started to notice that the level of engagement from Dow in all of the discussions that were going on collapsed as well. Dow executives stopped contact with us, discussions about the future just started to evaporate, and planning came to a halt. It was as though one family wanted to call off the marriage.

And the press didn't let anyone forget that Dow was paying a pretty penny for Rohm and Haas and questioned the value that they had assigned, particularly when stock prices declined for everybody. Quite frankly, I started to question whether this deal would go through under the original contract. There were several drivers for my question, including the sudden silence on the part of Dow to continue integration planning, but the most critical was the concern raised when the Dow venture with Kuwait Petroleum fell through in December 2008, putting into question where Dow was going to get the $7 to $8 billion of equity needed to finance the acquisition. So in a matter of months, new questions reared their heads regarding the value, the availability of funds, and then the speculations regarding whether Dow should renegotiate the price or just cancel the agreement and pay the break-up fees.

To our mind, we were not going to renegotiate the price. Once we decided to explore the sale of the company, we contractually stipulated three things. First, this was going to be an all-cash transaction. We did not want another company's equity. Second, once we agreed on the terms of the deal, certainty of closing was a key element of the agreement. Finally, we assured ourselves that there would be no "material adverse conditions" for closing that could derail the deal—conditions either on the part of Rohm and Haas or externally in the marketplace. As part of this, there were to be no financing conditions on closing the transaction that could disrupt or upset the deal. So from a legal standpoint, Rohm and Haas was in the driver's seat. The only condition was that the deal must get antitrust approval from the U.S. and Europe. We knew that Dow had sufficient remedies in order to go to closing. The only question was the timing. To address that, we had included the stipulation that beginning 24 hours after the last regulator approved the deal, if Dow did not close the deal, there would be a penalty. We called it "ticking fees." We had included this condition to get the approval process accelerated and make all the compromises that they needed to make in a timely manner.

We had what I would call an airtight contract. And, in fact, when the media began speculating about the deal, it turned out that in reality, very few of them really understood how tight this contract was and that the breakup fees were not an option because there were no conditions spelled out for the deal not to happen, unless, of course, the regulators didn't approve it. It was basically a deal without a fallback for Dow, because as soon as the antitrust approvals were received, the clock starting ticking. The agreement stipulated that the deal would close within 24 hours. That was it. It could go beyond six months up to nine months if Dow wanted to pay the penalty every month, but our shareholders really couldn't lose value under any scenario. The critics simply did not understand the power of our contract.

Some investors, such as John Paulson, did. He bought Rohm and Haas at $70 a share and hung in there until the end and made sure the deal closed. Rohm and Haas went from $46 to $74 on the day of the announcement then drifted down to the mid-$50s because of Dow-generated talk about whether the deal was going to close or have to be renegotiated. By the end of 2008 Dow said it could not go forward with the deal as originally agreed. That spawned a period of great uncertainty—unnecessary, ill-conceived, and ill-advised in our opinion. We did get European Union approval just before Christmas 2008. So that hurdle was cleared. We had full expectation that a week after that we would get approval from the U.S. Justice Department. But it was delayed and delayed, and then we learned that while Rohm and Haas was cooperating with Dow, Dow, behind the scenes, was going back to the Justice Department and suggesting that they should delay or block the deal. Dow did that because this was the only condition that could cancel the deal. That would then trigger the breakup fees, a path Dow evidently thought was a better option than acquisition. The negotiations had turned into a kabuki dance.

The Rohm and Haas board met in December 2008 to review all these events. I had just come back from my surgery literally three or four weeks before. We had planned the December meeting to be the last time the Rohm and Haas board would meet. We had had, in fact, a celebration at the Barnes Foundation museum, including not only the incumbent board of directors but also all retired board members. While our deeper concerns feared otherwise, we acted as though this deal would go through. But at the same time we were preparing for the possibility that it could go sideways and could be contentious. Our advisors decided to start planning for the worst, and the board was very supportive of what we had to do if the deal didn't go through or Dow reneged.

It turned out to be a prudent and prescient decision. By the end of December, it was clear that Dow didn't have the money to close the deal. There was no indication from them that the deal was going to go through. So we turned our sights on early January. We were expecting imminent approval by the U.S. Justice Department and hoping against hope that Dow would come to the table, and we would close during the second week of January.

In the meantime, Dow Chairman and CEO Andrew Liveris called me and said we needed to talk. He flew to Philadelphia, and we met in my office—the two of us and two general counsels, Dow's and Rohm and Haas's. We wanted the facts: What had happened to Dow's business and what happened to the deal? They said they just didn't see any way they could close the transaction, even if the U.S. Justice Department approved it in the next week or so. They told us they didn't have the money and that the banks they had been counting on to loan them the money were now in dire straits. Even if the banks had the money to lend, the performance of Dow was such that they wouldn't be able to meet the covenants, and if they renegotiated the loans, the cost of borrowing would be prohibitive. Dow said they would have to announce bankruptcy.

We continued to meet over the next several weeks to monitor where things were. One meeting occurred on January 8, 2009, the day the company had organized a farewell reception for me in the lobby. There I was with Kamla saying goodbye to the hundreds of employees who had come downstairs to pay their special respects one last time, while Dow representatives were upstairs still talking about whether the deal was going to go through or not. It was all very strange, if not surreal—pent-up anticipation and excitement about the acquisition on the one hand and a dying deal on the other. It was an odd moment, to say the least.

Throughout all these meetings, Dow insisted that they still wanted to do the deal, that they saw Rohm and Haas as a valuable asset, but that they needed time. That was all well and good, but finally I had to tell Dow, and by "Dow" I mean my colleague and friend Andrew Liveris, that if Dow did not close this deal after the U.S. Justice Department approved it, then there must be careful, consistent, and accurate communication from both our organizations explaining exactly why. I told him I understood the financial dilemma Dow was in and the fact that he needed time for things to stabilize. But once we received approval from the Justice Department, I said, there must be a joint release spelling out Dow's intention and the Rohm and Haas board's agreement to close the deal within six months and that that the clock would start ticking regarding the penalty. Liveris demurred.

I forget his exact words, but he replied that he could not or would not agree to such a communication or agreement. He could not go public, he said, because he couldn't ensure that he could close the deal in six months' time. And so I said we should continue to find ways to figure out when he could do it, but that if he didn't offer any alternative, I would have to go to my board and proceed legally. This legal procedure was the homework that our advisors had already started and the path we feared we would have to take. I concluded by saying to Andrew that I knew he needed time and that hopefully the economy would improve and he could close the deal that he and Dow's board were contractually obligated to do. But if they had to, I told him, they would need to sell other valuable assets that would give them enough equity to close the deal and renegotiate with the banks.

The stakes were high and growing for Dow. There was a real possibility that they would have to sell their highest-performing assets, including Dow Agricultural Sciences and Dow Corning. But I could see, and had to tell him that I knew, nothing was really happening, and that was unacceptable. It turned out that the Federal Trade Commission and Justice Department approved the transaction in the middle of January, and the 24-hour clock started.

We basically parted company at that early meeting in January saying we couldn't reach an agreement on the deal. Our intention in holding the joint communication was to give Dow time to close the deal and still be within the terms of the contract. Had we not had a promise of a specified timeframe, we would have been in breach of our own obligations to our shareholders. I think in my last phone call to Dow about their intentions, they came up with language that said basically nothing of substance, essentially something to the effect that they could close the deal at their discretion. So I said, "Andrew, you know, this is the worst communication I've ever seen. It says nothing. There isn't really much to talk about here, so if we can't agree on anything, there's no point in continuing the conversation." That's when all the hard work and homework we had done came into play. The following morning we informed our board that we had decided to file suit in the Chancery Court of Delaware for expedited hearings. We asked for the expedited track because there was another clock running—Dow's financing availability deadline from its banks. If the deal did not close by June 30, 2009, the financing agreement Dow had would expire.

Simultaneously with the decision to file suit, we wrote an open letter to the Dow board from the lead director of our board admonishing Dow and its leadership for its inactions and failure to meet its obligations under the terms of the agreement and fiduciary responsibilities to its shareholders. It was candid and unvarnished. We said in no uncertain terms that we expected them to honor their contract. The letter is a matter of public record, and it stated our case and Dow's contractual obligations in the boldest of words.

"It's Not Over 'Til the Fat Lady Sings"

The litigation, since we had a bullet-proof contract, went fairly smoothly, though like all litigation, it involved a lot of people, their time, and, of course, lawyer fees, for both Dow and Rohm and Haas. It was an expedited process and it involved something like 60-plus depositions in a period of three or four weeks. In addition to the tens of millions of dollars in legal fees, this totally destabilized the workforce as well as our customers, who were starting to have some doubts and concerns about the integrity of the dealmakers. These dynamics drove the urgency to bring the deal to a successful close. We were all hurting ourselves, I knew. At this point the board asked me to see the company through the process, which I agreed to do, despite my needing to convalesce from the prostate surgery. Pierre had been running the company, so my schedule was pretty clear at that point. I had left the office on the 18th of December 2008 with the view that I was gone and I was not coming back. So when I agreed to begin again, managing this litigation, including the relationship between the key investors and the board along with the family, all of a sudden I was back in action at the beginning of January 2009. By then I had given up my office and my administrative assistant and was rightfully out of the loop on the everyday decisions being made. So my primary task and focus was now getting the deal done.

I have to say this was also a very awkward period. I had been chairman and CEO for ten years, had retired, and now had been asked back by the board. Can you imagine an outgoing President of the United States coming back to the White House to handle official business after the new President had been sworn in and inaugurated? It was a little like that on the corporate level for me. But I had agreed and promised to do my best to bring the deal to a close. As part of that, I talked with our lead independent director, Sandy Moose, on the phone for a couple of hours every day. My purpose here was to keep the board completely informed. So Sandy and I jointly handled that role. It is not easy to get the board together for even a call with just a few hours' notice, so we agreed to split calling the board between the two of us and to let them know individually every two or three days how events were unfolding. And in all those calls, we would have the advisors as well as Pierre Brondeau, president and COO, Jacques Croisetiere, CFO, Bob Lonergan, General Counsel, and my public affairs counselor, John McKeogh, participating. This was a very hectic time for all of us.

Meanwhile, there were our employees. We still had a company to run and some 15,000 employees who depended on us for updates. We did written, video, and face-to-face communications to help fill the gap. In addition, I went to the company cafeteria every day for lunch or for my coffee in order to see as many headquarters office employees as I could. I tried to act normal and positive, but it was difficult. The biggest question had been why we were selling the company. When they digested the reasons the Haas family wanted to divest their shares and diversify their holdings, employees had started getting excited about the prospect of being part of a larger company with more resources. Now, all of a sudden, it appeared Dow didn't want us, and by pushing to get the deal done, were we risking the wrath of Dow and bad treatment at the end? There were a lot of fears and questions.

Obviously, as Rohm and Haas employees they were concerned about their future within the organization and wanted to learn their fate as quickly as possible so they could move on if need be. Our response to these questions and concerns was that first, we have an obligation to our shareholders, who will approve this transaction, to see this deal to conclusion. Second, the answer to the question of why we don't reduce the price is that we are not permitted to even if we wanted to. Dow had the means to conclude this transaction in a reasonable period of time, and we had an obligation to our shareholders. Failing that, we would have myriad shareholder suits filed against us. And third, Dow was paying a premium price for a premium asset that would be a major part of Dow's transformation from just a commodity company to a specialty chemicals company. While they might be angry and upset with the Rohm and Haas board and me, it would be stupid of them to be vindictive to the employees of Rohm and Haas. That's what I said and that's what I believed.

I was not communicating with Andrew at this time. I would say the communication between us stopped probably between mid-January and the beginning of March 2009. There was really nothing for us to talk about at this point. The judge had granted us an expedited hearing, so there were depositions going on throughout this period. And the court was very responsive. Among state courts, the Delaware Chancery Court is a significant and important dispute-resolution body that has become the most important decider of corporate law in America. Given the overwhelming number of companies incorporated in the state, the court hears scores of prominent cases each year, and the decisions by its judges help shape the course of business law.

But this case was different. The judge's view was that this was a business issue that should be resolved between the parties. As a Chancery court officer, he was obligated to resolve the issues on the legal merits, but he thought they paled in contrast to what appeared to be intransigence on the part of Dow to do what he, the judge, knew it was supposed to. In other words, he didn't want to waste the court's time dealing with this. It was an airtight contract. Dow's defense was that they didn't have the money, and if the court insisted that they close the deal, they would be forced into bankruptcy and thousands of jobs in the two companies would be destroyed. That's a moral hazard defense argument, not a legal one, and as such, it is outside the court's jurisdiction. The judge said that if forced to, he would decide on the legal merits of the case. And he told both companies he didn't want to have to do that. He wanted us to settle our differences ourselves.

My sense is there was a bit of speculation that Dow's board and Liveris were working behind the scenes to liquidate assets as well as thinking about how they could run the company if they acquired Rohm and Haas. They didn't want to part with these assets, for sure, so they were looking at a number of scenarios to finance the deal. The reason I believe this is that I received an e-mail or phone call or both from Andrew in early March, indicating some movement on their side. And then on our side, John Paulson, whose arbitrage play had made him the largest shareholder outside the Haas family, became a *de facto* major party to the transaction. So there was a confluence of factors pushing to resolve the issues—from Dow's side and from ours.

When I got Andrew's communication, I called him, and he said, "Raj, shall we give this one more try, and can we meet in New York?" He suggested he would bring one of his directors, Dennis Reilley, former president and CEO of Praxair, whom I knew and respected, and meet as "principals." I said fine, but that I wanted to bring our lead independent director, Sandy Moose, with whom I had worked since becoming chairman and CEO and had known for many years before that. I trusted her implicitly. Andrew agreed, and the following day, we met in New York—just the four of us. My first words, after exchanging pleasantries, were to express how disappointed we were when we considered how we had started these discussions initially and where we found ourselves today.

Andrew really didn't protest much. You could see he was both angry and embarrassed. He said, "All right, so what can we do?" And I think that was the question and mindset that came to convince the Haas family and charitable trusts and Paulson & Co. that maybe there was a new path to completion, a path that led to doing the transaction in the form of perpetual equity, meaning that the sellers take a good part of their proceeds from the deal as basically deferred shares with a big coupon. The big plus for Dow in doing it that way was that they could then borrow the money from the banks and therefore close the deal. But the secret to this was that we needed to convince the rating agencies not to downgrade Dow to junk status, because if that happened, all the bank commitments would be gone, and Dow would be in an even more precarious financial situation because they couldn't borrow money at market rates. So we agreed to join Dow management, meeting with the credit rating agencies and asking them not to lower Dow's debt rating to junk status in the event the deal closed without additional equity infusion.

Why did Dow agree to this? I think Andrew had taken a hard look at all the factors and came to the conclusion that closing the deal, if he could do so without selling off Dow's most profitable assets, could work. First, he knew he was looking at an unfavorable decision from the Chancery Court because the contract was so rock-solid in Rohm and Haas's favor; second, he was looking at a downgraded credit rating the more time passed, especially if the court decided against him and his bank covenants expired; and third, the economy looked like it was recovering, so if he could get bridge financing and some additional preferred equity, as he had done from Warren Buffett, he could close the deal.

The financing meetings started with John Paulson's basically saying, "I will take all of my $1 billion in perpetual preferred shares with a very high dividend payment." The second piece involved the Haas family trusts' taking $2 billion of its $6 billion in perpetual preferred shares similar to Paulson's. These were the considerations we were discussing while preparing for the expedited hearing on March 8th. We all went down to Wilmington, Delaware Sunday night in preparation for Monday's hearing, where I was to be the first witness. We stayed in one hotel and Dow's people stayed in another. At 6:00 am on Monday Andrew called me and said, "Raj, it looks like we are close to having an agreement to conclude the deal under the original terms. And I will call you, but perhaps what we should do is to go to the judge. They were supposed to start the hearings at nine, and let's see if we can see him. If we can see him at about 8 o'clock and tell him that the two parties are getting close to an agreement, maybe he would agree to move the start of the hearings to a later time in the day."

The judge heard our request and granted it. Coincidentally, the Dow Jones Industrial Average was showing no improvement, hitting 6,500, the lowest point of the market at that time, with Dow Chemical closing at $5.70/share that day. So, from that standpoint, there was little light at the end of the macroeconomic tunnel, though our own deal looked optimistic for the first time in six months. Coincidentally, at the price Dow Chemical closed that day, the Haas family and trusts could have bought Dow and had money left over! Dow's market cap that day was barely $6 billion.

At 4 o'clock on the afternoon of March 8, 2009, we went into the judge's chambers and presented the agreement we finalized that day. We stipulated that both Dow's board as well as its senior management had to sign the agreement and they did. We agreed to allow Dow time to get all the financing in place by the new closing date, which would be April 1. The closing effectively ended my duties as chairman and CEO of the Rohm and Haas Company. Right after the signing on April 1st, I went for a week to our Florida home and upon return had a message that Andrew had a gift for me. He sent me a case of very elegant Australian wine. We had dueled both as adversaries and partners, but we parted as friends. I've seen him at least a half dozen times since then, and he is always very courteous, polite, and friendly. He knows that I respect him as a businessman, and he knows I did what I had to do and he did what he had to do. Our relationship survived the battle.

N.B. author's note: I related much of the boardroom drama with Dow Chemical, replete with white-knuckle deadlines and threats of litigation, in the *Harvard Business Review* (https://hbr.org/2010/11/how-i-did-it-rohm-and-haass-former-ceo-on-pulling-off-a-sweet-deal-in-a-down-market) and in an interview with *Directors & Boards* (http://directorsandboards.com/DBEBRIEFING/December2009/RajGuptaarticle.pdf but in much greater detail here.

My parents, Phool Prakash Gupta and Rukmini Sahai.

At age 5 in the garden where we lived in Bareilly, India.

In Paris, France, circa 1985, a confident, rising
executive still proving himself.

Our daughters, Vanita and Amita, circa 2000.

A Gupta family reunion with our mother, my
brother, sisters, and spouses, 1988.

Kamla with then-candidate Obama in 2008.

With presidential candidate Hillary Clinton in 2008.

A "diverse family"— Kamla and I with Dr. Charlotte
Sumner, Amita's spouse, Dr. Amita Gupta, Vanita Gupta,
Esq., and Chinh Le, Esq., Vanita's husband.

Our next generation--grandchildren, left to right, Austin Raj Gupta, age 5, Rohan Gupta Le, age 4, and Chetan Gupta Le, age 7.

U.S. Attorney General Eric Holder sharing an emotional good-bye with Vanita and well-wishers at his retirement farewell event and a proud moment for her father. Photo by Zach Gibson/The New York Times/Redux

PART III

Moving On—My Career after Rohm and Haas, My Family, and Reflections on the Lessons of My Life

WHAT'S NEXT?

"When a thing is done, it's done. Don't look back. Look forward to your next objective."
—George C. Marshall, American soldier and statesman

Weighing Options

After the Dow acquisition of Rohm and Haas, Karol Wasylyshyn was again helpful to me at this transitional time even though physically, emotionally, and psychologically, I felt I was ready to leave. She reached out to me and said, "Raj, I have seen a lot of successful transitions, and there is a framework that might be helpful to you. Don't think about what you did or didn't do at Rohm and Haas, think about what it is that you want to do now, what it is that will challenge you and something that you would enjoy." I had been involved with a number of non-profits. For a time I served on the board of St. Christopher's Hospital for Children in Philadelphia. That was in fact my first board of trustees assignment. I also served as a trustee of The International House and the Chemical Heritage Society based in Philadelphia, and for a while I was a trustee of Drexel University. These experiences and work with non-profits allowed me to see how that would work for me and also what I wanted to do next.

Five broad conclusions surfaced as a result. One is that if you grow up in a corporate world you really come to relish your ability to build something measurable based on a mission and objectives coupled with your own actions rather than hearing about someone else's and then commenting or offering an opinion. Another was that in terms of contributing to causes I believe in, the best thing I can do is to contribute money rather than time. I had no problem writing a check for worthwhile projects, so I believed that my money in the case of non-profits could add more value than my time. Third, I thought the area where I could add the most value in terms of my time was in the for-profit world wherein I could learn about diverse industries at the same time. I had a good head start. I was already on the boards of Tyco and Vanguard and had just been elected to the board of Hewlett-Packard, which I consider to be the original Silicon Valley company, so they would remain my focus.

The fourth revelation was the need, I felt, to disaffiliate from my engagement with the chemical industry in order to give myself complete independence on whatever I wanted to do. Dow wanted me on their board, and DuPont reached out to me once they knew that I was not going to Dow. A number of other peer companies contacted me, including Sherwin-Williams, a leading coatings customer of Rohm and Haas. The more I thought about and weighed these chemical industry offers, the more I realized that accepting them would compromise my own management style and way of doing things—which is what I told Andrew Liveris when he asked me to join Dow's board. I didn't want to be second-guessing the man who had acquired the company I had been with for 39 years and run for ten. And if I joined another chemical company board, I might know things about its competitors that I didn't think would be ethical to know as a board member. The chemical industry is a very close community. People know each other very well, and many of their businesses and supply chains overlap. Another consideration was that I wanted to enter the private equity world. That would allow me a fuller degree of freedom to still be in the chemical industry where there might be interest but avoid the kind of potential conflict of interest that serving on a competitor's board would have or suggest.

And separately, and perhaps the deeper reason for not joining another corporate board or continuing in some way with Dow, was that my own family was growing. My daughter Vanita had re-married and given birth to our first grandchild, Chetan, in November 2008 and, having just gone through a bout with prostate cancer, I wanted to spend more time with my family. If I were going to truly balance work with life, then indeed the lives of now my grandchildren had to take precedence.

8

A New Life in Private Equity— Not All PE Firms Are Alike

"Don't be intimidated by people who seem to be experts. Hear their points of view and get their judgments. But at the end of day, you've got to make a judgment because it's not their life that's going to be affected so much as your future."
—Robert Dallek, presidential historian

So now I had to put my post-Rohm and Haas life plan into action. Clearly it was the end of a significant chapter in my life and career, and I had to think about what was next. I had given a great deal of thought to what kinds of activities I wanted to pursue, and that centered on serving the business, for-profit sector personally and the philanthropic sector through monetary contributions. I was already on several important public company boards, so that became a springboard for starting my post-Rohm and Haas life.

In addition, I put out some feelers to private equity firms and got nice responses from KKR, the Carlyle Group, Blackstone, and Apollo, among others, and I met with each of their principals. They certainly knew who I was after the recent headlines and consummation of the Dow deal, and so I had a captive and interested audience that, had I just retired from Rohm and Haas without the Dow acquisition, perhaps might not have been the case. I was certainly familiar with private equity firms, as many of them reached out to Rohm and Haas about doing deals. I knew the operating formula whereby they buy an asset at an attractive price, turn around the business, use leverage generously, lower costs, then flip the company at a handsome profit. I came from the side of a public company that saw the world differently—building business over the long term with limited use of leverage.

PE firms manage entirely differently. They typically have 50-100 professionals who manage tens of billions of dollars' worth of assets. Their philosophy of how they pick and choose their targets, how they manage, and how they track the progress is a very sophisticated and precise art if not science. So there was plenty to learn, I thought. Their way of doing due diligence, of valuing the company, and of determining what needs to be done are different from what a typical manager does in a public company. First of all, they look at perhaps 20 to 40 deals before doing one. And once they get in, their approach and metrics are also different. Everything is speeded up.

Yet, in some ways I would say PE firms do things better or at least more efficiently than the typical large public corporation.

First, they have a shorter time horizon (typically three to five years) because to them, time is money. They're always thinking about their exit strategy in order to maximize the time value of their investment. In a corporation, executives buy companies and invest for the long term, and sometimes focus is lost. The acquisition(s) get commingled with other assets in the portfolio and are lost in the shuffle.

Second, PE firms don't lose sight of the bottom-line objective. They have very clear expectations in terms of the sales growth, margin improvement, and return on capital in any investment they make or in the companies they're involved with.

And third, I would say they do better due diligence or at least suffer from fewer distractions or emotions about a business than their public company equivalents; they are much more engaged as a shareholder than is a typical public company shareholder. They are looking at shareholder value (theirs) all the time.

While I came to understand and appreciate the process, it didn't quite resonate with me that that's what I wanted to do. All my life I had been a builder rather than a kind of financial engineer, so it wasn't just making money and then more money that motivated me; it was more about building something. But I began talking with them, probably in January-February of 2009, and I had a conversation with Ed Breen, chairman and CEO of Tyco International, whom I knew from being on the Tyco board.

Ed came out of a technology background as president and COO of Motorola and CEO of General Instrument before that, and he had a lot of experience with private equity firms. He said, "Raj, I know this firm called New Mountain Capital, and I know Steve Klinsky, the founder and CEO, who is a good friend, and he and I worked together in the past. They are thinking about the materials space as something of interest. Before you make up your mind you may just want to go see Steve." So I took Ed's advice.

Steve Klinsky is not your typical PE leader, or not like the big ones anyway. He started New Mountain Capital in 1999 and runs the firm with a philosophy of building businesses and not just flipping them in some specified timeframe. "We don't just do financial engineering," he said. "We have a long-term time horizon. And we think the materials space might be an interesting space for us to look at, a space where you have a lot of expertise and experience, not to mention the fact that Ed says you are good guy. So we would like you to join us as an advisor with a retainer and then a year later we will assess the situation and see if it is working for both of us. And if it is working, we'll continue, and if it's not we'll part as friends." That was fine with me, so I said yes, I'd join the firm, which I did in the summer of 2009.

I liked Steve's approach. You can't just speed up the conveyor belt of a company and expect that therefore everything will be done faster. Time has consequences—on decisions as well as outcomes and people. It was clear from where the firm was and where it wanted to go that Steve and his team needed me. He hadn't done any transactions in materials-science-based companies, and that's what Rohm and Haas was basically—a materials-science specialty chemicals company—and so I could make a contribution to their team.

The important point here for me was that I didn't want to come in as a one-off kind of former CEO. I've seen those guys. They have had a great career, have made a lot of money, know everyone in the organization and the industry, and then all of a sudden they're thrust into a wholly different kind of enterprise where time horizons are shrunk, metrics are tight, and performance is everything. They're like fish out of water. They don't know anyone in either the firm or the company they have taken over, nor do they share any common history or experiences. And then, all of a sudden, they have to deliver on a well-laid-out, three-year plan. That often means the customers, employees, and suppliers end up getting a big haircut so the numbers will work. That wasn't for me. But New Mountain Capital was.

Our first acquisition was the former Mallinckrodt Baker chemicals company near Philipsburg, New Jersey, acquired from Covidien in 2010, whose products served the pharmaceutical, biopharmaceutical, research labs, and electronics industries. We re-named it Avantor Performance Materials. I serve as executive chairman and support the management team. I have two different roles here. My first obligation is to New Mountain Capital, where my role is to help them identify target opportunities and open the door to make connections at the right level, using perhaps my network in the corporate world. I then follow up with helping them with the due diligence—all part of my work as a senior advisor to New Mountain Capital. And then once they make their investment, such as in Mallinckrodt Baker, I help recruit the leadership team, and finally, I make sure the results are on track. New Mountain made two other acquisitions in the chemicals space—in India and in Poland. Both acquisitions are integrated with Avantor.

Already I have learned many lessons and different operating and managing styles. First, New Mountain Capital's leadership interacts with me in a very different way than, say, the Rohm and Haas board interacted with me. It's different with each private equity firm, depending on how they choose to engage with the target company. In some cases, it would be having a representation on the board with the board really having an operational function, not your typical board of directors meeting once a quarter. Operating boards' members are usually on the phone every day, watching over the CEO. New Mountain's model is that there is a senior member at New Mountain who is basically the champion of the acquired company, and s/he engages with the company at multiple levels on a day-to-day basis. The New Mountain Capital advisor, like myself, is engaged with the company CEO, and the CEO runs the company.

I will confess that had I seen and been more immersed in this approach and learning earlier in my life, I would probably have been a better CEO of a public company. I think there is a lot to learn from the PE model of operating. You cannot put everybody in private equity in the same bucket and say all are bad or all are good or all are in between. And a corollary is that private equity firms do need experienced and prudent advisors. First, they bring reality to the management process. You can't have just smart MBAs and consultants as part of the private equity advising process. That person has to know the challenges and grunt work that needs to happen in order for the business to operate. And second, the advisor needs to understand your stakeholders and shareholders in terms of where they are coming from and how to engage with them.

In my own case, I now wear a lot of hats—chairman, senior advisor, board member of PE-owned companies, and board member to four broad-based, shareholder-owned companies, Tyco International, HP, Delphi, and Vanguard—all very different organizations with different cultures, issues, problems, challenges, and opportunities. So I have to be able to ask and answer tough questions about justifications, rationales for strategy, resource allocation demands, people selection, and new business decisions. Making these decisions and seeing the mix they bring to a company, its culture, and its stakeholders have certainly made me a better board member in a public company. Some decisions have involved repairing reputations, some in reshaping a company's culture to get back to what they once had, others in assisting employees who have lost everything—their equity, bonuses, salary increases, even the guarantee of a job tomorrow—and others in sustaining and supporting a company's success and continued development. They're all different and require a different set of questions.

Looking Back on the CEO's Job
After Joining a PE Firm

What would I have done differently as a CEO if could apply what I have learned from a PE firm?

I would have thought differently about investments and the time I spent doing them, and I would have established greater accountability, whether it was an internal investment project or an acquisition. In big corporations someone sponsors the acquisition or big investment project, falls in love with it, and is promoted a year later. Then top management changes, the acquisition is frowned upon, and all is lost. Everybody loses in that scenario—the employees of the acquired company, its customers, and the firm's shareholders who financed it. In a private equity situation, accountability and visibility reign supreme. There is much more clarity in terms of your outcome and accountability. You don't buy something because you fell in love with it, at least not by itself. It has to make sense on its face or it doesn't happen. We fell in love with some businesses at Rohm and Haas that we shouldn't have bought or been in. Then it becomes like the old joke, "What are the two happiest days for a boat owner? The day he buys the boat and the day he sells it."

I would also fine-tune the standards in terms of the level of due diligence, and the questioning would be far more intense than what we typically did regarding the financial discipline required to make it profitable and sustainable. Furthermore, I would overlay another level of scrutiny. By that I mean I would have the decision process driven by clear sight on value creation. The public company isn't under that ticking clock, but it still needs to do a better and more disciplined job of setting expectations. Clearly, public companies need to bring managerial wisdom and prudence to the process.

9

BOARDS: THEIR IMPORTANCE AND ROLE IN CORPORATE GOVERNANCE

"Mention the phrase 'board of directors' to the average investor, and they are likely to conjure up images of nicely dressed men and women standing around a mahogany table, smiling congenially. Now, ask the investor to describe the primary responsibility of the board of directors and very few will be able to give you a definitive answer."
—Joshua Kennon, financial advisor, investor, and author

Creating Sustainable Value for Boards

I have come to see private equity firms in a whole new light, and also, as I navigate my life post-Rohm and Haas, I have come to see the role and responsibilities of board membership in new and expanding ways. One of my mentors and now good friend, Jack Krol, has played a big role in that process. Jack recruited me to the Tyco board. He has taught me a great deal about boards, and I value his insights. Those insights, I believe, would be useful and insightful to anyone who has interest in corporate governance as well as best governance practices.

Jack is the former chairman and CEO of DuPont, and he served with me on Tyco International's board from 2002, when Jack was lead director, until 2008. He also served as chairman on Delphi Automotive's board from 2009-2014. Jack made history with Ed Breen, who took over Tyco

International in 2002, when former CEO Dennis Kozlowski and his CFO resigned after being indicted and later convicted of fraud and embezzlement. Ed and Jack basically threw out the old board at Tyco and installed a new board in order to save the tarnished and hugely indebted company whose former executives' lavish lifestyles and criminal behavior all but sank the conglomerate. I was one of those new board members recruited by Jack and Ed. Ed is currently non-executive chairman of Tyco and Jack is a former director. Jack joined Delphi Automotive as board chairman in 2009, the company having just emerged from a messy spin-off from General Motors and four years in bankruptcy. There he built an entirely new board to include a seasoned blend of executives from the electronics, IT, finance, specialty chemicals, auto manufacturing, and related industries. I was part of that new board as well. Following are excerpts from Jack's thoughts and observations, including what criteria he looks for in recruiting a board member, a board's obligations to the company and its shareholders, and his assessments of me as a board colleague.

I first met Raj when I recruited him for Tyco's board of directors. He came highly recommended as someone with impeccable character and credentials. Everyone who knew him gave him very high marks, including the companies that recruited him to serve on their boards. That's basically why I recruited him for Tyco's board. He did an outstanding job there. Over time, it became more and more apparent to me how strong and consistent his leadership skills were, and we have grown to be close friends in the period since. I'll focus my remarks on what is required to be an effective board member and to potentially become chairman, and how I feel Raj meets those criteria.

What do you look for when you look for someone who can run a board? The first question I always ask is: What's the track record or success of this person? What does he or she bring with their experience that this board can use? These are important questions to discuss with a wide range of sources. An hour with the candidate is not sufficient. That's only a snapshot. His or her track record over the past 10 or 15 years is the backdrop to the interview that is most important.

How does the assessment process start? First, review business experience and results. How broad was the experience? Does it fit the board's needs? Every board should have an up-to-date list of backgrounds needed on the board. For example, at Tyco, which was a conglomerate, we recruited several CEOs from different business backgrounds. At Delphi, we recruited several CEOs and others with automotive backgrounds.

In all cases, people with financial backgrounds are necessary, preferably CFOs. The rest depends on other specific backgrounds needed.

A very important criterion is a record of high integrity, ethics, and trust. An issue in this area would be reason for rejection.

You also need to focus on the candidates who will best fit with the board—someone who will have the respect and confidence of board colleagues. Is he or she a team player or likely to be divisive and controversial? There's a balance here that's important. You want someone who has the conviction of their opinions, but is collaborative with the other directors. The candidates should have consistent temperament and style and be comfortable with their place in life. We're not looking for the next President of the United States or someone focusing on becoming chairman of the board. We're looking for an individual who can listen as well as offer judgments and is able to come to a consensus. Raj fits the above and brings both leadership and social competencies in his management style.

In addition to a core set of competencies, the ideal board candidate has to have the energy and drive to put the time into really understanding the company's business model so that he or she can contribute on both the strategic and operational side. As part of this two-sided perspective of the company, it's important that the candidate listens well and can draw out the board's thinking and ideas. This entails asking probing questions, what-ifs, turning the logic around and coming at it from different angles, all to bring out the best thinking of the board and get them all involved and engaged in the questions and issues to extract the best conclusion.

The issues that get to the board's attention are the tough ones, so they are important as well as sometimes very thorny. What makes Raj particularly suited to serve and lead a board is that he brings these skills to a discussion in a very quiet, almost invisible manner, and is persistent in getting consensus. These are highly desirable skills, very important to board membership, and absolutely essential for board leadership. The only observation I would have of this is that sometimes, not always, but sometimes, particularly in reaching tough decisions, there is the need for a board member to be a little louder than softer and more forthcoming about his views. Raj has the kind of temperament that boards need. He's smart, strategic, and even-tempered, not to mention gracious and generous. His ego is very much in check. He is a modest man by all measures and that is an important competency for a board member, much less a CEO. In his way, Raj generally gets consensus on thorny issues.

The above are the qualities that prompted me to have him join the Delphi board in 2009. Of course, I had the opportunity to observe Raj on Tyco's board where he served on the compensation and HR committee, took a very complex situation surrounding compensation to the board, and got the board in line. It was not easy at Tyco, because in those days following the scandal, there were people on the board who didn't see the company as objectively, I think, as Raj did. We basically needed to overhaul the company, including the compensation program. We made Raj chairman of the compensation committee. Today the board runs very smoothly, thanks to Raj, Ed Breen, and their board colleagues. Raj led the compensation committee to develop a leading compensation program. He did an outstanding job.

Raj was a member of that new crop of board members in 2009 whom I recruited. As we did our board evaluations, I called each individual sitting board member and asked two questions: First, who is making good contributions to the board and who might make more? And second, I asked each to name one or two board members who would be a good candidate for chairman. Raj generally came up at the top of the list. So, from my standpoint and eventually the consensus of the board, Raj was the right person. Raj was named chairman effective March 1, 2015.

Raj used his experience at Tyco and working with another board member, Sean Mahoney, to resolve a complex situation at Delphi—compensation. Delphi emerged from bankruptcy in 2009 after having been spun off from GM in 1999. Delphi began to flounder, leading to bankruptcy in 2005. Led by two hedge funds, Delphi's debt was acquired by Elliott Management and Silver Point Capital as well as other investors, and it continued to operate. The debt was exchanged for ownership by the hedge funds as part of the bankruptcy exit plan in 2009. This was a very delicate, serious, and debilitating financial period.

Hedge funds had their own ideas on compensation which were not totally consistent with what the board wanted to do on the way to becoming a public company. We had to build on changes that were made during bankruptcy and couldn't just march into being public without further overhaul. It is the same thing with the board. Second, hedge funds wanted to staff most of the new board with financial people. This was not a recipe for taking the company public. They're very smart people, no question. They can analyze a company and know exactly how and where value is created. But generally they don't have experience on the operational side, i.e., what has to be done when decisions are made. Things don't happen by themselves.

I argued that we needed a board that could bring the company public, and that meant allowing us to pick people with different backgrounds in industry. We ultimately agreed that we would have one person from the hedge funds and one from General Motors on the board and that others would have industry experience, bringing strategy and operational expertise.

We went public in late 2011, and it went very smoothly because we had a balanced board, a convincing strategy, and had begun to execute and get results. Part of the success of the company required an appropriate compensation program. As chairman of the committee, Raj had to deal with that. He got help from others on the board, some of whom were close to the hedge fund managers who had to be convinced to accept the new program. It was up to Raj to make it happen, and he did. He's a tireless worker. If he takes on a project, *you know it's going to get done and it's going to get done in depth. That's another reason why we recruited him to the Delphi Automotive board.*

What Makes Raj Tick?

So the next question might be, what makes Raj tick? My observation is that he's a person who is very quiet and modest and when you're around him, you wouldn't think that this guy has got overdrive in him. It's the first thing you notice when you get to know him, though. He just has it. And it's bone-deep. It's part of his fabric, his character. He's willing to work very, very hard at whatever he does in order to make you a success. He puts in whatever time it takes, whatever meetings he has to go to, whatever he has to do in order to try and make the project or venture a success. I think this was in his DNA or from his early upbringing in India and his time in the U.S.

I'm not sure what was in his mind when he first came to this country or when he started his career in finance. I don't think he ever had a vision that he would become CEO of Rohm and Haas someday. I think he saw his career in stages, wanting to take every opportunity that came to him and make the best of it he could. His focus was on whatever assignment he was given, and he does that to this day. That's what got him to be a successful CEO and board member.

When I was at DuPont, I counseled people who were always looking at the next job by saying, "Don't look up the line. Do your current job as well as you can and get results. You'll be recognized, I assure you. That's the best chance of getting whatever you want to be—a general manager, CEO, or whatever you're best fitted for." As I was coming up through the ranks, I saw people who were concentrating on who they knew, what were the right parties to go to, and what DuPont family members to get to know. I told them they were focusing on the wrong things. And you know what, most of these people left the company. They never made it. They probably felt they weren't moving fast enough or had hit the ceiling. They thought they should have been CEO after a few years with the company.

I never saw Raj that way. With Raj, it's about getting the job done that he's working on and trying to settle issues collaboratively. That's how he managed his career, I'm sure, and that's how he tackles tough assignments now.

Something else that I think makes Raj tick. He always tries to get consensus. He tries to resolve issues collaboratively rather than contentiously and then have divisions. And by the way, those divisions linger. I know. What happens is that the next time you want to reach consensus, it's even harder because of the bad blood from the issue before. Kind of like the fiscal cliff negotiations that went on between the president and Congress. Everybody thinks they're right. And they dig in.

The last thing I'll mention is the reason I think board members have to understand the business to add value for the shareholders. I served on an insurance company board and realized that to add any value I had to understand the business model and how the company made money. It was very different from the chemical business. And it took some time.

The lesson here for any board member is to learn the business, the way it makes money, the culture, the values, its unique language, and the leverage that a company has in the marketplace in order to constantly focus on the areas that will result in growing the value of the business. It's as simple and as hard as that.

Much of being a good CEO and a good board member is discipline—self-discipline and cost discipline while growing the portfolio and taking advantage of new products and new markets. But there's more, and that's where company leadership and board leadership come together. The same criteria that drive successful company management drives board membership: integrity and trust, excellence, teamwork, and accountability. We look to choose the CEO according to those same criteria that I look for to recruit board members.

That's what we did at DuPont, what Raj did at Rohm and Haas, and what we are doing at Tyco and Delphi Automotive and the other boards I serve on. We look for board members who know the business or invest the time to learn the business, and can bring

> *value to board decisions. That's where a board can help management the most—giving good advice.*
>
> *I've served on 11 corporate boards, each one teaching me something about managing companies, or industries. I've learned a lot. What's next I don't know, but having worked with Raj is one of the highlights of my career. He's a remarkable man. I'm proud to know him and call him friend.*

Corporate Governance in an Age of Uncertainty

It's not just Facebook, Google, and Twitter that mark a changing world tied to social media. The once-hallowed institution of corporate boards has been transformed by shareholder-rights activists and the media covering their protests and calls for voting down resolutions for higher executive pay and negating director nominations where company wrong-doing is alleged, or where a company has underperformed its peers.

The call for shareholder rights is being heard from the canyons of Wall Street to continents across the globe, especially in major, publicly held companies where additional eyes and ears are listening to and taking to task boards that don't hold accountable their CEOs. The assumption is that a board will act independently and its directors serve as a check and balance, like good government, in reining in a CEO's power or potential misbehavior or abuse, or in curbing outsized egos that could lead to harm or hubris or both. In addition, boards are expected to add their advice and expertise to that of top management when big decisions affecting the shareholders are concerned. This has not always been the case, as recent history has shown.

The Enron scandal in the early 2000s and later, the Great Recession of 2008 with its litigious aftermath, signaled that all would not be as before, as calls for greater transparency and stricter adherence to corporate governance guidelines and policies sent shock waves through many, but certainly not all, publicly-traded company boards of directors, overturning decades of deferential cronyism. Other boards are seeing a natural evolution of pressure from stakeholders, including institutional investors, for greater transparency in company decisions, executive compensation, safety records, and cost containment, as well as the talent and recruitment function.

In other words, the traditional board model is changing. I have served on boards comprised of a diverse mix of industries, CEOs, and organizational aims. I've been on more than a dozen public, private, and non-profit boards over the course of my career (see table at end of chapter), and indeed the change in board behavior, make-up, and shareholder responsiveness is in turn consequential, much-needed, and tectonic in its significance. The topic also raises several important questions for consideration.

I use this section to offer my thoughts and recommendations for how boards can align their functions with their traditional obligations while also updating their roles in the harsher light that transparency is demanding of them and the companies and shareholders they serve. In the wake of the Great Recession and the governance issues that were in many instances intertwined with business practices that contributed to that financial crisis and its aftermath, change was required.

Context, Certainty, and Undeniable Trends

Over the last decade and a half, two important considerations emerge. One is the nature of the change that has overtaken boards and the other is how these changes differ among non-profit, for-profit, and private and public companies. My observations are generic rather than specific to the boards on which I serve.

Boards reflect the character and culture of the companies they represent. Those that are entrepreneurial have characters much different from traditional, publicly-owned companies. Serving on the board of Facebook, Google, or other social platform or start-up companies is going to be a vastly different experience from serving on IBM's or HP's board, as I do. Yet, the leaders of each of these companies is living in a very unpredictable and even volatile world, and there are some commonalities that unite them (and therefore their boards) that are worth thinking about in order to create what I call a sustainable value.

One important set of questions and issues pertains to the board level and the other set to broader organizational leadership. The commonality serving all board members, whether serving on the board of Apple or a private start-up, is that board directors are the representatives of the shareholders. Within that overarching and common obligation, I would say that there are at least five categories of boards.

The first category is comprised of the boards of private companies. And for private companies, the board serves pretty much at the pleasure of the owners. A second category of boards exists in private companies that are owned and run by private equity (PE) firms. These boards are comprised largely of PE firm members. They are basically the extension of a company's senior management. They don't just ask, they actively help govern and manage.

A third category constitutes a family-owned or family-controlled public company where families are in the background, either conspicuously or inconspicuously. Some board members are members of the family. They are major shareholders, and they occupy important roles in the company's major decisions and therefore need to be briefed on big events or educated in depth on company issues. This was the case at Rohm and Haas Company where the Haas family and its trusts owned 30 percent of the outstanding stock.

A fourth category is the very-well-diversified, public shareholder company, which is what the majority of large corporations are. And the role of the board and how boards interact with the CEO or the shareholders is very different yet again. Increasingly these boards of large public companies are under pressure to be diverse, highly competent in their fields (and the company's), and engaged in the company's strategic objectives and ethical behavior from a compliance standpoint.

A fifth category is emerging in the Silicon Valley companies like Facebook, Google, Twitter, LinkedIn, or other typical social media or tech companies whose boards allow the companies' founders wide berth in making decisions separate from board input or consensus. Google accomplishes this with two classes of shares. I would label this category "boards of newer technology companies," as Google refers to itself in this action, and wherein perhaps the nature of the technology necessitates a speed of action not possible with the collaborative and deliberative decision-making process that typical public company boards bring.

I think in the first three categories there is no doubt that the board really interacts with the shareholders and the owners in a very direct way. And it varies in each of those situations. However, in the fourth context, which is what the majority of U.S. public companies or the global public companies are, where there is no family as a major shareholder, typically there is really very little contact between the directors and the shareholders.

With the exception of the fact that directors are elected by the shareholders, almost all the communications with shareholders takes place with management. Clearly that is changing over such issues as executive compensation, proxy access for the shareholders, and on other issues where shareholders are demanding a voice. The question that this poses is, should the boards engage proactively or reactively with shareholders on these issues? Today that dialogue is nonexistent. And that's the reason why boards and public companies largely remain mysterious and byzantine institutions to the public.

As to what boards do, why they are there, and why we never hear from them (or hear from them only in situations where there is some kind of panic or a crisis) we know very little, because the fact is that times of panic, crisis, and scandal are generally the only times when the board gets to see the light of day. Boards come under public scrutiny for many reasons—a company's poor results, bad people decisions or acquisitions, excessive executive pay, cover up, or fraud. Otherwise, the board seems to be living in a kind of la-la land.

The question I ask, as do others, is: What's going on in board rooms? What are these people thinking? Typically the question is asked of large public companies wherein boards impact big decisions involving acquisitions, divestitures, or change in strategic direction. But is there a dual obligation here? How can boards evolve in the context of where the world is going and communicate those directions with shareholders? Obviously it's important for board members to have as firm an understanding as they can about the company's future, its competitive threats, and what some of the trends are going to be which drive those things. Clearly, the pressure isn't going to go away, so what does a well-intentioned board do? In a way I would say there is a parallel here between what the board and management need to think about in order to run the company or organization and how best to create long-term shareholder value. And the first order of business in that regard is the selection of the board members.

A board, just like the management, has to have a set of objectives. There is no reason that a board should not have priorities and objectives; there is no reason that a board should not have performance management; and there is no reason that the board should not engage with the shareholders. The question becomes: How do you build and instill accountability and at the same time increase transparency? The issues here are what boards themselves can do in terms of the selection process, how they can deal with a non-performing or dysfunctional board and by extension, a non-performing director, without washing the company's dirty laundry in public, and still be communicative. Along these same lines, what should be the best practices for the board process?

What the answers to these questions seek to do is "demystify" the board as well as make it more effective. What are the prerequisites of an effective board?

A New Board Model:
Board Selection and Establishing Best Practices

The first step in my opinion is for an existing board to define its mission and identity. Who are your shareholders and how will you manage them, particularly in a public corporation where you do not have a majority shareholder? In today's world, large public corporations are dominant forces. They comprise the Dow Jones Industrial Average and make up the S&P 500, many of whose shareholders or "owners" are employees, directors, and long-term value investors in the form of actively managed index funds. If you look at the top 25 stakeholders together, you will find that the majority of U.S. companies have long-term shareholders owning 60-70 percent of the company. The board and management have to ask themselves if any of these shareholders represents hedge funds or activist investors. So the question of "Who owns you?" is very relevant today, as is the question of whether the focus on quarterly results is overblown in the context of who the "real" owners are today. Should the boards and the management reassess the focus on quarterly results in light of its owners and if so, how? What should be the message to the Street and other stakeholders? These are questions related to defining what a board's mission is.

Some boards are taking a proactive stance in communicating their mission publicly. In 2012, ExxonMobil presented a corporate Webcast on the issue of executive compensation. The panel consisted of the board chair of the compensation committee, the head of HR, and a compensation consultant. They discussed the philosophy of executive compensation, on what basis the CEO is paid, and how pay and performance are linked. The purpose was to take some of the mystery out of the issue. Hewlett-Packard, on whose board I serve, also has a well-articulated approach to shareholder engagement. We have a proactive approach with all our major shareholders to discuss governance and compensation issues. I applaud such a step. The next question might be what tools are available for demystifying other board functions and communications with shareholders? What are appropriate communications, and what avenues, elements, platforms, and topics are best suited for such a dialogue process so that the board, its members, and its function are demystified? The other side of the coin is to wait until there is a crisis and to communicate in a reactive mode. I think recent history has shown us that that is a bad idea.

The second consideration is how board membership is decided. The entire board selection process has completely changed in a majority of cases. The once-credible perception that board members are really buddies of the CEO, or are friends and acquaintances of other board members, is fast disappearing. Almost every company that I know of today uses a recruiting firm to fill its board. Every one of them draws up a profile of the mix of skills that they need on the board. The profile process is largely run by the non-executive chair or the chair of the nominating governors' committee. They work independently of the CEO, and while the CEO is part of the process, the CEO is not the sole decision maker. In the old days, boards and CEOs relied on networks—who knew whom, who liked whom, etc. The call went out and that was it. It was an "old boy network." Today it's much more deliberate. In my own case, when I joined the HP board, I didn't know a soul on the board.

When I was CEO of Rohm and Haas, the process of selecting a new board member took almost a year. Fortunately, the CEO selection and vetting procedure, at least for the companies I am familiar with, is much more efficient today than even ten years ago. The board selection process has also become much more practiced and professional than before across a wide variety of companies, a change which is better for the company, its top management, and its shareholders and stakeholders, in my view.

"Kicking it up a Notch"
Boards Today are Required to Do More

A well-crafted board selection process not only assures a steady and tailored talent and recruitment process, it also better prepares board members for the increased time and expertise required of them in terms of what the new board model entails. Historically, each board is supposed to have three mandatory committees—an audit committee, a compensation committee, and a governance committee. But that model has expanded. Depending on the industry, you may additionally have an investment committee, a risk committee, a technology committee, and an environmental, safety, and health committee. So now, board members may sit on more than one committee and have concomitantly more duties and decisions to review and evaluate.

Another critical element of the new board model is the self- and 360-degree assessment. By that I mean that the board is looking at its members individually and in cooperation with the whole board and management. This is a relatively recent phenomenon, one that has been actively transformed by the same sentiment as Food Network host and chef Emeril Lagasse famously says about his Cajun cooking, "Let's kick it up a notch." In fact, the latest thinking is to ask for management feedback as to whether the board is really being helpful and successful in what they need to accomplish, and whether individual board members are being constructive or not constructive in the role that they play. So it's not just a self-assessment by the board members but it's also a feedback process for management. In many respects, this is similar to the Japanese automotive production line—management is part of a continuous improvement process with a self-assessment board. Kind of a board room *kaizen* practice.

Four Criteria for Board "Best Practices"

Boards, like companies, must be engaged in best practices in their four main functions 1) CEO selection; 2) getting the strategy alignment right; 3) flawless execution of the strategy; and 4) monitoring culture and compliance. Let's take them separately.

Number one is selection of the CEO and talent management. If you get this wrong, you can really put the company at risk or on a bad path. In that regard, I would offer this piece of advice from long experience: A CEO from inside is less risky than an outsider. All the data show that the person whom you know is more predictable than the one you don't. Establishing a board that has a well-structured assessment process for evaluating a cadre of high-potential, top leaders over time is better than shopping for someone when the pressure of time and perhaps other exigencies distract board members from identifying and selecting individuals with proven, long-term core values, honed and sharpened by company experience. This may not always be the case, as fresh blood or fresh eyes are sometimes needed, but it is mostly so.

The second critical function of a board is getting the strategy of the company right. Because there are so many moving pieces, the board needs to be very objective, thoughtful, and reflective, looking at the long-term mission of the company. This is a function that affords the opportunity for the board to bring its strength and multiple perspectives into making pivotal decisions—whether it be an acquisition, merger, joint venture, disposition of assets, major R&D, or capital project—and not just to rubber-stamp management's idea.

The third area where I think the board's role is critical is in assuring that the company's strategy and goals are executed in a way that creates value for the owners. One of the core competencies of leadership is being accountable for bottom-line results and meeting or exceeding goals and expectations. This includes performance at the top and performance across the organization in achieving what is expected and committed to. The other side of execution is the know-how to get there—knowing how the businesses work, measuring the competition, and matching them to the company's own resources, processes, and priorities to assure continued profitability and viability in the marketplace.

The fourth area is culture and compliance. Culture is how a company works together toward common goals, and compliance is the act of doing that lawfully, honestly, and ethically. Together they are the way a company solves problems and achieves its goals. The board is part-owner in that process because it holds core values as well—creating a culture that is supporting a high level of integrity and also complying with the law. In doing so, the board has the implicit obligation to assure that the company's mission and objectives are unimpeded by contradictory behaviors or management practices of saying vs. doing. Boards therefore need to pay close attention to culture and compliance.

If boards do these four things right, they will generally be achieving their purpose as well as serving the shareholders well.

I would add that depending on the situation of each company, a prudent way to improve the functions of the board is just putting down three to four key priorities for the current year as a way of determining what the board should focus on. Include the rationale for each item and its alignment with what management's objectives are. Both the board and management have dual accountabilities, and in this way, the board is shifted from being solely the overseer of the CEO's performance to being an accountable partner. I think CEOs have an obligation to deliver against their own priorities and objectives, but at the same time they have to be aligned with the board.

Communicating with Investors

Another dimension is the importance of the process whereby the board engages with shareholders, a top line priority, in my view. Monitoring culture and compliance is often where outreach to investors comes in.

Most companies understand their obligation to shareholders. And yet, we really must address the issue of why boards are not better understood by the public and the media. We not only need to raise the bar and keep raising it in terms of the roles and responsibilities within the board, but also we should shed light on where some companies go wrong, particularly when the board, in partnership with the CEO, doesn't satisfy the four criteria of good board practice. Annually, shareholder advisory organizations, such as ISS and Glass Lewis, issue a detailed report on governance, compensation, and performance of public companies. A fairly high percentage of shareholders follow their recommendations on voting. So, for example, if ISS and Glass Lewis recommend voting against management proposals, boards (typically the non-executive chairman, lead director, and chairs of the governance and compensation committees) will engage with major institutional shareholders to tell their side of the story. Proactive outreach by boards can have desirable impact.

Boards Matter

In summary, having good board practices not only makes a better board, but more importantly it also allows the company to succeed in the marketplace. It allows companies to concentrate on what they're good at versus being dragged down by expensive and time-consuming efforts to correct weaknesses. Let me be clear here: corporate boards are not management surrogates. Business is too complex, and that's not what boards do. The board provides oversight and partnership. But it needs to dig into details when things are not on the right track, and it can do this job only if there is implicit trust and transparency between the management and the board. A lot of this is dictated by the CEO and organizational leadership. That's why the need for a transparent, open, productive relationship is so important, and where it doesn't exist, changes should be made.

Obviously there are situations and scenarios where board action is made difficult, such as when a CEO is all-powerful, has done a good job, or the board is just reluctant or afraid to challenge him. This only reinforces bad management, because withdrawal of participation by the board means the CEO can become more independent, more over-confident, more demanding, and perhaps more greedy. Unfortunately, lack of participation also isolates the board from what is really going on in the executive suite and what's going on in the company. An isolated board is in no position to judge its CEO or, for that matter, to realistically compensate him or her for performance. Ego often dominates, and many times a CEO will focus on compensation as the single scorecard for his or her value and become somewhat obsessed by salary and perquisites in comparison with others.

When a board sees these signals, it should go outside for additional advice, whether it's an independent compensation consultant, an outside auditor, or an independent legal advisor.

Sometimes the warning signs come too late, as when the company's performance slips precipitously or there are major defections in the senior executive ranks. To avoid such late-alarm situations, boards need to be alert to early warning signs and have a plan in place in order to engage in the discussion and decision-making process to save, correct, or mitigate the situation. More importantly, adherence to best practices enhances shareholder wealth, company profits, employee and customer satisfaction, and reputational excellence. In that scenario, everybody wins.

Raj Gupta Board Directorships

ENTITY	DATES
Public Companies	
Tyco International Ltd	2005-present
Rohm & Haas Company	1998-2009
Hewlett-Packard Company	2009-present
Delphi Automotive PLC	2009-present
Agere	2001-2004
Technitrol	1998-2003
Airgas	1997-1999
Unisys	2000-2001
Private Companies/Organizations	
The Vanguard Group	2002-present
Affle	2008-present
Avantor	2010-present
Stroz Friedberg LLC	2011-2013
IRI Group	2011-present
Not-for-Profit Organizations	
Ujala Foundation	2008-present
Drexel University	2001-2007
Eisenhower Fellowship	1999-2011
Chemical Heritage Foundation	2003-2006
Conference Board	2009-2013

10

BACK TO THE FAMILY

"You don't choose your family. They are God's gift to you, as you are to them."
—Desmond Tutu, human rights activist, Nobel
laureate, and retired Anglican bishop

I began this book with stories of my family. I return to my family again now, but this time I will let them speak for themselves. Following are excerpts from interviews conducted with the three most important women in my life—Kamla, and our daughters Amita and Vanita.

Kamla Gupta has played an absolutely critical role in my life as my wife, soul mate, and mother of our two daughters. Without her, I would not have achieved what I did or had the happiness and support that she came to represent. Her strong family values, her willingness to pick up and move whenever my bosses afforded me an opportunity somewhere else in the world, as well as her keeping our home and family together despite my being away so much, comprised the glue that kept our family, our marriage, and my career intact. It is important that Kamla speak her mind in these pages because she is so essential to my story—our story—in America.

Kamla Gupta

"Philadelphia is my home."

"Music was my refuge.
I could crawl into the space between the notes
and curl my back to loneliness."
—Maya Angelou, author, poet, dancer, actress, and singer

I grew up in Aligarh, a city about 90 miles southeast of New Delhi, a town famous for its Aligarh Muslim University. I was the middle child of nine children who included seven girls. My father was a businessman, and my mother stayed at home and raised the family. I was a good student and majored in music and political science at the university. I was devoted to my parents, and when my father died suddenly after my marriage, I was devastated. I still cannot talk about him without crying.

As with other young women of my generation, when I became of age, my parents arranged for me to marry a young man suitable to them and to me, a process that may be more accommodating than many Westerners believe. There is a go-between, and this person tries to make the match successful, so he listens to both families and both the intended bride and groom. With me it was the same. When he mentioned Raj's family and Raj as particularly suitable, he discussed it with my father, and I was certainly aware of that. When I met Raj, I thought we would make a good couple, even though I did not know him at all. But I had a good feeling, and we seemed to share a lot of the same interests. So we went ahead with the marriage, and soon after, Raj was on his way to America to study at Cornell. I had always wanted to go to America, so this decision on his part was more than fine with me. It was a dream I had always had.

I arrived in America, in Ithaca, after Raj had already spent a semester. It was the winter of 1968 and I had to get used to the snow and ice. We lived in the married students' graduate dorm and soon after I got a job as an Avon Lady. This helped me learn English and get to know more people. I would have kept at it, but I got pregnant, and when I slipped on the ice one day, Raj and I came to the conclusion that I should not continue to work and risk another fall, or worse, endangering the baby.

When Raj graduated the next year, he couldn't believe how many job offers he got. He was afraid he wouldn't get any, and he got five! We chose the offer from Scott Paper Company in Philadelphia. Raj had an uncle there and we felt that would be a good move, so we packed our belongings and moved to Ridley Park, just outside of Philadelphia, and settled in an apartment.

Shortly thereafter I gave birth to our first daughter, Amita. We had a nice circle of friends, and Raj was getting a good start at Scott. He liked the company and his colleagues but told me that he had some concerns about the future of Scott Paper and wanted to look at other opportunities. That was when he learned about an opening at Rohm and Haas. He interviewed and then was offered a position in the Finance Department. He liked the company and his bosses immediately and felt very sure he had made the right decision.

During those years I was mostly busy raising our daughter and making a good home for Raj. He worked very hard and started taking classes at night at Drexel University for his MBA, so early on we kind of naturally divided the duties of work and family—Raj was pursuing his career and studies while I took care of the home. But these were happy times, and often I would have his Rohm and Haas colleagues over for dinner. I liked to cook, and Raj was a good host. It was something we both enjoyed.

After a while, Raj was asked to take an assignment in London, so we moved to the U.K. London was not easy for Indians then, especially in the early 1980s when we first moved there. People were nice to me on the surface, but I never got the feeling they wanted to make friends with me. Certainly it was not like the U.S., where I felt people genuinely liked me and wanted to get to know me better. It may have been because India had been under British control or domination in one form or another for over 300 years and that history lingered. I don't know really. And then Raj was transferred to Paris and that was a whole different experience for us and me, as well as the girls. I liked the French and they liked us.

When I look back on our years in Europe, it was a learning experience. It was learning, really, how the other world lives, and how different cultures interact, but I wouldn't want to go back there to live. I never wanted to live in Europe or for that matter another place in the U.S. Philadelphia is my home. It's got everything. It's near Washington and New York. It's both cosmopolitan and comfortable. It's a great place to raise a family. You get the best of everything.

Raising Two Indian Daughters in America

Raj and I were blessed with two beautiful and intelligent daughters. They adapted to our living in Europe and in the U.S. They had no trouble whatsoever wherever we lived. We were lucky to be close to good schools—the American School of London, the American School of Paris, and back in the U.S., the Rose Tree Media Schools in Media, PA. So both girls experienced very diverse educations, cultures, and schoolmates growing up. While I would have preferred they had gotten more Indian culture, I was glad they got to learn about so many others. Both girls did extremely well in school—both Amita and Vanita finished near the very top in their respective classes. Vanita even got to speak in front of 500 people at her high school graduation, which made us very proud. I am so proud of them both. They did not need our guidance. The only wish we had was for them to become professionals in whatever field they chose, and they did. I didn't want them to be like me—to stay at home and cook and clean. But that was not an issue with them.

I did have one wish, however. I would have liked an Indian partner for Vanita. She did marry an Indian man. It didn't work out. And I probably shouldn't have urged her so strongly to marry him, but I thought he was brilliant, he came from a nice family, and if there are some things to work out, everyone can adjust just like Raj and I adjusted. So that's what I told Vanita, but it didn't turn out that way. Things turn out the way God wants.

It was different with Amita. She had a different lifestyle and that was very difficult at first to absorb. It was very tough on me.

Not so for Raj. Raj is more adaptable to everything, but for me it was very tough. They were a difficult few years for me, first with Vanita's first marriage not working out and then Amita's choosing a female partner. I think it's a cultural issue for me. I'm Indian, and I will never change. The values of being an Indian mother are not easily altered. There are even jokes and cartoons about it. But I had to cope with their situations, and I did. I know they appreciated the effort I made, and I think we are a stronger, closer family as a result.

Looking Back and Ahead

I built a whole new life in America. I don't keep in touch with the people I grew up with in India. When Raj and I go back and we're in the town where I grew up, I might see a cousin who was also my best friend, but that's it. I live here now. Looking back on my life as a mother, I don't have any regrets, but I wish I had been less restrictive as a parent. Quite frankly, I wish I had allowed my girls to go to more parties and socialize more with their friends in high school. I guess I was too strict. When they went to college, they could do anything they wanted to, but maybe I should have been more open to that when they were growing up. Maybe I was too much the Indian mother.

But the girls are doing fine. Raj is doing fine. He's a strong person. His work is his passion. And I support that. He'd be an unhappy guy if he stayed home. He loves working. And if he's happy, I'm happy. And now we have the foundation, Ujala, that is focused on health care and education. He's done good things with it. And he made a gift to Cornell in the name of his parents for biomedical engineering scholarships to deserving Indian students. I am so happy that we are doing so many good things. I think the giving back is an important part of his life now.

I'm also concerned about India as a country, about its future. My older daughter is a physician and specializes in infectious diseases, and she is doing a lot of work in India. But India needs a lot of help in a lot of areas. Our foundation is doing its small part.

There is so much poverty, so much malnutrition, so much need for education that if we can do something good like creating the schools for children who otherwise have no means of education, then we are making a difference in people's lives.

The other area where there is a great need is in political reform. Corruption is so widespread, it is slowing progress and hurting development. There is need for political change so that young people want to stay, grow their business, educate their children, and build a life. India's caste system is slow to go away. People don't talk about it, and for sure the segregation that defined the Indian social system is less pervasive, but it's a legacy that India is still trying to resolve. But it's slow. Progress is being made, but the system is kind of self-perpetuating because the kinds of jobs many people find themselves confined to take, like manual labor or certain kinds of household jobs, are constricting. That's why universal education is so important. It opens doors. It creates opportunities. It allows people to have a better life than their parents.

Our parents were very important in our lives, and they worked very hard to give us a better life. In some cases they paid a price. Raj's father never took bribes or did things under the table. There was always in India a vast scale and scope of male and female inequality that I saw and experienced. So when people talk about the double life, it's true. There's always a balance. Nothing comes automatically. When I sit in a room, people are making judgments, either consciously or unconsciously, about me. Before it used to bother me. Now it doesn't. I feel very confident about who I am and what I stand for.

There were instances when I was out to dinner with Raj and his business colleagues and they all ordered for themselves and I was left to sit by myself because I was a vegetarian and didn't eat what they did. Everyone was eating and having a good time except me. No food came for me. I didn't speak up because these guys were Raj's bosses, and nobody asked and nobody seemed to care. I saw it with other business wives as well. Back then I was very shy and very careful of not offending anyone. Evidently, so was Raj because his bosses were there.

I said something to Raj afterward. I told him he should have said something. Today that would never happen to me no matter where we had dinner—at a little restaurant by ourselves, or at the home of the Prime Minister.

It took time for me to come to this confidence, and yet it was something I think I had growing up. I was the first child in my family to go to English school. My father was very proud. I always wanted to learn. I took courses every summer. I didn't want to sit home and do nothing. And I loved music. I played the Indian drums you hear when you listen to Ravi Shankar play the sitar. Those are called tabla drums. No one else in my family played tabla drums. And we exposed our daughters to musical instruments when they were younger—flute and piano. While they didn't continue, they did have that foundation in music, which I think is very important for all children. Music gives you a basis for many disciplines, and it gave me immense pleasure and sense of myself.

I guess I would sum up my life as the Indian wife and mother who tried to be a good wife and a good mother and now grandmother in my adopted home of Philadelphia. I am still a woman who is curious, wants to continue learning, and lives life one day at a time. I wouldn't want it any other way. I am very happy.

A Conversation with Daughters Amita and Vanita

"A daughter may outgrow your lap,
but she will never outgrow your heart."
—Anonymous

What's it like growing up in three different countries, being Indian but raised as Americans, and being the daughters of a U.S. corporate executive and a traditionally-reared, Indian mother?

The short answer is, "It's not easy;" and it's even harder when one daughter, a global public health physician, professor, and research scientist in infectious diseases chose an untraditional lifestyle, and the other, a feminist, took an activist path as a civil rights attorney, divorced an Indian man her mother had hoped she loved, and married a Vietnamese civil rights attorney. While both daughters took different paths with different people, they taught Kamla and me many lessons about something I thought I knew a lot about—diversity.

Here is the candid assessment in their own words about what it was like for my daughters growing up in our household, or maybe I should say households because we moved at least five times with our oldest daughter, Amita, the Johns Hopkins physician and researcher, and four times with Vanita, her younger sister, recently named to head the Civil Rights Division of the U.S. Justice Department. Amita and Vanita spoke to my co-author about their lives, their parents, and the lifestyles and careers they chose. These are excerpts from that conversation relevant to my story and to theirs as part of our family.

What It Was Like Growing Up in the Gupta Household

Amita: I'm the older one. I remember from an early age, my dad was very attentive to me. This was in the early 1970s. I knew he was very busy. I can remember back to when he first started working for Rohm and Haas, I would sit with him and he would open up the newspaper and teach me how to spell words and tell me what they meant. He really loved that, and I'm sure he would have made a great teacher if he had chosen academia as a profession.

The other thing I remember about him when we were growing up was his love of sports. He got me playing sports at a very early age. I think it was a way he could enjoy spending time with me and be outdoors at the same time. We would start with ball-throwing and working with the racquet and then playing tennis. He does the same thing now with Vanita's little boy, Chetan. First the tennis ball and racquet and soon I'm guessing the tennis court. Chetan's just five years old now, but he'll be on the court soon, if I know my dad.

I think our household was very loving. I had a very happy childhood—free and not overly strict. Although my parents had rules, I never felt overly controlled or encumbered by either of them. I just have very fond memories of growing up. And I know that later on when Vanita was there, I spent more of my time with her when

170

my dad got busier and busier at work. But I still remember our family vacations and his spending time with us. He would play tennis with us every weekend. But it was funny the way it would always happen. If we were on vacation, the first thing in the morning when we got up, he would say: "OK, let's go." It would be 6:30 or 7:00 a.m. "Come on, let's go play tennis because it's going to be too hot to be out there soon." We'd say, "Oh, dad. It's so early." But we'd go and have a nice game. And that's one way we really bonded—playing sports. He and I had a very special bond sharing weekends together for many years. He's always valued his time with me—my mom did, too—but my dad particularly.

School and Studies and the Lettuce Project

My dad never pressured us—either Vanita or me—in our schoolwork. But I felt a real pride when we did well. Although maybe we were lucky in that we excelled at school, and he was always very supportive of our career interests. I remember in college I was struggling over whether to pursue engineering. I wanted to be either an engineer like my dad or to study medicine, which I was thinking was a better choice for me because I liked the people aspect of it. But I had gone to MIT, and he was very happy because it was such a great engineering school.

So when I finished I didn't think I wanted to continue in engineering. The ironic thing is that I didn't know then that my dad went through the same dilemma when he finished his master's in operations research at Cornell. Anyway, I decided to switch gears and ended up going to medical school. But I gave engineering a real effort. I even worked at my dad's company a couple of summers.

When we were in Europe, Rohm and Haas had this fantastic lab on the southern coast of France in Valbonne, overlooking the Mediterranean. Not too shabby! I did polymer research which turned into my undergraduate thesis. Very interesting project, actually, and quite technical. It had to do with the organoleptic and strength properties of this particular polymer. Organoleptics are the properties of a chemical or food that relate to its taste, color, odor, or feel. So it was like testing the taste properties as well as the strength properties of this particular polymer that they were making for commercial products.

Vanita: Don't forget the lettuce project.

Amita: Oh, my God, the lettuce project! I was in high school and had a biology project. My father helped me set it up. He got me an agricultural product used on lettuce. He was very interested in the science of it, but it was an herbicide. So at home, near Paris, I took over somebody's derelict garden, and I literally planted all these controlled rows of lettuce and placed the herbicide product on another row and let it grow. So I would take the lettuces and then typically desiccate them and weigh them to see at the end of the day the weight difference between those that were herbicide-treated and those that weren't. It taught me a lot about agricultural science.

But he was always interested in what I was doing and incredibly supportive. Initially, when he was hoping I would go into engineering, he tried to see if I was interested in the business side of it because I had told him I wanted to follow in his footsteps—major in engineering and get an MBA. We were very similar in a lot of ways. I love him very, very much.

Vanita: My sister's right. My dad is the kind of person who would find ways to educate us indirectly, so when he was teaching us it was always a kind of game or fun time. Even though I think that my dad and his siblings grew up in a tradition of sitting at your desk for six hours every day studying in a structured and disciplined way, that was not my father's way of raising us, nor my mother's. He would be reading the International Herald Tribune and then find words and have us do spelling and then he would go upstairs and let us continue. He developed an intellectual curiosity in us as opposed to kind of hammering stuff down in a rote kind of way.

Now that I'm a parent, I can see the wisdom of that. The more important thing is to develop a curiosity, an intellectual curiosity more than anything else. Throughout our growing up, I think he really felt it was important to be engaged with the world that in some ways is not traditionally Indian, and he would encourage us to watch the news and would ask us questions about what we saw afterward. I think that there were lots of little things that he did along those lines.

But I grew up very consciously being South Asian in Britain. I think that my mom felt that way a little bit more socially. My father was basically a product of corporate America, and he has a very interesting analysis of being a minority in England and in France in a very traditional corporate setting where brown faces didn't usually rise to the top, or they weren't seen in management positions.

And I certainly see this and did from early on. I developed a consciousness and for better or worse, my sister and I were both politically aware individuals. We used to get into lots of arguments about it with my dad. He seemed more tolerant of prejudice than we were. Maybe it was a generational thing or even political. We were very progressive, more to the left of center than my father.

But I have to say it was fun to argue with him in front of his friends. I think they actually goaded us sometimes. I think my father's and mother's friends loved to see these two feisty young ladies going at it about economic or social policy. I grew up thinking I knew so much. I think sometimes my dad was a little bit embarrassed by it because my father is not one to rock the boat or be confrontational. I know he has to have strong opinions at work and in a corporate setting, but his personal life is different. He doesn't like controversy or conflict.

To tell you the truth, I think his daughters sometimes pushed his buttons in terms of challenging the status quo, and doing it often in front of his friends. And I think he was very proud of it, but then at times kind of said, "Oh, my God."

The Daughters and Their Mother

Amita: My parents have a very interesting marriage from the standpoint of how they managed us. When Vanita came along there were two of us to fend for each other. Quite honestly, my parents argued a lot. I think they are very different people. They communicate very differently, but they are amazing to me because they had an arranged marriage. They barely knew each other in India or even when my mom came to the U.S. to be with him in graduate school. They basically embarked on a lifelong journey beginning as strangers, and so for that reason they had a lot of things to work out and perhaps are still working them out.

By comparison, we grew up in America with a very different notion of love and what a long-term relationship is, certainly different from our parents'. We had an incredibly happy childhood, but I felt the conflict a lot and I got involved in it. Our mom and dad have a relatively traditional marriage in terms of my mother's staying home and raising us and my father's traveling an enormous amount, especially when we were living in Europe, in France and in England. And so I actually developed this protective thing about my mother. That would sometimes create its own challenges between my father and me, but I also think that my father is not a traditionalist in the Indian sense. They have a more American setup in their marriage, but my mother is incredibly fierce about her opinions and is no kind of wilting flower. So I think that's part of why it could produce its own level of terseness and tension, but also a very loving relationship between them.

Learning Outside the Comfort Zone— The Experience of Living in the U.K. and France

Vanita: Yes, my mother is someone who has lived life very passionately. I feel temperamentally more like my mother. I think Amita is more like my father. But they were great parents and when we did anything or went on vacation together, there was always a huge amount of learning going on. Sometimes the vacations were a drag, to be honest. They would take us to the best places but there was nothing for kids to do. We'd go to Scotland to visit castles. We'd go all over France. Yet, the amount that we learned from traveling and living in all of these places was enormous. One thing I will say about my dad is that he is a firm believer in that you learn the most when you're outside your comfort zone.

And I think my father lived his life that way because he was the only South Asian or minority person in most of the locations he worked. There were probably occasions where it was a negative thing, but by and large, my father is someone who really thrives on that challenge and being out of his comfort zone, and I think he is really tough, which explains, kind of, the fact that both daughters chose to do untraditional things with our traditional professions of law and medicine. What can be more traditional in a sense? But my sister is doing HIV/AIDS and infectious disease work at Johns Hopkins and goes to India all the time. I am a civil rights lawyer doing criminal defense work. And I think my father and mother have taken extraordinary pride in that. I have never actually felt that they wanted to redirect me or suggest I go to work for a big Wall Street law firm or that Amita head up a department in a big hospital, clinic, or medical school. They were happiest when we felt fulfilled.

Amita: We moved to England when I was eight years old and Vanita was three in 1978. That was actually in the middle of the 4th grade for me. So half of my 4th grade was at this new school. I still remember moving and actually my first day at my new school. I was nervous in the sense that I felt like, "Oh my gosh, this is a completely new experience." But I think my personality is very adaptable, so what I remember is being really excited by this new place that I was going to. I didn't feel forlorn or upset or angry or any of those feelings. At least I don't remember feeling that way. We spent five years in England, so I was there from 4th to the end of 8th grade. From England, we moved to France from when I was in 9th to 12th grade. After I graduated from high school, I came to the U.S. for college. We were in an international school, so I would have to say I think we got an incredibly good education. Not just from a curriculum standpoint but in the people we met. They came from all over the world. It was an American school in Paris, and in England the school had a lot of American expatriates. I think that being educated in Europe was probably the best education we could ever have had in terms of living in other countries.

Vanita: I also had my first taste of racism when I was in England. I remember very clearly being shouted at, "Paki go home; go home Paki." They would say that to my face when I was on the street. That was during the raceriots between South Asians and skinheads in Brixton. There was some serious looting.

And then there was the incident at the London McDonald's. My sister and I were both there with my mom and my dad's mom. I was six years old at the time in 1980. We had just moved to England. My sister has kind of blocked out the experience, but I remember it very clearly. It's actually my first memory that's not so happy. But I just remember being in a regular McDonald's and my dad's mother was visiting. She used to come periodically from India, and it was very exciting because we had no extended family in Britain. Going to McDonald's was always challenging for my mom, who's a vegetarian. It was almost funny. She would order, the food would come, and then she would have to say, "No, you have to take the meat out; if there's meat on the bun, you have to remove the bun." It was, like, this 10-minute order and we would all think, "Oh, my God, what is she doing? We'll never eat."

So that day, we got the order and were sitting down and there were some skinheads at a table nearby. Margaret Thatcher had just gotten elected and there was a rise of this kind of ultra-right wing, neo-fascist group that was all about trying to make Britain all white. And they were sitting at the table next to us and they just started throwing French fries at us and yelling, "go home Pakies." It's weird because I remember the incident, but I don't actually remember what we did. What I kind of recollect was that we turned our heads, and we ate very quickly and left. But that kind of behavior was not uncommon. Britain was engulfed in those riots and we were not the only Indians to be victimized by it. It was a weird time.

Amita: The impact on me was that it made me very aware of my skin color. I think up to that point I wasn't really aware that I was that much different in terms of my friends and classmates. In the States, I don't really remember ever making that distinction, and I think it was really telling because we were treated so differently abroad. When we moved to France, it was different again. In France, Indian culture was really exoticized and respected and thought to be really this beautiful, old culture. I felt very differently treated than were those who came from North Africa, because Algeria and Tunisia were former French colonies and India was a

176

former British colony. Former colonials bring a certain stigma that people from other countries don't. So it was a very different approach to how I was treated in each of the countries where we lived—the U.S., Britain, and France. In the U.S. I was Indian-American. Americans tend to be comfortable with hyphenated people. It's used all the time and mostly respectfully, whereas in England I felt like there was always an undertone of other people's being very aware of my skin color, particularly when I was in the white environment, and especially in places that could be perceived as snooty or snobby. I just remember that the event in McDonald's changed my self-identity, and how I felt other people saw me, and even how I saw myself in the world.

Vanita: It's an important story for me. It's the reason I'm doing civil rights and why I care about black people in America. It's my own coming of age, of racial awakening around my own racial identity. I think that it definitely shaped or had an impact, but it was wasn't just that one incident. I think there were a lot of different incidents about being South Asian in Britain. There is a huge community in Britain that is very class-diverse, and there are upper-class South Asians, and there were very poor South Asians. When you go to Heathrow, the airport, for example, that's where all the cleaning folks are largely Indian or South Asian, and when you go to the doctor's, you could very easily have an Indian physician.

Bottom line—when I was growing up in England I became very conscious every time I went to a restaurant. I kept asking myself, "Are there any other people who look like me?" I'd ask myself the same question when I'd go shopping or go out. It started very young. I actually felt that way in Britain, but I felt that way even more so in France because there were a lot fewer people who looked like me in the stores or restaurants and, of course, they spoke only French. Ultimately, I really do believe that this put strength in my upbringing. It took me out of my comfort zone in thinking about being both an outsider and somebody who was young enough to be able to adapt. I had parents who learned French in their 40s and became incredibly immersed and enmeshed in a very French social scene. This was quite extraordinary, I think, and unusual.

A lot of my friends' Indian friends just stuck with their own, even in the United States.

My sister was in college throughout the second stint in England, and we never had a white British family that we were friends with, ever, even though my parents are very outgoing. In France, they cracked the French scene. They were doing all the parties. But it never came together for them in the U.K. despite their both being very social. I don't think the whole time we were there—nine years—we were ever friends with one white, British family. While my father is introverted in the sense that he doesn't share a lot of personal information with other people, he loves to be around other people. He draws energy from other people. He loves playing sports with other people, socializing, going out—both my mother and he love it.

Vanita: When my father says he doesn't think he has a lot of friends, I think what he's saying is he doesn't open up and tell anything very deep about his feelings or if he is stressed out about something; he would never let people know that. He has tons of friends, actually. But the only time he expresses his deep feelings is actually with us, his daughters. I'm sure he shares things with our mother that we don't know about, though. Although our mother and father are totally co-dependent, they couldn't be more different about their likes and dislikes.

Amita: First of all, my dad is out in the world and very socially engaged with lots of corporate acquaintances, and he is intellectually stimulated by his business obligations. My mother doesn't get her energy from intellectual challenges. She's not as interested in the detail about things as my father is. He wants to know facts and figures. My mother doesn't crave that kind of detail. She certainly adapted to my dad's interests, such as sports. She never really played many sports as a girl but then found that in order to spend time with her husband, she had to learn tennis. She also learned golf.

Vanita: My mother is very ambitious. In that way, they're both very similar. So when she learned tennis, she wasn't just going to dabble in tennis. She became a competitive tennis player. In golf, the same thing. My mom so often would say she wished she had worked or done something that engaged her more fully, because looking back, I think she feels she missed something in her life. She didn't feel inferior to my dad, but I think that she sometimes felt that other people saw her in a certain light. Plus, it's hard for her. She's surrounded by three people who draw a lot of energy from their work.

Amita: And not only that. We're hyper-educated. We went to the best schools. But our mother's no dummy. She finished college and then basically became a mother. She went to a small college in India and studied things like art and dance. She's very artistic. Our father, on the other hand, is not a particularly good dancer. He is not particularly musical. He likes to listen to music, but he's not a very artistic person in the right-brain sense. He's more analytical.

Vanita: They have different things that they enjoy. My mom will create this incredible garden and work really hard at mastering all the principles and practices and crafting it beautifully. So they've both kind of modulated their interests to adapt to each other. My mom kind of stretched herself to do the golf and the tennis thing, which she genuinely enjoys, and my father has stretched himself personally to meet and appreciate my mother's interests. On the one hand it works extraordinarily well, and on the other, they can also butt heads.

My father leans on my mom probably more than people think. My mother has very good intuition about people and people's motivation. Sometimes it is very weird. It feels like she has a sixth sense about some things. She knew that I was dating my current husband, Chinh, before I knew that I was dating him. But I think that my father has, over the years, maybe even more recently, talked to her about personalities and people for her opinion. And he would value what she said.

Amita: He wants to hear what she has to say. He doesn't always follow what she says but he wants to hear it, consider it, and often have her voice as part of his final decision where it's appropriate, especially about people.

Coming of Age—Going from Girls to Young Women

Vanita: I think my dad was a spectacular father. He had two daughters whose intellectual curiosity he worked very hard to develop. There could have been a lot of the kind of Indian feeling of "I don't have sons so I'm going to raise my daughters traditionally." My father was never like that. I never, ever felt like a second-tier child, was never made to feel that he wanted a boy instead of a girl. And I think that's a real credit to him and how he raised us. We were going to have every opportunity and we were going to be challenged in every way. He was not the type of father who would ask, "Did you do your homework," or at report card time, scrutinize it for how many A's we got. He was a busy man, but he always made time for us. He obviously had to read a lot, and he had to travel, especially as he got more responsibility at the company. There were a lot of times when I wouldn't see him for a whole week or more. He'd been in Asia or traveling in the U.S.

I remember one trip he'd made in the U.S., traveling for two weeks to something like 12 cities and he picked up a t-shirt for me from every single city. I ended up with 12 different t-shirts. I'm sure he had fun while he was doing that but it was the kind of thing that was really cool for me. I'm thinking, "Louisville, Kentucky, where the heck is that?" But when I'd ask him, he'd sit with me with a map and look up where those cities were. He traced his trip for me. And then in high school, I had a slightly tougher relationship with him that I think in part was because I was going through a lot of changes. I was also very moody. I guess I was going through a phase. I became very protective of my mom. I think I had more challenges in high school than my sister did and my father was gone a lot more, so I bonded with my mother. This was when we were in Britain for the second time in the late 1980s. He was running a global business and was very busy and traveled a lot. I think I was becoming a feminist then, and I was very political. For example, if I didn't like the way my dad was talking to my mother, I would tell him. He was very understanding and patient with me about it.

Maybe I was already developing into a civil rights lawyer, I don't know. It was a coming-of-age thing, I think. There really was nothing that anyone could have done about it, frankly. He was really more patient with me and Amita than he was with my mother or his brothers and sisters about things. He does have a temper, that's for sure. But he never raised his voice with us.

Raj as Father and Communicator

Amita: When he gets upset with us or when he used to get upset with us, he expressed it in writing. He writes it down and sends the letter. We'll get one every couple of years.

Vanita: He pours his thoughts out in those letters. When I was in the process of leaving my first husband, I had been married for just eight months and it just wasn't working out. My mother and I could not talk about it. She was completely emotional about the whole thing, and my father knew how unhappy I was. My mother was personally invested in the survival of the relationship. My father, on the other hand, was very logical about the whole thing. I remember he took me out for coffee. He said, "I want to sit down and talk to you," and he asked me some very pertinent and straightforward questions. And then he told me, "I support you. Your happiness is the most important thing to me." It was almost a year that my mom and I struggled, and she was not happy that my father said that. It was the single most important conversation for me around that time for sure. It was a very hard decision that I was making, and I knew how much it hurt them both, but just to have my father put that out there, and be very clear about what was the most important, was a huge thing.

My relationship with my father evolved over time as I got older. I noticed it first when I went away to college. I think I was becoming more mature and was at a distance from them. That allowed me to see what they gave me. I also missed them. They were in England, and then when they moved back to Philly, I would visit them a fair amount. I had friends who would come home and see me at my parents' house. And it was like this lens I started to see them through.

Amita: I knew my father's mother but not his father. He died when I was very young. We loved our grandmother. She was amazing. She was a role model of her generation. She was athletic. She was like a supermom; super confident on many different subjects. She raised six children. She's the one who gets the credit, I think, from all six of them, really, for the way that she sat and spent time with them and was incredibly attentive to their lives and their concerns. And her four daughters all went to graduate school. She clearly was the matriarch. When she used to come visit us, we would play Scrabble and she'd kick our butts. And she was better in badminton than we were!

Vanita: She was always reading. She was really cool. We would both spend time with her, and with Uncle Arvind. He was really the family liaison. We are very close with him. He's pretty amazing. He's like the family archivist. And he's a real chatterer. He and my dad are very different.

Amita: I think Arvind is the glue that keeps the family together and kind of wants to make sure that everybody's okay. And he is also the one who lived right down the street from my grandmother. I think my dad's big sorrow and regret—even though he had money and he had helped to build her a house—is that he didn't spend enough time with his mother.

Amita: Her death was very painful to him. We were all hurt, but I think it was a kind of turning point for him. I don't remember ever seeing him cry, but I remember him sitting on the bed just crying after he heard that she'd been killed.

Vanita: He used to have a terrible temper but by then he had changed and was so vulnerable. It was such a violated way for her to go. She was murdered in the house that he'd given money for her to build, and she took so much pride in having this home. She was so proud of him. It makes me upset when I think about it. It was so horrible.

And she was very independent. Every one of her family wanted her to live with them and she was insistent: "No, I have my house. I have my garden. You can come visit." But I think her death really did change him. I'll never forget when it happened. It was May 1992, and I was just graduating from high school. My father's family is very close, very supportive of one another. There's a lot of love, a strong connection. But my grandmother was a very strong woman and my father was deeply attached to her.

Amita: My dad left home when he was 16 to enter boarding school and kind of left the family in a way. And maybe he feels a little guilty, I don't know. He doesn't naturally call his brother and sisters. My mom picks up the phone to call each of the siblings. It's just not his style, I guess. Yet, he gives his love to his daughters. He will call us up to check-in in a way that he doesn't do with anyone else. Nobody else, I think, can get that kind of time from him.

Vanita: And now, forget about us. It's the grandkids! It's all about the grandkids! But it wasn't always that way. I think my father is fundamentally a very practical person, and this is how my parents are very different. My father is a very practical and practically-driven person. He struggled with my situation. He also really struggled with Amita's for a little while, but then at some point when he makes a decision, he doesn't look back. And that is not the way that a lot of people are. That's not the way my mom is. He always looks forward with things. He's an optimist at heart. So if there's adversity that comes his way, it is not to say that he doesn't feel pain. He does feel pain. He feels extraordinary pain. I remember one time when my sister's photo was in Time magazine.

Amita: It was a rally in D.C. in 1990 or 1991 when I was in high school. It was the Indian equivalent of a gay rights pride event.

Vanita: And my father saw the photo, and we were in Europe at the time, and he locked himself up in his room for about 36 hours. I had never seen him to do that before.

Amita's Dilemma—"Where do I fit?"

Amita: Yes, that was a very big deal. And I guess, interestingly enough, to their credit and to my credit, I didn't end up trying to be something that I wasn't.

I was still in college and probably 19 years old. It was the first time they had to deal with it. I played tennis, and my tennis partner *actually fell in love with me. At that time, I wasn't really kind of thinking that way, but she came to visit. She had written all of these letters, and my mom read my letters. And she knew that she was coming to visit, and my parents sat me down and said: "So, do you have something to tell us?" I said: "No, no. I have nothing to say." So then they asked: "What's going on?" Basically, they said: "Is something going on with your friend?" I said no. I denied it all along. I just remember their kind of trying to say: "Look, this is a passing phase. We can get you psychiatric help." I kept saying, "No, there's really nothing you can do."*

But it wasn't like I was comfortable with myself. It took a long time to actually be comfortable. And then we didn't talk about it for a few years. When they came to Boston when I was in medical school, I never even told them I got arrested for assisting anti-apartheid demonstrations at MIT. I never told them any of that because I didn't want them to worry or be unnecessarily concerned. In fact, I had been on the front page of the paper, and I never told them because the last thing my dad ever needed to know was that this was public knowledge.

Vanita: But he would have cared.

Amita: They would have been fine with that. But, you know, I was still very stressed out. In college, I wasn't sure about myself, so I dated both men and women. I was trying to figure out what I was. Then I also got very politicized by HIV, because at that time it was the late 1980s or early 1990s when people were dying from HIV, and I volunteered at Aids Action. The guy I was doing the hotline with died a few months later, and I was really affected by all of this and trying to see where I fit in. I kept asking myself, "Am I or am I not?" And then, I think, by medical school, I knew. I had dated a guy right between college and medical school. By the time I had gotten to the second year of medical school, I sort of said: "You know what, let's just face reality." I didn't talk to my parents about it. They were still in Europe or they had just moved back when I started medical school. And they came to visit me in Boston.

Vanita: But it was after they had gone to Provincetown with Amita that this whole thing kind of came out. It was a very happening place and I think my parents were kind of freaked out by it.

Amita: Yes, well, one event in particular kind of set the stage. The guy who was waiting on us at the restaurant was wearing a condom around his middle finger, getting us breakfast. So by evening, everyone was quite tense.

Vanita: I didn't have a clue that they were so tense.

Amita: I was totally unprepared, and I think at that point they confronted me and asked what is going on. Who are you dating? Are you gay? I sort of totally cracked, essentially. I ended up, not by my own volition, just finally telling them what was going on, what I was. I was mostly upset that the conversation did not happen on my own terms. It happened in my room. I was confronted, and I had to tell them.

Vanita: I don't know whose idea it was, but I think it was more my mom's idea. She had had a sixth sense about it. We are a family that generally discusses things. It's the four of us where stuff just comes out. My husband's family is different. They know about their own dramas but they don't talk about them. But in our family, we have it out.

Amita's Lifestyle and Vanita's Divorce— Testing the Bonds of Family and Culture

Amita: I remember just bits and pieces of when I told my parents about who I am and that I'm gay and what that meant, because honestly it was a very difficult moment, I think. This was a very long and complex journey for me, and I didn't think I was given the opportunity to explain it on my terms. I felt like I was having to tell them something when I was not ready to. But they, particularly my mom, were so persistent in trying to get it out of me that I told them. And that was hell for me. My mom cried all through the session, she was so upset. My dad was also very upset but then had the additional responsibility of having to take care of my mom and her grief about it. And Vanita, poor thing, had to just, I think, hear it through again. She knew when I was in college.

What sticks so clearly in my mind, though, was the letter that I got from my dad. I was 25 at the time. I remember exactly. He had written this letter and he basically expressed all of his thoughts about it. Before, all I had gotten from him was how upset my mom was and how angry she was. The letter from my dad basically said, "This is difficult to take in. I worry that this kind of lifestyle can be very hard for you, and I'm not sure you really understand what you are getting yourself into." And this was very painful to read, but I still tried to understand it. My sister probably struggles with this as well. The letter was my father's way of pouring out feelings and to some degree saying that while he didn't really understand it, he recognized my difficulty and my pain around it. He said that it would take time for him to try and accept it, that he would try his best to do what he could to be a loving father, but it was tough.

So he put that all on paper. I remember being so upset and just crying on the bathroom floor, just weeping away as I was reading the letter and just being really touched, but at the same time knowing how hard this was for them and not wanting it to disappoint them but at the same time, not wanting to be dishonest as to who I was. And it was interesting because Vanita and I lived afterwards for a year together. It was at the end of medical school. We shared the apartment where my parents came and visited in Boston. Vanita and I had a nice year together. It was great.

Vanita: Oh, it was amazing. I had just graduated from college and had a year and a half in Boston. I delayed going to law school for two years.

Amita: So we lived together and I remember then I had to make a decision about where I was going to do my residency. Obviously, there was a subconscious decision-making on my part because I struggled a little bit. I thought, well, I could stay at Harvard or I could go to their teaching affiliate hospital, The Brigham and Women's Hospital. Those are great programs, or I could go out West and be 3,000 miles away. I obviously chose to go out West to San Francisco to the UCSF Medical Center which is ranked among the top programs in the country.

So I prioritized them among my own choices, UCSF first and The Brigham second. And I remember when I got my envelope—and again this was where my mom's sixth sense kicked in—she sort of knew I was going to be making a decision that she was not going to be happy with. It was Match Day, the day you find where you're accepted for your residency. I had my sister with me and I opened the envelope and said, "Well, I got my first choice," and I was really excited and so was Vanita. Then I think my mom either called or we called her a half an hour later. Then I was in tears, really upset because my mom was so angry at me for having decided to move so far away as well as for what else was going on in my life and what going to San Francisco would mean in that regard. She thought I was lost; there was no going back to the closet or whatever.

That was all very upsetting to me. I don't remember my dad's reaction. He was essentially silent, I think. They came only once or twice to visit me the entire three years I was there. I would come East to visit, but they, I think, only came out to San Francisco a couple of times. And one time when they did come—and my sister wasn't there—I was really busy. I lived in the moment, not to mention not calling them very much, either. Anyway, we were scheduled to have dinner. And I'm saying to myself, "How am I going to have them meet the person I was dating then—who is my partner now—Charlotte. And I didn't say anything to them about, "You are going to meet Charlotte." So I had two friends of mine—one who is Indian-American, Ashish, whom I went to medical school with and whom my parents knew and liked and who is brilliant and another friend, Jonathan, who was a residency friend. So I had these two male buffers at the dinner along with Charlotte and my parents. Charlotte was clearly gay. I remember my father's being unable to look Charlotte in the eyes. He did this little court game. He did not look at her in the eyes at all, whereas, my mom tried. But then my mom would speak in Hindi to Ashish and she'd be, like: "So, who are all these people?" And of course, I know Hindi and am listening to all these side conversations going on at the table. I think my parents saw through the buffer strategy pretty quickly, but they didn't say anything about it. As a matter of fact, we didn't talk about Charlotte really until we had our marriage ceremony in 2006, which really changed things.

I remember that it was essentially a tough process. We really didn't talk too much about it. At the same time, slowly, I think, through a lot of patience on my part and I guess to some degree on their part, I just sort of gently chipped away at it. I also made the decision to move back to the East Coast so that we (my parents and I) could be closer. (Charlotte's parents are New Zealanders living in New Orleans.) So I moved back in steps. First, I went to CDC (the Centers for Disease Control) in Atlanta for two years, and then ended up coming to Baltimore. So it was a gesture on my part to be closer to my parents, which I think they realized to some degree.

They were certainly very happy that I was going to be closer. But again, it was always really a difficult conversation to have. It took a long time for my dad to even really be able to understand what this was all about. He kept calling Charlotte my friend. You know, if Charlotte came to some affair with family they would introduce her as a friend, so our relationship was kind of minimized. And meanwhile, my parents were dealing with Vanita's divorce, so at that point, when Charlotte would show up they would know, but we just didn't talk about it.

Vanita: Yes, they knew and then they started to accept it. There was a huge acceptance of the fact that my sister was gay. But my sister and I would often have a battle because I felt that my sister expected too much from my parents, and I had felt like I was the one who had always been the buffer through all the trials and tribulations going back ten to twelve years when she was in Boston and then San Francisco. I was the one who was always seeing my parents and constantly communicating with them.

Amita: That's true. You did all the hard work.

Vanita: They would pour their hearts out. They would initially say: "Can you talk to her? Can you change her or tell her?" Of course, I didn't want to, because I felt very strongly about my sister and her identity and her life. I also was very cognizant of what they were going through. So I tried to compensate for what they felt about my sister by visiting and calling them more. When I was in college, I called every other day. And I would go home a lot more.

Amita: She felt she had to do the right thing.

Vanita: Yes, I did. I felt obliged, and I also think I wanted to play that role a little bit. But I actually felt like Mom and Dad started to really accept Charlotte in a way that was pretty significant, maybe a couple of years in. I have to say, the distance that my parents have travelled is amazing. Charlotte is just like any other sister or daughter-in-law.

Amita: And as I said, the ceremony was the culmination of a lot of factors. Before that, I think their context for Charlotte was that there was still a level of discomfort around her.

Vanita: I also know that they didn't tell their friends, so they weren't able to get any comfort or positive feedback from them when they could have. Instead, it seemed like they were trying to hide something. They didn't try to hide it at home, but they did with their friends.

But from my vantage point, I think two things resulted from my divorce that may have affected my parents' transformation about my sister. First, they saw that Amita was really happy and that further aggravating the situation was not worth it, but they were still kind of in the closet. And then came time for Amita and Charlotte's ceremony. With me, they had thrown this huge, beautiful wedding, inviting everyone they knew, and then literally, within a year, I had left the marriage. That marriage had been a huge cushion and feeling of relief and pride for my mom as well as my father. My first husband was perfect on paper—Indian, great parents, everything. And so I tried to stay in the marriage for as long as I could, even though I wasn't happy. We weren't well matched.

Amita: I told my sister that I didn't think he was right

Vanita: I know. I was even in counseling with him before we got married. But my mom kept saying, "Love isn't just this Hollywood romance. You have to work at it." She just has a totally different view of marriage than I do. But I'd had a college boyfriend for 4½ years, and I knew what it meant to be in love, and this wasn't it. But anyway, it was a tough time for me. I was professionally at the top of my game. I had just litigated the Tulia case in Texas. I was travelling the country and in the newspaper all the time, and then

I would go home and feel like energy was being sucked out of me. Eventually, I knew I had to reconcile these parts of my life and I did that.

But I think the ceremony for Amita and Charlotte was so powerful because my dad's sister Aparna from Michigan came.

Amita: Yes, and she decided at the last minute. I think this was to my cousins' credit. I felt pretty close to my aunt who lives in Michigan. When my parents lived in Europe, they would send me over to the States where I would spend summers with Aunt Aparna and my cousins, and they would take really great care of me. I tried to tell her gently that we were going to do this, that it's going to be a party, and that she didn't have to make it a big deal. But I told her that this was important to Charlotte and me, and we would love for her to come. Then I even said that if they wanted to invite anybody, they could. I just wanted to make it as easy for her to come as I could. At that point, I had decided to invite my cousins because my four cousins from Michigan are really cool.

I have to give particular credit to my cousins Divya and Priya. They really made a case to my aunt. I remember getting an email back then saying that she felt a little strange about it and why would I want to have something like this. Initially, I had been told that she wasn't going to come. And then I think literally four days before, she decided to attend.

Amita: But I do remember, interestingly enough, the difference between my ceremony and that for Vanita's wedding. For Vanita, all of the family from India was there and there was all this hoopla. Of course, I would never expect that they would do that for me, but I remember I was in my room getting ready for my ceremony, and my mom and dad never even came to the room to check up on me and see how I was getting dressed or anything. I was left to my own devices to complete the entire planning. They gave me a check. They helped pay for the ceremony, which was very generous. But it was very different. To them, basically, this was our own doing. Even Charlotte's parents were also shy about it. They didn't invite any of their friends. But I do remember as a result of that whole thing—my parents and her parents—our families were completely transformed by the event because I think, in part, they realized that we are a very loving couple and were surrounded by incredibly loving people, and this had an effect on them.

Vanita: My mom at the ceremony got up and did something that she did at my ceremony. She put Amita's and Charlotte's heads together and gave a blessing. At my wedding, she did the same thing with me and Chinh. It was amazing.

Amita: Everybody said "Woo!"

Vanita: My mom did that. It was just crazy. It was actually crazy. It was a very transformative event. In front of 200 people at this full-fledged reception. To see that was really something.

Amita: And since then, my parents have been like night and day. It's incredible. They're amazing. I can't ask for a more loving family, and the other amazing thing is, when Vanita got married for a second time, to Chinh, some of their relatives, many of my parents' siblings, were invited. A lot of the family came over to our [Charlotte's and Amita's] house which is really a huge deal.

Vanita: Huge!

Amita: So that was really the first time that many of the extended family came to know as well about Charlotte and me. I have to give my parents a huge amount of credit because it's not something that you sort of take lightly. When you look at both of us—between Vanita getting divorced and marrying a Vietnamese-American and my choosing a nontraditional lifestyle, and the most amazing thing, having a child (I had an anonymous donor and got pregnant)—my parents have been nothing but extraordinary.

Vanita: And with my husband, my dad's the same way. I think that my father and Chinh took an immediate liking to each other. Chinh and my father go out and enjoy food and wine. He is so relaxed around him. Chinh is the Legal Director of the D.C. Legal Aid Society and my father is the chairman of one company and sits on the boards of a bunch of others, and they're best friends. Chinh had to make adjustments as well because he was coming from his own idea of what a CEO of a Fortune 500 company was like. So it was an adjustment for both of them.

Vanita: My father is the kind of person who works hard and plays hard. He's very confident but he's also very grateful to the people in his life. He knows how to talk to people on any level. He can talk to the President of the United States, but he can also talk to the person who is working in manual labor. He always shows everyone the utmost respect. I don't think it is ingenuous at all. In my case, he suddenly started wanting to know much more about Chinh's family from when they were in a refugee camp in Vietnam in 1975 after Saigon fell to the Communists. My father wanted to know the whole history. He wanted to learn as much as he could. So I feel like these are different pieces of what makes him tick. On the one hand, he had a tough time with my sister's being gay and my going through a divorce, but he has enormous pride in us and he's been very generous to us both and to our families.

Amita: I feel the same way. I think he feels real pride in us and wants to tell his own story and to pass it on to his grandsons. He's always worried about his health and that he might not be around when they graduate from high school. He wants them to know him. And of course, he likes to write what he thinks. It gives his thinking clarity and this book is allowing him to do that.

Vanita: Yes, my father was really affected by his cancer but he's always been someone who's been very concerned about his health and his mortality because his younger brother had an umpteen number of heart attacks and strokes. My uncle had a heart bypass when he was in his 30s.

Amita: Yes, he had terrible health problems.

Vanita: And then his own father died at 60. I remember in England my father's being rushed to the ER having chest pains that were basically panic attacks.

Amita: Yes, he was having chest pains and he was thinking he was dying, and so we were, in the middle of the night, thinking the worst was happening. Later, when he was diagnosed with prostate cancer, Charlotte and I got quite involved. I knew there was good therapy and treatment available and I wanted to get him the best. I even had him come to Hopkins and meet one of the most famous prostate surgeons in the world. Yet, in retrospect, it's hard to know what to do because prostate cancer is one of those cancers that actually we don't know what the best approach is for treatment. It's very complex, particularly when you're in this middle category, which my father was—not advanced—and so it was a very stressful time for him. That was when he was having to negotiate the Rohm and Haas sale and at the same time worry about what his cancer meant for his own mortality and his family. My dad has never been one to fret over his health. He takes good care of himself. He gets up every day and exercises. He's always been in good health except for the panic attacks. He was the most disciplined person I know.

Amita: No matter where he was in the world, he would get up and he'd exercise, and he really took good care of himself. (I wish I'd gotten that gene.) So when this happened and he had all this other stressful stuff happening, it just made him feel very vulnerable and just scared.

Vanita: And I was about to have his first grandson. He had the prostate surgery in October 2008, and I gave birth at the end of the November. There were a lot of things going on.

Amita: And it kind of made him feel very mortal. It's something that takes control away. And he was someone who's used to being in control, and taking charge, and knowing exactly what decisions to make. So I think that was tough for him. The cancer's gone, but he's had some long-term side effects from the surgery. Still he's done remarkably well.

Vanita: If you didn't know he had it, you couldn't tell at all. He loves playing golf and tennis. And like everything else in his life, he doesn't let much get in the way of anything.

Amita: But I do think he felt incredibly vulnerable during the whole process.

Vanita: Yes, that and then the injury on his heel—a chronic wound that came from when he fell off a golf cart and really hurt it. It took a really long time to heal. But it's fine now, and he's in good shape from all his exercising. But that heel injury took him out of action for six months, and he was pretty affected about it. He has this balance where he works hard and plays hard, and when one part is out of sync it really affects him.

Amita: I would say, from a physician's perspective, he is occasionally a little bit of a hypochondriac, worrying about the worst possible thing. I think one time, he told me this one small symptom, and I said, "Well it could be this or it could be that" and of course he picked the worst possible outcome. And then he apparently was up all night worrying about it. My mom was a wreck. But that's the way he is—he takes the worst case scenario and then gets driven crazy by it.

Raj's New Role as Grandfather

Vanita: I will make another observation. His relationship with my son, his first grandson, who's just a toddler, is amazing. My dad kneels down to get down on his level, makes eye contact with him, and just loves being with him. They're really buddies. My father has this absolute, constant desire to be around him. It's the greatest thing about having a kid. To see what he brings out in my father. I think both my parents—my mom and my dad—waited a very long time and now all of a sudden they have three grandkids to play with. But with my older son, in particular, he and my dad are two peas in a pod. My son will call my father and ask when they're going to McDonald's again. They are just inseparable.

Amita: I'll tell you a story about something that happened with my son who was about six months old at the time. One day, I needed a few hours of help and my dad said: "I'll come down." And he did. He drove down to Baltimore from Philadelphia. He left at 5:00 a.m. and arrived by 7:00 a.m.

Vanita: And this was without my mom.

Amita: He came by himself and took care of my son. He changed his diapers and gave him bottles. I was gone for 4-5 hours and he did the entire thing himself. And my mom was incredulous: "I don't think he even did that with you." I loved it. He said: "I'm coming. I'm into it." So that goes to show you how much he values being a grandfather. He just loves it.

Intelligence, Humility, and Pride—
Raj's Legacy to his Daughters

Vanita: The other observation is about his ability to explain very complex subjects in terms people can understand. Not too long ago we had an event at the house and my dad was talking about the digital revolution so that everyone in the room could understand what he was talking about. I know how smart my dad is, and I have these moments where I listen to him and say to myself, "Look at this guy. He's not just smart, but he can even translate it for me and for people who have no technical background."

And I'll say something else about what makes him special and is a key characteristic of his—his humility. When I was in the New York Times a lot when the Tulia, Texas case [46 people, 40 of them African-Americans, were falsely arrested on trumped-up drug charges, and the case was overturned as a result of the NAACP's work, subsequently made into a documentary] was getting all that publicity, my dad started making copies of the articles and sending them to his friends. I know this because I was getting messages about it from people I didn't know all over the world. That's my dad. He'll do it for his daughters, but not himself. He never puts on airs. He tries to make everyone feel important and valued. I don't even think it's a conscious thing with him. I think it's just how he relates to people in the world. And there are a lot of people in his position who are not like that. Not like that at all. He's different.

Amita: Right. He's very ambitious, but quietly so; and he's humble. I mean, and what's cool, he's an interesting combination, sort of a rare combination of being driven but yet being humble, in terms of his motivation. He loves his craft. He wants to be really good at it, but it isn't at the expense of anybody else, and he doesn't need to tell everybody else about it.

Vanita: I think they've raised us with very good values that way. It's true that my parents have always provided for us. Now at this stage in their life, they are able to provide even more for us, but I think they never wanted us to grow up with a sense of entitlement. And it's been very important to them. And we've always worked and done all the chores in the house. They obviously didn't have everything that they have now when we were growing up, but even now I think that they instilled in us that we have to be self-made people, regardless of their station in life. I think that's something that my sister and I don't even really think about because we are so work-minded and career-minded on our own; we're not ones to say, "Oh, if we had a lot of money, we would quit our jobs."

I can only feel really good about where I am right now and feel lucky that both sets of grandparents are alive and have such invested and active roles in my kids' lives. I think my father since his retirement is anything but retired and plays such an important role in his grandchildren's lives and in other lives as well. My father is still incredibly active. I think that he needs to continue that way. Sometimes I think that my mom was initially concerned that he wouldn't stop, but I think working is what makes my father tick.

I think my parents were always accepting of our choices. I could have gone anywhere when I graduated from law school and I chose the NAACP's Legal Defense Fund, and I think they were kind of thinking about where that was going to go, but at no point did they discourage me or try to dissuade me from what I wanted to do. They were always proud. They always supported me. And that's saying something, because this was not part of their world at all.

Amita: I also feel incredibly lucky and feel very full in terms of my career path. In some respects, while I'm a physician, I've gone into academics, so it's not entirely nontraditional, but I'm at a very good place. I get affirmation in what I do. On the other hand, I wouldn't say that I'm the best at what I do, by any stretch. I'm more of a plodder, and in an environment such as Johns Hopkins, there are people who are absolutely, unbelievably brilliant. They are a quantum leap from where I am. There are people there making amazing discoveries. That's not who I am, and I never saw myself like that. I've always been very good, but I'm not on that level. But on the other hand, I think I'm a really good people person. I have a really nice team. I am building a program in India that I've taken over from my mentor that I'm putting my stamp on. I have people I mentor in terms of residents and fellows, and I really enjoy that part and like the team-building aspect of it. I like the human interaction. I feel like I can wake up in the morning and feel good about what I do. I work on important and neglected diseases such as tuberculosis and HIV and maternal child health issues that are of global importance. So whatever I do, I don't worry about the fact that I'm doing something that isn't meaningful or isn't interesting. I like intellectual stimulation, but at the same time, I also don't obsess about it. I feel like I'm not someone who is singularly obsessed about my career. I actually really enjoy just hanging out.

Vanita: I feel like the thing that the three of us have—and in totally different sectors—is that all three of us have this need to feel like we are in the mix and feel that our work is meaningful in some way. And that's why my dad doesn't want to retire, because he needs that stimulation

That and our families are what really drive us both as well as my father. When you might feel bogged down with a lot of administrative work, you know that there's a greater purpose to it, and I think that's something that we like to be part of and have those higher-level conversations. We feel like we're moving lives, each of us in our very own spheres, but it's not without ambition, obviously. I feel good that I am Deputy Legal Director of an organization at the age of 36. It's something that unifies us. It's a trait that we've probably gotten from our dad, and there are times when we feel lackluster and kind of discontent and we feel like we're spinning our wheels a little bit, but we try to keep our eyes and focus on the bigger picture. And that we have each other.

Since that conversation, Vanita was nominated by President Obama in October 2014 to be assistant attorney general for the Civil Rights Division and the top civil rights prosecutor for the U.S. Department of Justice. As such, she is the first woman, the first person of South Asian descent, and the youngest person ever to receive the appointment to lead the 50-year old division. This comes at a time of increasing incidents and evidence of racial bias and an intense debate over the role of government, law enforcement, and the rights of minorities perhaps not seen since the civil rights movement of the 1960s. Vanita's background in criminal justice reform will serve her well as the Justice Department works with cities and police departments nationwide for greater community collaboration and in reform efforts to address mandatory minimum sentencing laws. This is but one part of the division's wider role and mission of expanding opportunities for citizens across all of American life; preserving the infrastructure of democracy; protecting individuals from exploitation, discrimination and violence; and expanding the tools to protect citizens' civil rights. Here is an article about Vanita's appointment: (http://www.huffingtonpost.com/2015/05/06/vanita-gupta-doj-civil-rights-division_n_7190982.html)..

Amita, who has received recognition for leading cutting-edge, U.S.-India collaborations to fight infectious diseases such as AIDS and tuberculosis, continues her work as a physician and professor of medicine at Johns Hopkins. Here is just one article on her work and efforts in fighting infectious diseases in India: http://main.ccghe.net/sites/default/files/assets/documents/Amita-True-Fighter-Article.pdf.

11

REFLECTIONS ON MY LIFE
AND LESSONS LEARNED

"Watch out and guard yourself from all types of greed, because one's life does not consist in the abundance of his possessions."
—Luke 12:15

"No one remains what he was when he recognizes himself."
—Thomas Mann, novelist, social critic, and philanthropist

On the American Dream

For me, the American dream starts with what it basically means to be an American. For all America's faults and shortcomings, including those it is living with now, it has the fairest system in the world for its citizens, a system that transcends their country of origin, their skin color, gender, or the God they worship. It creates the most even playing field in the world. I know there is luck and chance involved, but not primarily. The dream is not based on who your parents were, or how much money they came with or passed along to you.

The foundation of the American dream is fairness. It is what sets America apart from the rest of the world. We are a country based on the *rule of law*, three words measured in blood and treasure that stand today as one of America's noblest characteristics. It is to me what makes

America great. It is what allowed me to realize my potential. I was never handicapped by where I came from, how I looked, the color of my skin, the accent I spoke with, or the views I held. I was aware of my differences and was sometimes perceived as different, but I was not hobbled thereby.

The American dream is under assault these days. America's once wide-open arms are said to be closing, its membership disheartened and discouraged by the separation of the haves and the have-nots. Economic data confirm this widening income gap, and social scientists warn that if the trend continues, a life of stagnant earnings and diminished opportunities will hamstring those children of the once upward-climbing middle class. And yet, Emma Lazarus's words, inscribed at the base of the Statue of Liberty, "I lift my lamp beside the golden door," still describe what American liberty means to the immigrant from afar and to the immigrant who has made America his home—a door leading to unequaled opportunity for a better life. If one doubts the pull to be free and to escape either the horrors of war or political oppression, then one needs only glimpse the hardships of Syrians and other émigrés risking death on the open waters or undertaking treacherous pilgrimages to squalid camps in unfamiliar lands, as they make their way to a better life.

Even with all that's going on with the banks, Wall Street, legislative gridlock, and institutional skepticism, I still believe that there is no nation in the world that is anything like this one. And I, for one, don't think the system is broken. It's more a question of how we go about fixing what's not working, not tearing it down and starting over. Maybe we're learning more about capitalism than we thought it could teach us. Maybe it is vulnerable in ways we hadn't thought about. Maybe it needs more safeguards, more incentives for good behavior, or a clear reward/punishment regime for those who believe they are beyond the need to abide by the rules. But the system works. It is a system that allows those with ambition to improve their lives. I tread a line culturally still, but I listened and learned and took advantage of the opportunities given to me. I wear American citizenship with the pride it deserves, as do my daughters.

President Obama's election epitomized American democracy and egalitarianism, maybe even more so in the eyes of the world than in America, though certainly one had to be deaf not to hear the page turn as the news media and pundits hailed a promise fulfilled in historical terms. That, I think, goes back to reaffirmation of what this country is all about—irrespective of your start, you have a shot, what President Obama called "the audacity of hope." The great tigers of Asia—India and China—have eons to go before realizing the promise that America has achieved in the blink of time's eye. There is something in this country that allows you to flourish and find your way. But finding their way for those folks who are not "native" in the typical white-male-American-born sense is a winding and often uphill path, a path that America is still trying to clear so that all citizens have an equal shot.

On America

American middle class values set the model for the world. It is time again for America to redefine and give hope to those values in the 21st century, through jobs, infrastructure improvement, better schools and teacher opportunities, and more effective working partnerships between local, state, and federal governments and private industry. More money for basic research and more capital for entrepreneurial business, either through federal dollars or private philanthropy, are proven pathways to greater opportunity for all.

Re-expanding opportunity is of enormous importance because an entire culture can be dramatically changed by economics. When a growing portion of the middle class strata becomes jobless, or their incomes are shorn of power above just paying for necessities, the dream of a better life vanishes. The incentive to be selfless or generous to others is diminished. It forces people to put up walls—all sorts of walls—that tear away at the American fabric and the stuff that makes the American dream a reality. And to me, someone whose native society did not have a thriving middle class, the American dream is the source of America's strength—those who are born with modest resources, who see tomorrow as better than today, with pluck and ingenuity make the impossible happen. I assert that this strong belief is as much the source of America's diversity, its uniqueness, and its continuing self-inventiveness, as I believe it is India's potential.

And while America's higher education remains the world's best, its feeder system—many of its public high schools and elementary schools—seems lost in teaching-for-the-test vs. teaching concepts and critical thinking. That is the syndrome of lesser countries, whose Darwinian politics favors the elite and those strongest in both military and political power, and it should not be happening in our meritocracy.

The public trust in our institutions is now near historic lows, as the Baby Boomers, Generation Xers, and even Millennials have slowly but inextricably either slipped in stature and standard of living or failed to find promise in the future. As their fortunes have ebbed (or failed to be achieved), those of the 1 percent have skyrocketed. The middle class is the seed corn of American prosperity, and it is failing to grow. And in the process, the common citizenry's confidence in the politicians, bankers, and financial and political institutions designed to protect them has markedly fallen. According to a 2011 Gallup poll, Congress ranked last in public trust only slightly behind banks, big business, and HMOs.

Wall Street is the poster child for greed in business, no question. And when the macro-economic system threatens instead of improves, the "what" needs to be addressed along with the "why" and then changes and fixes instituted. The political and financial systems, the foundation of capitalism, are based on trust and confidence

What would I fix if I were in charge? First, it would be to infuse capitalism with a greater conscience. Capitalism has proved to be one of the great transformative ideas of the modern world. It has the potential and track record to bring out the best in individuals and the best out of the nation. There is certainly the temptation for those at its controls to game the system. That is the moral hazard. The challenge is to reward prudent risk-taking and decision-making. I would do all I could to facilitate what I see as increasing evidence that 21st century corporations will be different from those of the 20th century, different in the sense that they are becoming more innovative, accountable, and more engaged in unifying society rather than just making money for shareholders. Such a shift in the role of corporations to include a wider group of stakeholders who see a wider ecology of customers, employees, suppliers, and community does two things, in my view. First, it sharpens the sense of corporate responsibility to benefit more people and conserve the earth's resources, and second, by its nature, lessens the unintended consequences of greed and excesses, two traits that have, in my judgment, hurt capitalism and the global economy.

On Business, Wall Street, and Income Inequality

A professor once asked his ethics class why one shouldn't cross the street against the light even if there are no cars or policemen around. There was silence. Then he said, "Because a child may see you do it and think it's OK." Writ large, the story is important for two reasons. There are laws, regulations, and policies for their own reasons—to keep order, to protect people, to prevent harm to oneself—but the public obedience of those laws shows others that there is intrinsic meaning and value to them. Whether it's not crossing against the light or not throwing litter in the street, or complying with the SEC laws and regulations, or not gaming the market, organizations have a duty to themselves and their society to act ethically as well. If the CEO breaks the rules, then obviously the rules are not important and soon everyone breaks the rules, and the organizational culture goes astray. The system upon which our government is based is no less immune from the character and behavior of its citizens and leaders.

Jesus' parable about the preoccupation of acquiring possessions, quoted at the beginning of this chapter, is a cautionary tale as true today as then. In the case of Wall Street, the stakes are extraordinarily high because capitalism depends on a culture of credibility and trust. The telling cliché of the movie, *Wall Street*, that "greed is good" is both an excuse and a benchmark for many whose art and craft is doing an always bigger deal or making a market that qualifies him (and it *is* usually a male) into becoming a so-called Master of the Universe, as Tom Wolfe termed the trading tycoons in *Bonfire of the Vanities* back in the 1980s. Wall Street attracts some of the best and the brightest from America's universities and business schools, those able to ride the carousel of finance capitalism with its myriad and never-ending brass rings who, even if they should they fall off, land with riches unknown to the average American.

Wall Street has made a science of technical innovation and the engineering of complex financial instruments in the name of creating shareholder value, successfully distributing these products to investors throughout the capital markets. But when these products and financial instruments unduly exploit the market or introduce risk or uncontrollable leverage, Wall Street turns into a gambling casino and its investors into bettors. With any house of cards, if the liquidity congeals because the financial system is over-leveraged beyond what it can bear, it can collapse, as almost happened during the subprime mortgage crisis beginning in 2008.

What makes Wall Street's actions in the Great Recession and leading up to 2008 such a cautionary tale is not its creation of wealth for corporations or those who invested in prudent risk and finance capitalism, or even the creation of asset bubbles, which all markets experience. It's the way the bubbles were exploited and leveraged, not just by Wall Street, whose financial engineering exaggerated irresponsible leverage through designed-to-default bonds whose complexity only a select few even understood, but also by the underrating standards, the statistical rating agencies who looked the other way, and the lax financial standards that allowed unethical, illegal, and immoral practices to go unchecked.

It didn't have to be this way. The stock market is not a casino, and investing shouldn't be a legal form of gambling with other people's money. We're still digging out, and ominously, the permanent signs of the new normal suggest that traditional post-recession recovery will leave many more behind than were before. Nor should those who survived the Great Recession try to transform the recovery into a digital gold rush for insatiable consumers. Silicon Valley and venture capitalists should beware of start-ups just looking to make a quick buck and, indeed, raise the investment bar high in the entrepreneurial spirit of innovation and future shareholder value, and to "make the world a better place" or to "change the world."

I would suggest the focal point of both Wall Street and Silicon Valley and indeed business innovators and creators should be in the areas that the Center for Strategic & International Studies calls "The Seven Revolutions." These are:

1. Population—What effects will population growth/decline, aging, migration, and urbanization have on our future world?
2. Resource management—What changes will we see in food, water, and energy consumption/production?
3. Technology—What changes are we going to see in computation, robotics, biotechnology, and materials science?
4. Information and knowledge—How does the vast amount of data change how we learn and govern in the future?

5. Economics—How is our economic landscape changing?
6. Security—How do we balance state competition/conflict with the increased pressures of transnational threats?
7. Governance—What is the role of leaders, corporations, and NGOs in this new environment?

I'm clear about what's important to me, however. I think everybody pretty much wants to define how they want to live. As to those who in business stray from what they know or are taught to believe is right and fair, I think their behavior is largely a result of two dynamics: the pressure to win the game and the pressure to stay on top once one has won. It fuels the drive to feed Wall Street's insatiable appetite. I make no excuse for them, but in my view, they are not only letting themselves, their families, and everyone who trusted them down, but also they are causing the common man to lose trust in his valued political and economic institutions. That is the battle we are seeing now in the 99 percent movement in the broader political sense and the one that needs the greatest attention.

Great opportunities await technology, mobile computing, the cloud, and the Internet of Things. In a way, Silicon Valley, mobile computing, and the cloud are already changing the way the world is thinking not only about business, but also about technological frontiers that meld human and artificial intelligence in ways that we can only dream about not to mention ways that can solve real and seemingly insoluble problems. Business innovation and technological engineering are not threatening the system; they are creating opportunities that in many ways seem boundless.

The 21st century CEO will have to learn when and how to use the myriad tools and platforms of social media communication and to provide dialogue forums with employees, customers, shareholders, suppliers, and the public. It's a whole new world for corporate communications and one whose tools need to be understood and mastered. Social media is to the 21st century CEO what the microphone is to the politician. Be careful what you say because if it's on, the whole world hears it.

On Leadership

While my new career in private equity has certainly brought a sense of the timeliness of financial investments, my seasoning as a chairman and CEO has also taught me that CEOs need a patient but also watchful eye so that they can do the job they were hired to do while still fulfilling their obligations to their shareholders. It is an intricate process of maintaining dynamic tension, as well as trust, that must be delicately and skillfully managed if it is to succeed. It's a multi-dimensional process of giving opinions, guidance, mentoring, and listening as well as facilitating. It's something I spend a lot of time, every day, looking to improve. And people notice when you have made this effort, as a recent experience on the HP board exemplifies.

In 2011 we had almost an entirely new board at Hewlett-Packard, where I serve, a world leader in printing and personal systems and servers, storage, networking gear, and services for enterprises, with annual sales in excess of $100 billion. And when the time came that the board needed a lead independent director, the chairman wanted us to vote for someone we felt could best represent us. I was chosen. And the reason for that was, I think, first and foremost, that I didn't come with a personal agenda and that I would listen carefully and objectively to their ideas. They felt I could empathize with their views and therefore fairly represent them to management. Otherwise I see no reason to select someone like me, because I'm not the most vocal person on that board, and I didn't come from a technology background. I think they saw me as a person who would stand up for what's right and fairly represent them and the interests of HP's stakeholders. I was pleased and surprised to be chosen. In 2015 HP announced it was splitting into two companies, and I have again been selected to be the lead independent director for HP Inc., which includes printing and personal systems with sales in excess of $50 billion.

Another lesson I have learned is that you cannot reduce success to one single trait or set of habits. Success comes in different shapes, sizes, styles, and skill sets that are a function of the times and the life of the organization. For example, the people who are successful in turning around stressful situations have a different set of skills from those who are managing a predictable and stable organization. Apart from some fundamentals, such

206

as basic competence, managing a start-up or an organization in transition requires another wholly different skill set. Ben Horowitz captures these challenges and skills in spades in his book, *The Hard Thing About Hard Things: Building a Business When There Are No Easy Answers* (2014). When everything is falling down around them, leaders need to keep their heads focused, maintain priorities, and make hard and unpleasant decisions, all the while keeping the enterprise afloat and motivating the hell out of people to go out and sell more, discover more, and grow the business. Horowitz acknowledges that the process can grind you down, as he recounts it did to him in his own career. Sometimes you have to be incredibly autocratic and even brutal in decision-making. For these reasons, I think the real test of leaders is when they are under stress or the organization is under stress. That includes personal lives, too. Your real leadership traits show up when you have to choose between two negatives—the dire and the less dire. One method to achieve continued viability and survival is building organizational resilience, starting with resilient leadership, because the traits that make you successful are different depending on who and what organization you're talking about. And different times and circumstances call for different leaders.

Let me say one thing here that blends the personal and professional. You can't separate what you believe as a businessman from what you believe as a parent, spouse, or caregiver. The work/life balance isn't just something that is a measure in time spent at home or time spent at work, like a see-saw—parceling out so much for the business and just so much for the family. It's a way of seeing and living. It's being able to recognize the small activities of life, like attending a child's soccer or football game or play, and seeing them as important as a meeting on a pending merger. The meeting is important, no question, but to that child, that game or that event becomes part of who they are and who they will become. One can either choose to be part of that process or not. To me that is the work/life balance, adjusting one's time and attention to what's important in his or her life and then working at it every day.

Being a CEO is often a mixed blessing. You're proud of the individual achievement it signifies and the faith others have placed in your leadership skills, but you must make decisions that neither you nor the others are always in favor of or that do not advance the well-being of your stakeholders.

Sometimes, though, you are able to facilitate a business decision that improves lives, creates growth, expands the marketplace, and introduces new products and technologies.

When I was at the helm of Rohm and Haas I had the ultimate leadership job of my career. I felt fulfilled that I had achieved something rare and enviable, but it had not been a life-long ambition. I was the corporate leader of a significant chemical company that was proud of its products, its people, its customers, the good will it was able to generate in the communities where it operated, and its philanthropic gifts to other deserving organizations.

It also put into stark relief my own bouts with anxiety when I was younger, and later, trying to please my superiors with my mortality staring me in the face during my bout with prostate cancer. These experiences made me look at life and leadership in new ways, especially now that my grandchildren have come into my life. More money will not get me more time with my loved ones or a greater sense of well-being or happiness. The parable rings true for me as I hope it does for all people fortunate enough to have had material gifts in their life. Greed is not the answer. Greed is not good.

I was fortunate. I think that the moral guidelines that my parents and later my company, Rohm and Haas, gave me in terms of right and wrong had been espoused for many years by the company's founders and the leaders who followed Otto Rohm and Otto Haas. It didn't mean we did everything right, but at least we never did wrong knowingly. So it's hard for me to say doing the right thing is either an educational, philosophical, legal, or even religious sensibility. It's more. It's cultural and all the things a culture imbues. And I think there is an innate sense of right and wrong outside of our individual cultural upbringing. Scholars of religion have found that the one universal tenet and principle found in all the world's religions is a version of the Golden Rule: "Do not do unto others what is repugnant to you."

My other biggest learning here is about the tendency to push the limits. Pushing the limits has pros and cons. You always want to do better than before or to win in competition with others, but when you don't know what you're doing or are taking risks that push beyond accepted legal, ethical, or moral boundaries, you get caught in a trap, or worse, cause others pain and suffering. In that sense, organizational values can play a big role in your own behavior—both good and bad. Even good people with strong values can get caught in the trap if the organization rewards bad or unethical behavior. In that sense, organizations can provide a moral compass for their employees. There are so many opportunities and even distractions in the warp and woof of daily life at work that an organizational culture can influence (through rewards and punishments) both consciously and unconsciously. CEOs fail their stakeholders if organizational culture is not attended to with a vigilant eye and monitoring system. Corporate culture sets competitive benchmarks as well as behavioral boundaries.

It is very important to keep an open mind, surrounding yourself with good people who have the courage to express their opinions and are encouraged to. That said, it is very difficult for an employee, even a senior manager, to say to his CEO, "I think you're wrong and here's why." Someone of lower rank is always going to think twice before challenging his or her superior, but good leaders should want and ask for the best advice their lieutenants can give them for several reasons: first, the best idea is likely to win out, which is good for the organization; second, the leader builds confidence and collaboration with his senior people, and that's good for the leadership team as a whole; and third, giving real feedback and being challenged is a learning experience for the subordinate who might one day be in a CEO position, having learned the valuable lesson of how good ideas are born. They're borne out of challenge and not just inspiration. Organizations fare better with the leader who is not afraid to take the best idea, especially if it's not his or her own. I encouraged my colleagues to challenge me and clearly listened to and considered what they said. Sometimes I took their ideas; other times I didn't, but regardless, they knew it was important for them to weigh in on whatever was being discussed, especially if it was significant or critical to our operations or long-term strategy. That's what they're there for, in my opinion.

What is the ethical obligation of an organization and its leadership? Beyond a worthy global mission, the organization, be it start-up or legacy, industrial or service sector, can realize significant financial and wealth-producing opportunities in addition to addressing, mitigating, or improving life conditions of the many who live in shamefully debilitating circumstances. Part of that mission is for companies to stress high moral and ethical values in their desire to change the world or make it better.

And if you are able to do more good on balance than otherwise, perhaps you can say at the end of your tenure, "I helped the company grow; allowed the shareholders a reasonable return on their investment; provided decent, fair, and competitive salaries for my employees; made quality products for my customers; and contributed to human health and the environment." When Dow Chemical acquired Rohm and Haas in 2009, I was forced to do this summing up involuntarily. Now I do it for my life, voluntarily, with the benefit of hindsight and deliberation.

On India and America

In December 2010, we saw how closely connected the world has become when an amateur videographer made a film of a Tunisian street vendor yelling, "How do you expect me to make a living?" and setting himself on fire after he was repeatedly harassed and insulted by officials for infractions related to his little fruit business. The film of the gruesome moment was uploaded, went viral, and revolutions swept Tunisia, Egypt, Libya, and Yemen, sending a tidal wave of street protests through the Middle East in what became known as "the promise of the Arab Spring." The world was witnessing its first truly "mobile wave" revolution, and the Middle East was experiencing the inflamed hope of more participatory and democratic governments. That awakening has been regrettably deferred if not derailed by a growing radical Islam and a geopolitical instability fed by that region's myriad young, unemployed, and disenfranchised. We now have to add to this both the continuing civil war in Syria and its millions of refugees, the largest numbers since World War II, fleeing into neighboring countries, countries either bereft of resources to care for them or wary of their own civil discontent, or both, keeping the region in continuing crisis.

As an American with Indian roots and ancestry, I know full well the trap of government by the aristocracy and the cobwebs of poverty, political dysfunction, graft, greed, and choking bureaucracy. It is a pattern of government and cultural practice that are putting India's progress at great risk. Such are lead weights that hinder India's stake in the 21ˢᵗ century and hobble its demographic dividend.

I have always been cognizant of the great cultural divide that separates India from the United States, marked by profound differences in history, philosophy, customs, and religion. And I am aware, as well, of the even greater economic divide that separates the haves and the have-nots in each country.

The subcontinent of India, with its population of nearly 1.3 billion people, has wrestled for decades with its colonial past to achieve its great potential as the world's largest democracy. Home to 30 percent of the world's poorest, India is still wrestling with teeming poverty, a still-stultifying caste system, a lagging infrastructure, an under-serving health and education system, and fast-depleting groundwater aquifers, the source of 85 percent of its drinking water. Yet even so, the irrepressible will of its people to create a better life for themselves and their children prevails in India's unstoppable spirit of market innovation and entrepreneurialism.

Nations, like individuals, are the product of their history and development. India's long economic and cultural domination by the British has left indelible stamps, some positive, some leaving a legacy of what I would term cultural dependence. Clearly, India benefited by school and government influences in English-language learning and the parliamentary system. The huge sub-continent was thereby equipped with tools and infrastructure that have facilitated India's becoming the world's largest democracy, with competitive skills honed to lead and compete with the world's most advanced economies. India's economy itself can now boast that it is the world's fastest growing, surpassing China's.

The downside of British colonialism and long history of economic exploitation has, in my view, resulted in a loss of identity and self-confidence among many Indians which has taken generations to overcome. Post-colonial effects are not unique to India. Countries subject to long periods of colonial domination suffer from these same economic, cultural, and psychological residues, sometimes referred to as neo-colonialism. Much of Latin America and Mexico, Indonesia, the Philippines, and much of Africa have been impacted and still bear the stigma of colonialism, despite clear and bold attempts at development; dysfunction still prevails and, in my opinion, was fostered, and to a large extent lingers, because of its colonial past.

America, by contrast, was a child of the 18th century British Enlightenment. It was blessed with an open frontier, vast resources, and the will to see the world anew. Its Founding Fathers and their descendants put into practice their belief in Manifest Destiny, the driving, quasi-religious and political undercurrent that propelled unfettered growth, geographical expansion, and cultural conquest, along with an always-resilient optimism. Borne of European settlers who were intent on building a better society for themselves and future generations, the United States framed a government of laws, not men, and became a place where an individual's drive and hard work were the rungs of upward mobility. Shorn of caste and class as predictors of an individual's future, Americans were theoretically free to speak, write, or worship as they chose—that set a new standard of civilization.

But not without costs. Not all Americans came to see or experience the American dream, despite its egalitarian promise. Millions of immigrants had to weather personal, social, and even legal barriers that deferred if not denied them the ticket to a better life. America's other "Indians," i.e., Native Americans, fared even less well. And those brought here against their will, and cast into slavery, endured unspeakable pain before gaining their freedom and starting on the long road to full equality, a road they are still traveling.

Now, in the early years of the 21st century, India and America are both at crossroads. Both must confront their destinies in a world that is hotter, flatter, more connected, and now more asymmetrical than ever before.

America must rededicate itself to meet the challenges of an ascendant Asia and a destabilizing Arab world. The cost and burden of maintaining and deploying its military might and of protecting its oil-dependent economy as the wealthy get wealthier is deflating the buoyancy of its middle class and disaggregating its members. Its rising tide is failing to lift all boats for the first time in its history.

For its part, India has made enormous progress since gaining its freedom in 1947. Its post-independence period, championed by Mahatma Gandhi and more recently the economic reforms of 1991, have spawned an India that is better able to release the potential that its people possess.

In the desire to spur entrepreneurial growth and enterprise, Prime Minister Narendra Modi has already shown significant commitment to fulfilling potential by partnering with business to increase infrastructure development, digital commerce, and smart cities and by cutting red tape along a road still filled with stubborn obstacles and legacy practices. If China is the smooth-running, state capitalist clock that can tell its people and industries when they must act and how, then India is an ancient sundial, less precise perhaps, but more in tune with itself and more capable of tapping its rich possibilities. India remains at risk, however, from the shadows cast by its historical and hierarchical clouds. If further progress is not made, those clouds of its caste system, corruption, and poverty will obscure the overhead sun from guiding Mother India in the right direction, a challenge that economists Jean Drèze and Amartya Sen warn of in *An Uncertain Glory—India and its Contradiction* (2013). If these deprivations and inequalities are not addressed and reversed by its leaders and policies, India's progress will be threatened. While India may think, hubristically in my view, that it is superior to China, by comparison, China is progressive and highly disciplined in its steadfast march to economic supremacy, while dark clouds surround the world's largest democracy.

If I were to point to one thing in my native India as perhaps a reason for widespread, endemic corruption, it is that solid institutional foundations are lacking, in my judgment. And it goes back hundreds of years with the Indian princes selling their estates to the British—selling land and possessions and the intrinsic wealth of the country for money. And now corruption has almost become something that's condoned and accepted, almost an implicit way of life there. I see it when I go back; I read about it in the papers; and I see it in a few of my countrymen who have come to this country and achieved more wealth than 99.9 percent of their peers, but are tempted still.

I don't know if this trend is a new form of social Darwinism fostered by macro events or a response to shifting political awareness in the second and third worlds where impatience for a better life is creating cracks in the old social order. In 2000, the World Bank classified 430 million people as middle class. By 2030, there will be about 1.5 billion. In India alone, the ranks of the middle class will swell from 50 million to nearly 600 million despite its still grinding poverty wherein over 300 million Indians do not have access to electricity and over 90 million have no access to safe drinking water. Stymied, in addition, by a lack of education, healthcare, and adequate nutrition, India's poor, if they are to advance, will demand huge energy consumption, much of it coal- and carbon-derived, pitting India's development plans against global pushes for greener energy sources in the face of the West's worries about climate change. China's shift to infrastructure development is causing an even bigger draw on the world's natural resources. China is already the world's largest consumer of coal, steel, cement, and now oil. Its need for fresh water and its singular wealth of rare earth minerals gives it the world's largest appetite for global energy as it seeks to encourage domestic growth and economic development across all industry sectors. In the meantime, the still-thirsty first world continues to look for feedstocks that threaten the ocean ecology, fresh water sources, and forests in support of an ever-growing desire for a better life.

Russia and China are retreating into nationalist agendas and trumpeting anti-Western values in hopes they can stoke their own economic growth and regional hegemony while Europe, now at the brink of recession once again, wrestles with trying to keep its once mighty EU intact. The backdrop of this delicate balance in a connected, contentious, but still developing world is the threat to the global "commons"—its oceans, air, flora, and fauna—and to the promise of what the West does best—offer its people a first-rate higher education, an open and free society, a government of laws that protects its citizens, free and open elections, and most importantly, the promise of a better life not found elsewhere.

America's challenge is to continue to prosper at home and be a beacon to those less fortunate, providing safety and security for its own citizens, while still assuming the mantle of world leadership and offering options for a balkanizing world. India's is to take advantage of its demographic dividend during this period of globally low commodity and energy prices in oil, steel, and copper to bolster industry growth, company profits, and consumer spending and to realize its vast potential. Arguments made by many Indian economists, including Jagdish Bhagwati and Arvind Panagariya in *Why Growth Matters* (2013), conclude that a rapidly expanding economy is the best antidote to poverty. In that sense, America and India have much to gain from each other—a brightening economic outlook, common values of entrepreneurial spirit, a talented workforce, and a democratic and diverse population. With these come common challenges—depleting natural resources, aging infrastructure, and a multicultural society where race and class still hold unfair sway.

And last, both countries need a more functional and effective federal government. Clearly, India has the harder task here, but America has the same row to hoe. Both can learn and benefit from one another as both seek to adjust the balance of wealth: America by renewing and revitalizing its middle class by creating jobs, focusing technical training on high-value work, reducing the debt burden of college education, and reforming tax laws; India by seeking pathways for its poor to climb out of a dead-end life through education, better health, and nutrition. Both nations were borne of diversity and will, in my opinion, thrive because of it. As an ambitious student in India 50 years ago, to me the promise of America loomed like destiny. The reciprocation of that opportunity to thousands if not millions of others guides my life now. In that way India and the U.S. are bookends of what is and what can be—not just for each other but for the world and for the billions of people still in poverty, living on the margins of a life yet to be realized.

On Thinking English, Acting Indian

It was part of my cultural upbringing that you try to be subtle and not adversarial. In retrospect, I think it was confusing to people on the receiving end of my message. Over time, I have balanced subtlety with the need for direct action. With the new company that I'm building now, I can have frank conversations after a few months' time if need be, whereas before I might have waited for many months or even years. And I am more focused and clearer with my colleagues in terms of expectations and behavior.

But in *Imagining India* (2009), Infosys co-founder and entrepreneur Nanden Nilekani talks about the consternation caused when Indian businessmen appear to agree with their non-Indian counterparts and then do something entirely different, what Nilekani calls "thinking English and acting Indian."

Indians have been able to access and understand Western ways of doing business even though that does not mean they react or think the same way as Western business people. What Nilekani is saying, in my view, is that to understand what someone is talking about does not mean he or she agrees with it. My sense is that the consternation behind "thinking English, acting Indian," when uttered by native English speakers or Westerners, is their frustration with the two signals—understanding and agreement. My American friends who deal with the Japanese express the same frustration and therefore look for signals other than head-nodding to realize what their Japanese business partners are understanding, thinking, or perhaps have already decided.

I'll go a step further and say that I think one of the implications of being able to think in English and act Indian has allowed Indians to be more successful professionally in the business world, both here in the U.S. and in India, in contrast to, say, other Asians. Why do I say that? Because being able to think in English and acquiring many of the social assets associated with native English speakers, Indians have become adept at understanding and quickly assessing how the system operates in the West, and in particular, the American system of doing business—what is acceptable behavior, what are acceptable norms, and thinking strategically. Thinking English and acting Indian is therefore part of the double-life phenomenon and not, I would argue, unique to Indian-Americans, despite their early education in Western ways of acting and speaking.

Indians are very intuitive when just watching and understanding the Western business model. And then, given the increasingly complex and competitive world we live in, we are able to use our experiences growing up in India, where it is intensely competitive within a constantly changing, as well as chaotic, environment. To be able to synthesize and to figure out things is part of what we learned and part of the way the Indian system works. The ability to integrate the two systems is maybe somewhat unique.

Asking why Indian business people are becoming more successful both within India and globally is the theme of a well-regarded book by Wharton professors Harbir Singh, Peter Cappelli, and Michael Useem, *The India Way* (2010). It goes back to the same cultural concepts. Indians in India have an innate skill to navigate and intuit both Indian and Western cultures because of their growing-up experience and the resources and confidence they had to develop in order to manage businesses in a country with over a billion very diverse people. And with the passing of time and greater experience, they're becoming more confident in themselves and now have acquired the management skills to lead global companies. They possess adaptive capability.

It is a work in progress for many Indian-Americans, but their backgrounds, exposure to Western culture and language, not to mention higher education, are seen as tools to success. It is a process that Indian-Americans consider very important, if not key, to their success in America. I know it was to me on my American journey.

On Myself
The Double Life

The noted literary critic and theorist R. Radhakrishnan, in his widely-quoted and thought-provoking work, *Diasporic Meditiations: Between Home and Location* (1996), has defined the double life for Indian-Americans as a response to their marked differences of skin color, family background, and other ethnic and unassimilated traits. This, Radhakrishnan believes, creates a so-called double life for Indian-Americans who create an ethnic private life and an "American" public life, with very little mediation between the two. Yet this is not unique to Indian-Americans. It would be natural for other minorities, particularly those of color who stand out, even in a multicultural society like the U.S., to believe that there are only certain "ethnic" things they can do in public while reserving others for the privacy of their homes.

I never liked the term "the double life." I thought it conjured up visions of someone who adopted two personas—one for the public and one for his private life—that maybe were not authentic to either one or were designed to hide a secret.

As an Indian-American, I, too, have lived on the hyphen, and that influenced much of how I saw America. Coming to America was a fundamental disruption of my cultural ideas and values; how I interacted with others; how I behaved in public as well as in private spaces such as my home; not to mention my concept of myself. This, of course, was overlaid by my skin color and appearance, as it is for any person of color. My Indian history and culture, including its values, customs, and traditions, suffused my social behavior and world outlook. Raised in the Hindu religion, I also saw the world through a different religious lens than Christians might. In those early years in the U.S., starting in graduate school and my early career, I was renegotiating my commitment to being Indian with my desire to assimilate and transform myself to fit in and be part of the American community, a predominantly white man's world. I decided I was best suited to be the American businessman, but one with the conscience, moral compass, virtues, and values I learned and experienced in India. This would let me serve as a guide to my family and my colleagues.

I had some advantages others may not have. My study discipline and work ethic gave me confidence that if I worked hard and played by the rules and had some luck, I would achieve my dream. I also was lucky in that the arranged marriage which put Kamla and me together not only succeeded, but thrived, in terms of love and companionship and a shared commitment to help each other and raise a loving family. No doubt, Kamla saw her role and life in the U.S. as different from mine, because it was. I was the breadwinner and as such had to succeed in the external world and make sure my public "American" self was in keeping with what my American colleagues expected, even if it meant working late nights and weekends, and going through anxiety attacks. Kamla had to be everything else—Indian mother, corporate spouse, family communicator, advisor, soul mate, sounding board, and keeper of hearth and home.

In many ways, Kamla's double life was a greater navigational challenge than mine. Indian men see a dichotomous world of public and private behavior whose boundaries and borders are more clearly delineated than Indian women may experience. The world of work is clearly demarcated, whereas the world of home, for an Indian woman, is not just four walls but, indeed, a neighborhood, a community, a network of social relationships and links whose access she may not easily achieve, much less feel entirely comfortable with, despite the attempts by others to welcome her into their circles or include her as one of their own. Kamla raised our children as an Indian mother and provided the "Indianness" that she believed was expected of her and that she wanted to do. She felt she owed it to her daughters and husband. She understood that her daughters saw their world differently than she had seen hers as a little girl, and she wanted her daughters to assimilate with their American friends and acquaintances, as Kamla ultimately did, not to mention my business colleagues on social occasions. But clearly, her perceptions of that double life were sketched from how people reacted to her and the challenges she saw and felt as a result.

I won't speak for my daughters. They see America and their lives, including their "Indianness" differently, as they should. They have their own voices. But as their father, I realize that as second generation Indian-Americans, they don't bring the same sense of what a double life is or was for Kamla and me, a life we have lived and still explore and navigate today. Yet the America of divergent lifestyles, demographics, and opportunity has touched me and my family in positive ways I could not have anticipated, a subject I have explored in my story as well. It also touched me in ways that could have derailed my career.

"What Is It Like to Be Different?"

In Europe, it was different, but in this country and in the companies I have been affiliated with, I've had an immense sense of fairness and objectivity toward me. And this is what I admire most about the kind of culture we have in America and that we had at Rohm and Haas. What I mean by this is that my Indianness, while an obvious racial and cultural difference, was not a boundary or limitation to reaching my personal potential. It may have been there but it was never the gorilla in the room. To my knowledge, it *wasn't* there except on the rare occasions that I have shared with the reader.

My belief system is based on taking responsibility for how we interpret our experiences and on understanding what our preconceived notions and biases are and how much we allow them to influence us. When we first came to this country, my generation was primarily concerned with making it in America and proving our worth as good citizens, able employees, and contributing members of society in the common aspiration of achieving the American dream. And we certainly were aware of our differentness. But what was relevant to me then, in my view, is not relevant to Indian-Americans now. The world is different, the U.S. is different, and therefore the world of the Indian-American diaspora is different. At least that's my opinion, formed and reinforced through interaction with circles of young Indian-American professionals. They know they have made it. Their concerns are more focused on perceptions of white Americans' thinking they're arrogant. My generation did not have that fear. We were focused on proving ourselves first, and if we "made it," then being thankful and wanting to give back. My daughters' thoughts and the thoughts of their Indian-American friends and acquaintances are more relevant to this topic now.

When I talk to people, what I try to say is keep your conscience and mind clear and don't look at actions or decisions that reinforce that "default" racial and negative response that you have, because if you do, you are going to find yourself in a vicious circle of always interpreting everything in that light, whether it's about a promotion you didn't get, or an invitation you didn't receive, or a bonus that you felt you earned.

To me, mentoring works best when it is offered by someone who is perceived as the mainstream. If you're working for a Japanese company, it's the Japanese who are the mainstream. If you're working for an American company, it's probably the white man who is the mainstream. If they are your mentors, and by this I mean mentorship in its full meaning of a trusted, senior person who assists, guides, or advises a more junior person, then they will help you a lot more if they are not mentoring you solely because you're the successful Indian-American or successful African-American or successful woman. Why? Because a lot of natural ability gets discounted or hidden when the mentorship is based solely on ethnicity, gender, or race. When I was offered mentorship, I took it with the assumption that it was offered to me because someone saw something in me that had potential, not that I had fit a certain racial or ethnic profile. That is an example of taking responsibility for one's own perceptions.

What I learned and tried to practice was that diversity makes organizations stronger. I wrote a blog piece for the *Harvard Business Review* entitled "Overcome Your Biases and Build a Great Team," arguing that diversity is not only a moral imperative, it is a business imperative <u>file://localhost/(https:::hbr.org:2014:12:overcome-your-biases-and-build-a-great-team).</u> Those two themes are the primary lessons I have learned from life.

Being Spiritual vs. Being Religious

Some people chalk up my strong pro-diversity stance to a deep religious foundation or core. I'm Hindu. To be a religious Hindu I am not required to do prayer or some other kind of ritual for a specified time each week. What's more important for me is the Hindu philosophy of life—the importance of consciousness and memory, the spirituality of life, knowing oneself through self-mastery, the importance and distinction of the mental and physical senses, living within your means, giving back to others—all these ideas and pursuits are important to me as a Hindu. I still remember that every morning all six of us with my mother would say a prayer together at home. We would light a candle at the end of the day and sometimes we would pray in the evening as well. (We still do that, by the way.) When my grandson Chetan was a baby, I would sing some of the prayers to him, trying to get him to go to sleep. He's seven now, and, while he doesn't understand a word of Hindi, he can narrate 20 lines of prayer in Hindi like there's nothing to it. (Now, mind you, he can also converse with his paternal grandparents in Vietnamese. It's really amazing!) Today here in the U.S. we have a temple at our home. I probably pray there once a week. I'm not a worshipper in a formal sense, but I am definitely a practitioner of the philosophy of Hinduism. This very well might be my own rationalization or justification for what I don't do, but I think I get more out of the philosophy than the worship per se.

I suppose I am not a religious person so much as a spiritual one. I have not read the Bible or the Koran, but with the little I do know, I'm fundamentally sure they tell you the same things. No religion teaches you to lie or cheat or harm anyone. No religion tells you to treat people with disrespect. Even so, I am fully aware of the divide that separates Hindus and Muslims.

The tailwind of history is more powerful than any tank or even any individual terrorist, and we are realizing that tailwind challenge now. Anyone who looks to the global marketplace must see that the six degrees that once separated the world's population is shrinking fast in the wake of the world's more than two billion Internet users. As the world gets hotter, flatter, and more crowded, as journalist Tom Friedman so clearly describes in his book, *Hot, Flat, and Crowded: Why We Need A Green*

Revolution—And How It Can Renew America (2008), the seven revolutions described by the Center for Strategic and International Studies file://localhost/(http/::csis.org:program:seven-revolutions) and defined above are becoming increasingly important to the world's ecology, governance, ability to feed, clothe, house, and educate its inhabitants, and keep them from killing one another. They are shaping our destiny faster than ever before. We are now one click away from many of the world's seven billion people. To me, then, being strongly inclusive and pro-diversity is a matter not only of religion and morality, it is a practical response to the growing global community. My point here is that cultural awakening is both an internal and external process. It starts at birth and with family but adapts to life experiences.

Giving Back

I have set up a family foundation, Ujala, to focus on health care and education, both in India where education in poorer regions is urgently needed, particularly among young girls, and here, where my older daughter Amita, a physician at Johns Hopkins, is actively involved in fighting infectious diseases. In 2013, Ujala made a $1 million gift to Cornell University in memory of my parents, to be called the Phool Prakash and Rukmani Sahai Graduate fellowship in the Department of Biomedical Engineering. Cornell was my first home in the U.S. and laid the foundation for learning and growth throughout my career. I was just 22 when I came to Cornell in 1968 and my wife just 19, so it served as my introduction to U.S. culture, education, and the start of my married life. I owe Cornell a huge debt of gratitude for giving me the confidence and education I needed to start my career and be successful. The fellowship is named for my parents because, as I have tried to show in my story, they were singularly responsible for making all of us in the family independent, caring, and well-educated. They made us believe in ourselves.

I set up a similar scholarship for undergraduates from India in my mother's name at Drexel where I earned my M.B.A.

More recently our family foundation made a $3.5 million gift to the Johns Hopkins School of Medicine. Ujala is also active in supporting the

Academy of Natural Sciences and The Franklin Institute in Philadelphia. Science education and a multidisciplinary approach to problem solving are to me the pathways to greater innovation in all fields. It is but one small effort in hopes it will combine with others. Our goal is to contribute up to $1 million every year to organizations that meet the mission of the foundation.

I'll close as simply as I can. Life grants us opportunities to do many things. Youth speeds us on a certain path and then family, friends, and the infirmities of age slow us down and allow us the opportunity to reflect— on our lives, our legacy, our happiness, the paths we took and did not take. I am at that stage now. I have not stopped, but I have paused to take a look around my world and at myself.

I have been blessed with many people and things. I have resources that my parents would never have dreamed of having. With these resources comes the obligation to give back and to think beyond myself. I want to give back to those I know and those I don't know. Life is a gift, and as we navigate through its various paths and challenges we should always be cognizant that nothing is guaranteed or given without something required in return. I am at a point now where the giving back is more important than the "getting" and the "getting" is mostly the enjoyment I receive when I'm with my family, including now my three grandchildren. Through their eyes I witness genuine astonishment as they discover their world, a feeling we once cherished ourselves and one we continually wish for but that is usually obscured by the heavy cloak of habit and care we wrap our lives in as adults.

As the saying goes, there are no pockets in a shroud. We live and should judge ourselves by the good works and deeds we do, not what we just intend or wish. I am not a deeply religious man but I stand humbly in awe of the self-sacrifices made by those more religious, spiritual, or philanthropic than I. The journey for me now contains a different reward system, one based on living a meaningful life. I feel blessed with both paths taken and look forward to helping those less fortunate than I but who cherish the same dream.

12

THE SUMMING UP

'The only person you are destined to become is the person you decide to be."
—Ralph Waldo Emerson, American essayist, philosopher, and poet

I owe the reader what I owe myself. To sum up what I think I have stood for and follow as personal and professional compass points. There are only five, but five are plenty to tell me what's important to me both now and throughout my life. First, let me say that they would not have been made possible had I not come to America.

Here are my lessons and beliefs, writ briefly but strongly held:

(1) Sound education, strong family, and ethical core values provide the foundation for sustained, long-term success. Unfortunately not everyone can take these for granted. I had the good fortune of having two parents who believed in these three pillars and provided them for their six children.

(2) It is our individual choice to choose the organization we work for. To realize one's full potential, it is vital that we choose the organization that shares our core values and provides its own level playing field. I have been very fortunate to be associated with individuals and organizations whose value system and core beliefs aligned with mine.

(3) Finding the right balance between a healthy ego, self-confidence, and humility is key to individual success. The right work/life balance allows one to be a better learner, listener, and team player. Eliminating one's "default" response to situations will help one enormously in finding that balance, because getting self-imposed barriers out of the way paves the path to interpreting every one of life's experiences in the most objective manner and in living life in the moment.

(4) U.S. corporations (in particular large public companies) must shift their single-minded focus on short-term results and shareholder value. There is plenty of evidence that companies that generate Long Term Shareholder Value have a broader definition of stakeholders (customers, employees, communities, suppliers, and shareholders) and maintain a healthy balance between shorter-term performance and long-term investments.

(5) The United States of America, in my view, is rightly called the "Land of Opportunity." What binds its citizens is the "Rule of Law." Despite its flaws and shortcomings, in my experience this country provides the most even playing field in the world for everyone, irrespective of the color of their skin, gender, country of origin, religion, or sexual preference. It is a country that truly believes in meritocracy.

INDEX

A

accountability 69, 76, 96, 143, 144, 151, 156, 160
acquisitions 47, 50, 64, 65, 72, 74, 83, 85, 86, 87, 88, 89, 90, 94, 102, 105, 106, 108, 110, 118, 120, 121, 122, 137, 139, 140, 142, 144, 155, 159, 234
    Dow Chemical xvi, 104, 105, 117, 128, 129, 210, 233
    Duolite 64, 65, 74
    Morton 50, 85, 86, 87, 88, 89, 91, 92, 96, 98, 102, 105, 106, 114
"Acrylic backbone" 45
Agarwal, Aparna 4, 15, 24, 190
Aligarh Muslim University 6, 12, 164
Allworth, James xvi
American Chemistry x
American dream xii, xv, xvi, 26, 40, 199, 200, 201, 212, 219, 237
Angelou, Maya 164
arranged marriages 7, 14, 15, 32, 89, 93, 98, 173, 218
authority 16, 39, 64, 70
Avantor Performance Materials 142

B

Barnes Foundation 121

Bhagwati, Jagdish, *Why Growth Matters* 214
BisCME, CME 50, 51, 103
BNSD College 11
boards
    executive 98, 101
    membership 148, 151
    needs 50, 101, 102, 147, 148, 166, 167, 168, 195, 196, 197
    responsibilities 101
boards, *see* also corporate governance x, xii, xiii, 92, 129, 138, 139, 142, 145, 146, 148, 151, 152, 153, 154, 155, 156, 157, 158, 159, 160, 161, 162, 191
Bonfire of the Vanities 203
Borg-Warner 72
brain cancer cases, Spring House 103, 104
Breen, Ed x, 141, 145, 148
Brondeau, Pierre 92, 97, 107, 114, 125
bureaucracy 52, 210
Burns, Robert 108

C

capital x, xii, 49, 50, 54, 140, 141, 142, 149, 159, 201, 203
    investment 50, 89
Cappelli, Peter, *The India Way* 216

Carpenter, Arvind Dr. 51, 103
Celanese Corporate of America 37
Center for Strategic and International
    Studies 222
Chandra, Indu 4, 6, 9, 15, 24
Charan, Ram xiii
chemical industry 72, 138
Christensen, Clayton, *How Do You
    Measure Your Life?* xvii
Chua, Amy, *Battle Hymn of the Tiger
    Mother* 21
communications 51, 52, 73, 122, 123,
    125, 126, 127, 155, 157, 205, 235
    fundamentals 207, 217
    importance of 50
    reputation 11, 48, 53, 63, 77
    strategy 149, 187
control 9, 39, 47, 53, 67, 77, 92, 103,
    104, 165, 188, 193, 202
    in a crisis 50
    management 100, 102, 147, 149,
        151, 152
    personal 173, 178
Cornell University 222
Corporate communications (*see also*
    communications) 73, 205
corporate governance (*see also* boards)
    112, 145, 152
Cravath, Swaine & Moore 117
Croisetiere, Jacques 96, 98, 107, 111,
    114, 125

D

Dalai Lama 85
    "Follow the R's: Respect for self,
        respect for others, and
        responsibility for all your
        actions." 85
decision-making ix, xii, 19, 48, 66, 78,
    84, 111, 154, 162, 186, 202, 207
    closing plants 68

crisis management 52, 66
Delaware Chancery Court 126
Delphi Automotive x, xii, 145, 146,
    150, 151, 162, 233
digital revolution 195
Dillon, Karen xvi
Disney, Walt 26
diversification 45
    acquisitions 50, 88, 89, 102
    dangers 10
    due diligence 89
    managing 88, 152
    people issues 68
diversity xii, 19, 170, 201, 215, 220,
    221, 222
double life xvi, 37, 168, 217, 218, 219
Dow Chemical Company xvi, 104,
    105, 117, 128, 129, 210, 233
Drexel University 37, 137, 162, 165
Drèze, Jean, *An Uncertain Glory—
    India and its Contradictions* 213
Duolite 64, 65, 74
DuPont x, xiii, 45, 49, 117, 138, 145,
    150, 151

E

Elliott Management 149
employees 51, 52, 55, 57, 64, 68, 78,
    92, 96, 103, 104, 105, 106, 110,
    116, 122, 125, 126, 142, 143,
    144, 156, 162, 202, 205, 209,
    210, 219, 225, 234
encephalitis 9, 10, 60, 62
Enron 152
European Union, Euro zone 64, 121

F

Feck, Mark 75
Federal Trade Commission 123
Felley, Don 93, 99
fibers crisis 47, 49, 61, 94, 95, 112

Fitzpatrick, Mike 84, 92, 93, 94, 98, 113
Ford, Henry 66
France 18, 62, 131, 171, 173, 174, 175, 176, 177, 178
Friedman, Tom 221

G

Gandhi, Mahatma 212, 237
Giuliani, Rudy 67
Gregory, Vince ix, 45, 46, 48, 56, 57, 84, 91, 93, 99, 112
Grove, Andy 90
growth xvi, 46, 49, 50, 56, 57, 64, 72, 74, 76, 77, 85, 87, 88, 89, 96, 106, 140, 204, 208, 212, 213, 214, 222, 233
Gupta, Amita Dr. v, ix, xv, 36, 60, 131, 133, 163, 165, 166, 167, 169, 170, 172, 173, 174, 175, 176, 178, 179, 181, 182, 183, 184, 185, 186, 188, 189, 190, 191, 192, 193, 194, 195, 196, 198, 222
Gupta, Kamla 163, 164
Gupta, Phool Prakash 130
Gupta, Pramila 4, 9, 14, 15, 23
Gupta, Raj xi, xii, xiii, 134, 162, 233, 235, 237
Gupta, Sahai Rukmini v, 4, 130
Gupta, Vanita 133

H

Haas, David x, 116
Haas, F. Otto, Jr. 55, 112, 115, 116
Haas, Janet 115
Haas, John 91, 116
Haas, Otto 51, 55, 112, 115, 208
Haas, Tom 116, 203, 221
Hewlett-Packard x, xii, 138, 157, 162, 206

Hinduism 3, 221
Hoechst 45

I

ICI 45
IIT xi, 11, 12, 16, 17, 18, 19, 22, 26, 27, 28, 29, 31, 32, 37, 40
India xi, xii, xv, xvi, 1, 3, 4, 7, 11, 12, 13, 14, 16, 17, 18, 19, 20, 23, 26, 27, 28, 29, 31, 33, 40, 58, 83, 90, 99, 130, 142, 150, 165, 167, 168, 173, 175, 176, 177, 179, 190, 196, 198, 201, 210, 211, 212, 213, 214, 215, 216, 218, 222, 237
  caste system 168, 211, 213
  colonial past 211, 212
  Delhi 3, 17, 18, 31, 164
  demographic dividend 3, 211, 214
  Muzaffarnagar 3
  need for education, infrastructure, public health 168
  Reforms of 1991 212
  Utter Pradesh 3
innovation xvi, 39, 72, 203, 204, 205, 211, 223

J

Johns Hopkins University (*see also* Gupta, Amita Dr.) 237
Johnston, Bill 86, 92

K

Kennon, Joshua 145
Kimberly-Clark 38, 39
Klinsky, Steve x, 141
Kozlowski, Dennis 146
Krol, Jack x, xiii, 145
Kureha Corporation 72

L

Lagasse, Emeril 158
leadership ix, x, xii, 46, 59, 64, 66, 67,
    71, 74, 75, 76, 77, 78, 80, 84,
    85, 96, 97, 103, 106, 109, 112,
    113, 115, 118, 124, 142, 146,
    147, 148, 151, 153, 159, 161,
    206, 207, 208, 209, 214, 237
LeaRonal 86, 91, 92, 96
Levantin, Alan 70, 73
Lewis, Phil Dr. 51
Lippincott, Phil and Scott Paper ix, xi,
    35, 36, 37, 38, 39, 41, 83, 165
Liveris, Andrew (*see also* Dow Chemical
    Company; Rohm and Haas
    acquisition; litigation over)
    122, 138
Lochan, Arvind 4, 10, 11, 13, 14, 22,
    23, 51, 103, 182, 214
Lonergan, Bob 117, 125

M

Mahoney, Sean 149
Mallinckrodt Baker 142
Mann, Thomas 199
McDonald's (*see also Paki incident*) 62,
    176, 177, 194
McKeogh, John 51, 117, 125
McNabb, Bill x, 237
mentors ix, xi, xv, 16, 37, 40, 41, 45,
    54, 56, 57, 79, 80, 81, 94, 118,
    145, 196, 220, 237
mission and objectives 101, 137, 160
MIT 11, 18, 26, 27, 171, 184
Modi, Narendra 213
Monsanto 45, 47, 50
Moose, Sandy x, 94, 98, 125, 127
Morton acquisition 50, 86, 87, 89, 105
    decision 49, 98, 99, 101, 148, 149,
        152, 164, 165, 179, 181,
        183, 186, 187, 188, 193

Morton International 85, 88, 96
Mulroney, Jack 93, 99, 113

N

New Mountain Capital x, xii, 141, 142
Nilekani, Nanden 215
    founder of Infosys Technologies
        Ltd, chairman, Unique
        Identification Authority of
        India (UIDIA) 16
    Imagining India 16, 215

O

organizational values, culture, and
    resilience 203, 207, 209

P

"Paki" incident, U.K. McDonald's
    Restaurant 62, 175
Panagariya, Arvind, *Why Growth
    Matters* 214
performance xii, 65, 75, 76, 97, 103,
    105, 119, 122, 142, 156, 157,
    159, 160, 161, 162, 225
    feedback 189
    management and 149
    objectives 101
philanthropy and social
    responsibility 201
Porter, Michael, *The Competitive
    Advantage* 75
private equity firms (*see also* venture
    capitalists) x, 139, 141, 143, 145
Proctor and Gamble 39
prostate cancer xvi, 22, 118, 138, 192,
    193, 208
public relations 51

R

Radhakrishnan, R. author 217

Diasporic Meditations Between Home and Location. Minneapolis: University of Minnesota Press, 1996. (see also the double life) 217

Rodel, Inc. 92

Rohm and Haas Company x, xi, xvi, 64, 71, 90, 129, 154, 235
    acquisitions 50, 88, 89, 102
    European region 98, 110
    fibers crisis 49
    ion exchange resins 50, 64, 71, 83, 96, 114
    Philadelphia plant 51
    Spring House 103, 104

S

Scott Paper Company 36, 165
"seeing the girl," *pennu kannal* 14, 15
Seligman, Marty 78
Sen, Amartya, *An Uncertain Glory—India and its Contradictions* 213
Sendak, Maurice xvi
Shaffer, Fred ix, 49, 54, 55, 58, 79, 94
Shakespeare, William 3
Shipley Company 93
Silver Point Capital 149
Singh, Harbir, *The India Way* 216
Singh, Jitendra, *The India Way* 216
social media 53, 152, 154, 205
Spring House (*see also* brain cancer cases) 103, 104
Stewart, Jay (*see also* Morton acquisition) 86
succession planning
    evaluation 148

T

Teesside, U.K. 68, 69, 70, 71, 74
The India Way 216

"Think English and act Indian" (*see also double life*) 216
top management 48, 144, 152, 158
Tulia, TX (see also Gupta, Vanita) 189, 195
Tyco x, xii, 138, 141, 143, 145, 146, 147, 148, 149, 151, 162

U

Ujala Foundation x, 162
U.K. 58, 61, 62, 63, 64, 68, 69, 70, 71, 165, 174, 178
University of Pennsylvania 235, 237
Useem, Michael, *The India Way* 216
U.S. Justice Department (*see also Gupta, Vanita*) 121, 122, 170

V

values ix, xii, xiii, 5, 7, 20, 38, 41, 46, 49, 58, 74, 77, 88, 90, 105, 106, 110, 116, 118, 120, 121, 138, 140, 144, 145, 149, 151, 152, 153, 156, 159, 160, 161, 163, 167, 179, 194, 195, 201, 203, 204, 209, 210, 214, 215, 217, 218, 224, 225
Vanguard x, xii, xiii, 138, 143, 162
Varshney, Sujata 4, 14, 15, 24
Vassiliou, Basil ix, 73, 81

W

Wachtell, Lipton, Rosen & Katz 117
Wallace, Mike xvii
Wall Street xii, xiii, 77, 86, 98, 111, 118, 152, 175, 200, 202, 203, 204, 205
Wasylyshyn, Karol 75, 101, 137
Wharton School, University of Pennsylvania 237

Wilson, Larry ix, 46, 55, 56, 70, 73, 75, 78, 87, 88, 93, 94, 99, 112, 113, 116

Wolfe, Tom and *Bonfire of the Vanities* 203

Y

Yale (*see also Gupta, Vanita*) 55

Z

Zeneca LLC 86

Raj Gupta

Photo courtesy of Sharon Gunther

Raj L. Gupta currently serves as chairman of Delphi Automotive PLC, a global supplier of high tech components and software for the automotive industry. Previously, Mr. Gupta was chairman and chief executive officer of Rohm and Haas, a Fortune 300 company and an international producer of specialty materials, the first foreign-born executive and person of color to lead the century-old chemical company, now owned by Dow Chemical.

For more than 39 years, Raj Gupta applied the lessons of his parents to work hard, play fair, and seize opportunities that come your way as he worked his way up the corporate ladder. This is his story of the tough decisions he had to make on businesses and plants that didn't meet their targets, re-aligning businesses and managers to take advantage of high-growth opportunities, and putting the company on a competitive trajectory, all the while, as chairman and CEO, wrestling with the dot-com crash, huge currency swings, and an acquisition that needed pruning. It worked. From 2004-09 the company achieved a Total Shareholder Return of 17.3 % compared to the S&P 500's -4.8 %, a feat, among others, that had Rohm & Haas in 2003 ranked second on *Fortune* magazine's list of America's most-admired companies in the chemicals industry. Mr. Gupta takes the reader through the good times and the bad, the personal ups and downs, and the nail-biting at the end when the Haas family decided to sell their shares, leaving to Mr. Gupta the job of navigating the company, its customers, employees, and shareholders through acquisition by Dow.

Mr. Gupta offers some lessons learned, both personally and professionally, about what makes a CEO successful and a board of directors more effective. Throughout, he is measuring and raising the bar on what's important in his own personal life and how to give back to others. Readers will find many of Mr. Gupta's lessons to be applicable to their lives both inside and outside the workplace.

SYD HAVELY

Syd Havely was Director of Global Issues Management and a speechwriter for Raj Gupta at Rohm and Haas Company and currently teaches at the University of Pennsylvania in the Organizational Dynamics Program in the Graduate School of Arts and Sciences. In addition to his teaching and writing, he does issues management and crisis communications consulting through his firm, Havely Consulting, Inc. He co-authored, with Subaru of America co-founder Harvey Lamm, the improbable story of the how Subaru got started in America, *Getting Traction—The Subaru Story and the Entrepreneurial Mindset.* Dr. Havely holds a Ph.D. from the University of Pennsylvania and graduate degrees from Vanderbilt and Wake Forest and his undergraduate degree from Hamilton College. He lives with his wife, Jaime, in New Jersey, and is an avid hiker and cyclist.

Praise for *Eight Dollars and a Dream*

"*Eight Dollars and a Dream* tells of a remarkable personal and professional journey by one of America's premier CEOs and corporate directors. Raj Gupta, working with Syd Havely, offers a candid and captivating story, told with passion and special appreciation for how family, mentors and other leaders transformed him and how he in turn changed his world, a compelling account for all who are navigating a corner office, a boardroom, or their life course."

—Michael Useem,
Professor and Director of the Leadership Center,
Wharton School, University of Pennsylvania

"Mahatma Gandhi challenged us to 'be the change you want to see in the world.' Raj Gupta has lived a life that responded to this challenge. From his early upbringing in India to the top of the global corporate world, he shares his deeply personal journey through many decades, cultures, adversities and opportunities. And the Buddha said, 'The mind is everything. What you think you become.' Raj has become many things in his life. Grounded in the generosity, moral principles and work ethic of his parents in India, his mind has led him to great insights and success. Read his story and ask your own mind if you have become what you think."

—Bob Bollinger MD, MPH,
Professor of Medicine, Public Health and Nursing and Director,
Center for Clinical Global Health Education,
Johns Hopkins University School of Medicine

"Raj's story is the American dream writ large with a focus on what is really important in life. I have had the privilege of working with Raj for many years and have seen his qualities as a business leader firsthand. But I have benefitted even more by watching his example of how to lead one's life with dignity, integrity, and grace. This is a book that needs to be read!"

—Bill McNabb, Chairman and CEO,
The Vanguard Group, Inc.